MW01115536

Customer Centricity

Why It Is Critical to Your
Business and How to Measure It

Gareth Evans

GARETH EVANS

Copyright © 2016 Gareth Evans
All rights reserved.
ISBN-10: 1540334260
ISBN-13: 978-1540334268

Acknowledgements

My deepest gratitude and thanks to Graham, Ian, Nick, Jamie, Jay and Mark for giving me the encouragement and inspiration needed.

Thank you to my family and friends for being so incredibly supportive and to Daniela for being the best partner anyone could ask for.

Thank you to Kevin, Naeem and Casey for giving me my start and helping to cultivate the understanding, interest and enjoyment in business that resulted in this research.

Thank you to all that took part in the interviews for giving me your time, knowledge and insight.

Also thank you to my brother Michael for the beautiful cover design.

Finally thank you to Dr Sionade Robinson for giving me direction, advice and genuine care.

GARETH EVANS

About the Author

Gareth Evans is a specialist in Customer Experience and Sales & Marketing and is the co-founder of strategy consultancy Eastbound.

He has worked across start-ups and established corporates in the technology and recruitment sectors in London and Tokyo. He holds an MBA with Distinction from Cass Business School.

This book started life as Gareth's MBA dissertation and has been reworked for a general audience

www.weareeastbound.com

Table of Contents

List of Appendices

List of Tables and Figures

List of Figures

List of Tables

GARETH EVANS

List of Abbreviations

B2B   Business to Business
B2C   Business to Consumer
CD   Customer Dominant
CEM   Customer Experience Management
CRM   Customer Relationship Management
GD   Goods Dominant
IT   Information Technology
NPS   Net Promoter Score
SD   Service Dominant
TQM   Total Quality Management
UK   United Kingdom

Introduction

It has been called the age of the customer, a time in which *"the most successful enterprises will reinvent themselves to systematically understand and serve increasingly powerful customers"* (Cooperstein, 2013).

Digital disruption has brought about a change in the producer/customer dynamic. Reichheld (2011) states, *"we live and work in a web-savvy world in which customers have near-perfect information"*. Information is power, and digital technology gives access to it in a way unparalleled in history. As Forrester (2013) say *"your customers know more about your products, your service, your competitors, and pricing than you do."*

Some argue conditions mean it has also never been easier to start a business (Ramirez, 2011) and scale it to reach a global audience. Digital technology has reduced barriers to entry: the disruption of industries; commoditisation of products and increase in competition are happening at an unprecedented rate.

Access to information and an increasing abundance of choice means customers are free to take their business wherever they like. Traditional measures like *"quantity, quality, functionality, availability, accessibility, delivery, price and customer support"* (Mascarenhas et al. 2006) have, therefore, become hygiene factors (Herzberg et al.

1959, pp.113-119). They have *"become unspoken requirements, tickets to entry"* (Shaw and Ivens, 2002).

With this, there has been a stripping away of traditional sources of competitive advantage. What remains are the relationships companies have with their customers (Faber, 2012).

Competitive advantage then comes not from operational efficiencies but customer relationships. The development and management of these require *"improving the customer experience, taking the customer's point of view, and taking steps to measure and manage customer value"* (Peppers and Rogers, 2011).

This development of relationships for competitive advantage is why customer experience has been called the next competitive battleground (Pine and Gilmore, 1998; Kirsner, 1999, Shaw and Ivens, 2002, 2004, Klaus & Maklan, 2013; Sorofman and Thompson, 2015). It is also why *"only companies that put the customer at the very centre of their operations can successfully compete"* (Reichheld, 2011).

A Gartner study found *"by 2016, 89% of companies expect to compete mostly on the basis of customer experience, versus 36% four years ago"* (Sorofman, 2014). Econsultancy found 78% of companies agreed they *"try to differentiate through customer experience"* (Econsultancy, 2015) and Laufer and Parish of Forrester (2015) state *"from a once-nascent discipline, customer experience rose to the No. 1 priority for business and technology leaders in 2015."*

The financial benefits of delivering improved customer experience are evident. As Manning (2015) discovered there is a *"clear correlation between superior customer experience and superior revenue growth"* and a Harvard Business Review study found *"customer experience is a major driver of future revenue"* (Kriss, 2014). Rawson et al. (2013) clearly state - organisations able to "*skilfully manage the entire [customer] experience reap enormous rewards: enhanced customer satisfaction, reduced churn, increased revenue, and greater employee satisfaction.*"

Focusing on creating a valuable customer experience should be a business priority but its delivery is not straightforward - *"55% of large companies across selected global markets say the complexity of customer experience [is] the greatest barrier to improving customer experience"* (Econsultancy, 2016)

Defining customer experience is common in academic research, but there is little in the way of consistent definition for organisational use.

Businesses often view customer experience as the responsibility of a marketing function. Improvement of customer experience and the building of customer relationships is however a cross-functional responsibility. *"It can't merely be assigned to marketing if it is to have any hope of success."* (Peppers and Rogers, 2011) There must be organisational alignment and the customer placed at the centre of operations, which Loshin and Reifer (2013) define as customer centric.

Being customer centric is the only way to deliver enhanced customer experience and build sustainable competitive advantage. While academic research and management literature is extensive on customer experience, there is less research on customer centricity and its measurement.

This research will, therefore, answer the following research question:

- Can customer centricity be effectively measured?

The aim is to examine customer centricity for the purpose of delivering sustainable competitive advantage through enhanced customer experience. Based on the definition and derivation of customer experience and customer centricity it will propose a Customer Centricity Framework and Scorecard.

The purpose is to assist organisations with *"identification of priority areas for managerial attention"* (Klaus and Maklan, 2013) and provide a guide for senior management for investing resources in building a customer centric organisation for delivering improved customer experience.

Research Objectives

The research has the following objectives.

- To define the competitive advantage of customer centricity that comes from enhanced customer experience
- To identify and explore what elements contribute to customer experience
- To identify and explore common failures in delivering customer experience
- To develop a framework and scorecard which managers can use to evaluate their organisational customer centricity

Research Structure

The research will take the structure shown in Figure 1.

Figure 1 The structure of the research

Literature Review

Figure 2 Structure of Literature Review

Introduction

This section provides an examination of existing literature on customer centricity. It consists of three types of review: a *"historical review"* to examine the history of customer centricity in literature; an *"integrative review"* to *"generate new frameworks and perspectives"* and a *"theoretical review"* to explore existing theories (Saunders et al. 2016)

It will be structured as shown in Figure 2 and will cover: the definitions of customer experience and customer centricity; the history of customer experience; the customer centric business; the customer and the limitations of existing research.

The review was carried out using the following parameters (Bells and Water, 2014). Included was English language literature related to customer experience, customer service, customer satisfaction and customer centricity from the last 50 years. Literature was selected without geographical preference, although the English language selection meant a focus mainly on the UK and the USA. Included were relevant books, papers and media along with consultancy reports and management texts.

Customer experience has emerged as an area of focus not just for business to consumer (B2C) companies but also a *"critical concern for the vast majority of B2B companies"* (Schunck et al. 2015) and therefore the review was approached as a cross-industry study. Customer centricity requires alignment across organisations and it was therefore a cross-discipline review.

Definitions

Customer Experience

The need to define customer experience is important because "companies that have a definition for customer experience and use this definition in everyday decision making are more likely to exceed profit and revenue goals than those that don't" (Barnes et al. 2009)

The definitions[1] fall into three broad themes: business created; customer created or combination created. The themes and definitions are explained below in Table 1.

---

[1] *A summary of the definitions, sources and themes can be seen in Appendix A*

Table 1 Themes in the definitions of customer experience

Theme	Definition	Sources
Business Created	It is *rational/physical* and created by the organisation	(Kirsner, 1999; Grewal et al. 2009; Barnes, 2011; Manning & Bodine, 2012; Watkinson, 2013)
Customer Created	It is *emotional/non-physical* and it created by the customer	(Pine and Gilmore, 1998; Payne et al. 2008; Ghose, 2009; Grewal et al. 2009; Verhoef et al. 2009; Richardson, 2010; Lemke et al. 2011; Manning & Bodine, 2012; Klaus & Maklan, 2013, Econsultancy 2015; Grønholdt et al. 2015; Thompson, 2015; Weill and Woerner, 2013)
Combination Created	It is both *rational/physical* and *emotional/non-physical* and it is created by both the company and the customer	(Shaw and Ivens, 2002; Mascarenhas et al. 2006; Gentile, Spiller and Noci 2007; Grønholdt et al. 2015; Meyer and Schwager, 2007; Roberts and Alpert, 2010; Shaw et al. 2010; Lemke et al. 2011)

The definition of customer experience used for this research is a *combination created* definition

> **Customer experience is the emotional response** (Payne et al. 2008; Shaw et al. 2010) **a customer has to expectations being met or not** (Shaw and Ivens, 2002; Shaw et al. 2010; Thompson, 2015) **in every engagement with an organisation** (Meyer and Schwager, 2007) **at each stage of sales - pre, during and post** (Verhoef et al. 2009; GrØnholdt et al. 2015; Thompson, 2015)

Customer Centricity

Customer experience is the emotional response a customer has to every engagement. Customer centricity means to "provide the right environment and setting for the desired customer experience to emerge" (Schmitt, 1999). To maximise the customer experience in every engagement, the business needs to be aligned with "customer focus at the heart of everything" (Golding, 2015; Shah et al. 2006) describe the "path to customer centricity" and one "driven by a strong leadership commitment, organisational realignment, systems and process support, and revised financial metrics"

Customer centricity is shifting the responsibility for delivering customer experience from marketing to the whole organisation as shown below in Figure 3.

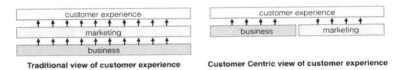

Figure 3 The customer centric view of customer experience

While the definition of customer experience in the literature is divided the definitions of customer centricity are more closely aligned. Customer centricity is placing the *right* customer at the heart of the business and aligning every decision and process around them (Fader, 2012; Loshin and Reifer, 2013; Hunsaker, 2013; Marjanovic and Murthy, 2015). It is Fader (2012) who gives the clearest definition and the one used for this research

> Customer centricity is a strategy to fundamentally align a company's products and services with the wants and needs of its most valuable customers. That strategy has a specific aim: make more profits in the long term

History of Customer Experience

To further understand customer centricity it is important to understand the evolution of the dominant logic and management concepts it has developed from.

Dominant Logic

Prahalad and Bettis (1986) defined the *dominant general management logic* (dominant logic) as *"knowledge structure and a set of elicited management responses"* that are *"expressed as a learned problem solving behaviour"*. That is

> *The way in which managers conceptualise the business and make critical resource allocation decisions - be it in technologies, product development, distribution, advertising, or in human resource management*

The history of customer experience covers three dominant logics:

- **Goods Dominant (GD) logic:** *"From a goods dominant logic perspective, suppliers produce products and customers buy them"* (Payne et al. 2009). This *"dominant logic focused on tangible resources, embedded value, and transactions."* (Vargo and Lusch 2004). The focus is *"making, selling and servicing."* (Payne et al. 2008)
- **Service Dominant (SD) logic:** This dominant logic is *"one in which service provision rather than goods is fundamental to economic exchange"* and it is *"focused on intangible resources, the co-creation of value, and relationships."* (Vargo and Lusch 2004). The focus is *"listening, customising and co-creating."* (Payne et al. 2008)
- **Customer Dominant (CD) logic -** *"positions the customer in the centre, rather than the service, the service provider/producer or the interaction or the system"* (Heinonen et al. 2010, Heinonen and Strandvik, 2015)

The transition is *"away from tangibles and toward intangibles, such as skills, information, and knowledge, and toward interactivity and connectivity and on-going relationships. The orientation has shifted from the producer to the consumer"* (Vargo and Lusch 2004).

SD logic (Vargo and Lusch 2004) is considered a marketing logic. For a business to be customer centric, there needs to be cross-functional organisational alignment. (Shah, 2006) CD logic however is *"a strategic issue, and not only a concern for marketers in the traditional sense"* (Heinonen et al. 2010) and therefore CD should be called a *business logic.*

Management Concepts

As the dominant logic has evolved from GD to SD different management concepts, have emerged. These started with *total quality management* in the late 1970s and moved to a focus on *service quality* in the 1980s. The 1990s saw the use of technology to bring organisation closers to the customer with *Customer Relationship Management* (CRM). CRM then developed into *customer experience management* (CEM). The latest evolution of this is customer centricity.

Total Quality Management

Total Quality Management (TQM) started in Japan and then came to the USA and Europe in the 1970s and 1980s. (Zink, 2007) It involves strategic management of every part of the organisation to *"focus on meeting customer needs and organisational objectives"* (Hashmi, 2016).

TQM brought forward customer satisfaction as a consideration, but it was still an internally focused concept. Klaus and Maklan (2013) write TQM focused *"on the provider rather than the value derived by customers."* It was the start of businesses becoming highly *"information driven in managing the operations side of the business."* (Woodruff, 1997)

Service Quality

With a transition to the SD logic came a change in management concept and need to measure service quality. (Parasuraman et al. 1985) Service Quality was *"an outgrowth of the total quality management movement of the 1980s"* (Klaus & Maklan, 2013).

Parasuraman (1985) discusses the challenges of service quality measurement being that services are *"performance not object"*, *"they vary from customer to customer"* and they occur in an *"interaction between the client and the contact person"*. The shift in dominant logic is apparent in this description. There is an acknowledgement the customer should be a considered party. Service quality also introduced the importance of *"the comparison that customers make between their expectations about a service and their perception of the way the service has been performed"* (Caruana, 2002).

CRM

With the importance of the customer emerging from Service Quality and the development of technology for business solutions, the two combined in CRM. CRM *"emerged in the information technology (IT) vendor community and practitioner community in the mid-1990s"* and is *"often used to describe technology-based customer solutions"* (Payne and Frow, 2005).

Payne and Frow (2005) argue, *"CRM is not simply an IT solution"* but *"involves a profound synthesis of strategic vision."* In practice, this is often not the case, and CRM is a software solution rather than a strategic mind-set. This is one of the reasons CRM projects have a high failure rate. In a Gartner study cited by Shah (2006) *"estimated global CRM failure rates [in 2001 were] 65%"*.

CRM needs to move from its position as just an IT solution to a *"cross-functional approach"* (Payne and Frow, 2005) and it *"has to result in the delivery of a valued customer experience"* (Peelen et al. 2009).

CEM

CEM emerged with the growing requirement of businesses to focus on building customer relationships. (Schmitt, 2003; Thusy and Morris, 2004; Sultana, 2008; Verhoef et al. 2009; Shaw et al.

2010; Teixeira et al. 2012; Grønholdt et al. 2015). Schmitt defines it as *"the process of strategically managing a customer's entire experience with a product of company"* (Schmitt, 2003).

It is more externally focused than the previous management concepts because it is focused creating *"value both to the customer and the firm."* (Verhoef et al. 2009) and *"is concerned with seeing the world through the customer's eyes...to understand what an experience truly means."* (Shaw et al. 2010)

It also brings to the fore the use of customer insight and customer information to shape the business. (Sultana, 2008, Teixeira, 2008)

The 8 characteristics of CEM (Grønholdt et al. 2015) are shown below in Table 2.

Table 2 8 Characteristics of customer experience management

8 Characteristics of Customer Experience Management	
Top management involvement	Customer insight
Customer touch points	Customer-driven innovation
Customer focus	Employee recruitment and training
Goals for customer experiences	Branding

Customer Centricity

The next stage of progression in management concepts and one in tandem with CD logic (Heinonen et al. 2010, Heinonen and Strandvik, 2015) is Customer Centricity.

Customer centricity can be seen emerging from development in the dominant logic and management concepts (as shown in Figure 4). They have over time gone from firm centric, looking *"within the organisation for improvement"* (Woodruff, 1997) to an external focus which is building customer relationships. As Loshin and Regier (2013) say *"customer centricity incorporates ideas, approaches, strategies, and tactics which have evolved over time in alignment with different industries' customer-oriented initiatives.*" (Loshin and Reifer, 2013).

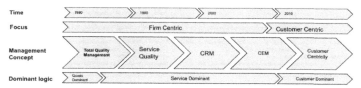

Figure 4 Timeline of the evolution of dominant logic and management concepts

Product Centric to Customer Centric

In a product centric organisation, a *"company tries to find as many uses and customers as possible for its product"* (Galbraith, 2005). They are, as Pepper and Rogers (2011) argue *"structured around the product and service that they create and sell"* and *"product innovation"* is the *"important key to business success."*

However *"in contrast, a customer centric company tries to find as many products as possible for its customer"* (Galbraith, 2005). The orientation, as Vargo and Lusch (2004) says shifts *"from the producer to the consumer."* The *"enterprise makes itself, its products, and/or its services so satisfying, convenient, or valuable to the customer that she becomes more willing to devote her time and money to this enterprise than to any competitor."* (Peppers and Rogers, 2011). The differences between a product centric and customer centric approach (Shah et al. 2006) are shown in Table 3.

Table 3 A comparison of the product centric and customer centric approaches

	Product-Centric Approach	Customer-Centric Approach
Basic philosophy	Sell products; we'll sell to whoever will buy	Serve customers; all decisions start with the customer and opportunities for advantage
Business orientation	Transaction-oriented	Relationship-oriented
Product positioning	Highlight product features and advantages	Highlight product's benefits in terms of meeting individual customer needs
Organizational structure	Product profit centers, product managers, product sales team	Customer segment centers, customer relationship managers, customer segment sales team
Organizational focus	Internally focused, new product development, new account development, market share growth; customer relations are issues for the marketing department	Externally focused, customer relationship development, profitability through customer loyalty; employees are customer advocates
Performance metrics	Number of new products, profitability per product, market share by product/subbrands	Share of wallet of customers, customer satisfaction, customer lifetime value, customer equity
Management criteria	Portfolio of products	Portfolio of customers
Selling approach	How many customers can we sell this product to?	How many products can we sell this customer?
Customer knowledge	Customer data are a control mechanism	Customer knowledge is valuable asset

(Shah et al. 2006)

14

The Customer Centric Business

Customer centricity as a dominant logic necessitates company-wide change (Vandermerwe, 2014; Heinonen et al. 2010; Fader, 2012). It involves complete cultural and organisational alignment around the customer to deliver improved customer experience. This is not seen in a product-centric business, even if they claim to have a customer focus, because Meyer and Schwager (2007) explain:

> Within product businesses...product development defers to marketing when it comes to customer experience issues...and customer service personnel tend to concentrate on the unfolding transaction but not its connection to those preceding or following it

Cross-functional alignment is a requirement in a customer centric business. (Payne and Frow, 2005, 2007; Payne et al. 2008) They need a *"deep knowledge of the customer needs, and this can only be achieved when all staff and departments in an organisation collaborate."* (Frow and Payne, 2007) Without *"integrating individual customer information into every corporate function"* the customer strategy *"cannot deliver optimum return on investment"* (Peppers and Rogers, 2011).

Customer Strategy

Econsultancy (2015) found that *"most companies see customer experience strategy as the most important element for customer experience success"* and the customer strategy is key to success (Berry et al. 2002; Payne and Frow; 2005; Bingham, 200; Barnes, 2011; Peppers and Rogers, 2011). This is because it *"cuts across functional boundaries and examines customer needs and behaviours holistically"* (Bingham, 2009) and is needed to *"establish a focus on the customer, a commitment to genuinely understanding the customer and a culture in which every employee believes that the customer comes first."* (Barnes, 2011)

Culture

Although customer experience covers every interaction with a customer, few people in the organisation *"give sustained thought to how their separate decisions shape customer experience"* (Meyer and Schwager, 2007) and this is why *"customer experience is not a technology problem – it's a culture problem."* (Crandall, 2016)

To address this Loshin and Reifer (2013) put forward the need for executive involvement, and the need for this is so essential to the success of customer centricity that Temkin (2009) suggests that senior management *"either get actively involved in customer experience transformation or drop it from their [organisational] agendas".*

There is a strong argument that engaged employees that *"clearly understand [the] strategy and direction"* and are *"personally committed to making it a success"* (Roberts and Alpert, 2010) are also essential to a customer centric business. (Vargo and Lusch 2004; Ghose 2009; Roberts and Alpert, 2010; Dixon et al. 2013; Goodman, 2014; Klaus, 2015) They are a key component of the *Service Profit Chain* (Heskett et al. 2008), which *"establishes relationships between profitability, customer loyalty, and employee satisfaction, loyalty, and productivity."*

Customer Experience Teams

There is agreement that customer experience needs senior leadership but there is a question over whether it requires a dedicated team. Duncan et al. (2013) say *"only by getting cross-functional teams together...and design solutions as a group... can companies hope to make fixes that stick".* Klaus (2015) argues the opposite of this and says, *"these individuals do not necessarily establish a central and cross-departmental team."*

Operations

Customer centricity is a *"set of strategies that place the customer at the centre of an organisation's operations"* (Loshin and Reifer, 2013) and it can only be successful it is it built into the business model (Thusy and Morris, 2004; Seppanen and Laukkanen, 2015). Peelen et al. (2009) argue that it should *"force organisations to rethink their processes, especially in the area of capturing customer information, processing and analysing it and defining how it can be put to use."*

Product/Service

The move from product centric to customer centric requires a change from expertise in product development to understanding what the customer wants (Fader, 2012). This means that *"research and development processes [should] be broken down and rebuilt"* based on the customer and *"product teams [should] be eliminated in favour of customer segment teams"* (Faber, 2012)

Customer centric built products and services should be developed that *"have emotional appeal, a value statement, and a personal identity"* (Mascarenhas et al. 2006). They should also, most importantly, be developed to be the least possible effort for a customer to use. They should have a low *customer effort score* (Dixon et al. 2014). As Meyer and Schwager (2007) *"the secret to a good experience isn't the multiplicity of features on offer"* and ease of use is seen both as key to delivering improved customer experience and building customer loyalty (Dixon et al. 2013; Watkinson; 2013).

Technology

Starting with the CRM movement in the 1990s technology has played an increasing role in building customer relationship and delivering customer experience. As Peppers and Rogers (2011) say *"technology alone does not make a company customer centric"* and integration between technology and the business is essential (Klein and Morrison, 2007)

Feedback and Insight

As Underhill (2009) says, customer experience is *"ask[ing] people what they think"* and customer insight in one of the core requirements of customer centricity. (Dougherty & Murthy, 2009; Ghose, 2009; Temkin et al. 2009; Barnes, 2011)

The inability to action customer insight and feedback is, however, what stops *"companies from becoming as customer centric as they should be"* because *"customer insight is worthless unless it drives change that increases revenue."* (Bingham, 2005)

What are needed are feedback loops whereby customer data is collected, interpreted and used to drive change in the product and the service (Peelen et al. 2009; Peppers and Rogers, 2011).

Customer Journeys

To be able to gather customer insight and feedback and to manage the customer experience, organisations must understand the channels their customer uses, their customer journeys and the touchpoint they have. As Thusy and Morris (2004) say *"CEM is the process of managing every step of the customer experience"* and Maklan (2013) say *"customer experience is generated through a longer process of company–customer interaction across multiple channels"* (Klaus & Maklan, 2013)

Personalisation

"Building the value of the customer base requires a business to treat different customers differently" and *"all customers, in all walks of life, in all industries, all over the world, want to be individually and personally served"* (Peppers and Rogers, 2011). Because of this, Loshin and Reifer (2013), argue *"the objective of a customer centric strategy is to deliver the optimal service to each customer on a personalised level."* Technology is the solution to be able to do this.

Measuring Customer Centricity

Peelen et al. (2009) discuss the need for a change in metrics as companies shift from *"value creation on a transactional basis"* to value creation during the entire buyer-seller relationship" but discussions of measurement in the literature are mainly around customer experience. They are also either marketing based or external measurements. For example Klaus and Maklan's (2013) EXQ measurement introduces *"a scale measure of customer experience"* but it does not provide a measurement for internal divisions to align for customer centricity.

Net Promoter Score (NPS) (Reichheld, 2011) is a very popular measurement for customer advocacy. Reichheld (2011) argues, "until your NPS results are just as solid as your financials, achieving the kind of customer centricity that will enable you to win the quiet revolution will remain an uphill battle". NPS does not, however, give measure to customer centricity but rather, as with Klaus and Maklan's EXQ, the outcome of it.

Customer Centricity and Competitive Advantage

Competitive advantage comes from the development of relationships because the "emotional bond between companies and customers [is] difficult for competitors to imitate or sever (Berry et al. 2002). Previously companies looked "internally within the organisation for improvement, such as reflected by quality management, reengineering, downsizing and restructuring" (Woodruff, 1997) they now need to look to their customer relationships, built through customer experience, for sources of competitive advantage.

These relationships can rebalance the power shift from producer to customer that comes from information. If as Forrester (2013) say "your customers know more about your products, your service, your competitors, and pricing than you do" then competitive advantage can not come from information on those. Instead information on customers, used to develop relationships and collected through enhanced customer experience becomes a competitive advantage. Figure 5 shows how relationships and competitive advantage changes with the amount of information each party has.

Pepper and Rogers (2011) say, "enterprises [should be] strategising how to gain sustainable competitive advantage from the information they gather about customers" and give a useful narrative.

> If you're my customer and I get you to talk to me, and I remember what you tell me, then I get smarter about you. I know something my competitors don't. So I can do things for you my competitors can't do, because they don't know you as well as I do. Before long, you can get

something from me you can't get anywhere else,
for any price

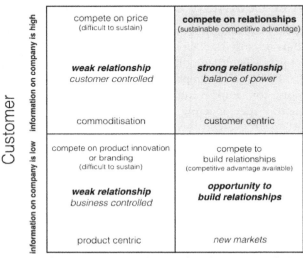

Figure 5 A matrix showing how the power in relationships and
competitive advantage change with access to information

The Customer

In a product centric worldview the customer is *"information processing"* and *"decisions orientated"* (Payne and Frow, 2007). The customer centric view recognises they are emotional beings and not pure rational thinkers. GrØnholdt et al. (2015) citing Balakrishnan (2011, p.222) say that this is the correct view because *"economic decision-making is 70 percent emotional and 30 percent rational."*

Pine and Gilmore (1998) argue customer experience is the result of an emotional customer because *"experiences are inherently personal. Existing only in the mind of an individual."* However Holbrook and Hirschman (1982) temper this view by saying *"abandoning the information processing approach is undesirable, but supplementing and enriching it with an admixture of the experiential perspective could be extremely fruitful."*

Expectations

Expectation management is a key concept in customer experience (Rowley, 1999; Meyer and Schwager, 2007; Barnes, 2011; Dixon et al. 2013; Watkinson 2013; Goodman, 2014; Crandell 2016) and *"companies should design the product and the marketing strategy to set and meet reasonable customer expectations."* (Goodman, 2014)

For Barnes (2011) meeting expectations is not enough, it should only be seen as a hygiene factor (Herzberg et al. 1959, pp.113 - 119) and not enough to create strong customer relationships

> The company that falls short of meeting expectations can be confident customers are already moving on to deal with one of its competitors. Meeting customer expectations is obviously of great importance, but it is not sufficient to move customers toward the establishment of genuine relationships.

If meeting expectations is a hygiene factor (Herzberg et al. 1959, pp.113 - 119) then should the goal of the customer centric organisation be exceeding them and creating *delight?* (Oliver et al. 1997; Finn, 2006; Palmer, 2010; Barnes; 2011; Dixon et al. 2013).

For some the answer is no, Palmer (2010) says *"delight may be a transient concept, because today's delights for the basis of tomorrow's basic expectations"* and for Dixon et al. (2013) *"delight is expensive"* and *"customers really don't care to be delighted by you as much as they want to just get on with their lives"*. Dixon et al. (2013) build on this by saying that *"once you're consistently meeting the expectations of the majority of your customers, you've already done the most economically valuable thing you can do."*

Customer Goals

In the product centric organisation, a product is made and a customer is found (Payne et al. 2009). Consideration is not necessarily given to the wants and needs of the customer and *"they often solve the wrong problems, improving their products in ways that are irrelevant to their customers' needs."* (Christensen et al. 2005)

In a customer centric organisation understanding what the customer wants is at the heart of the business. However *"what we say is often not really want we want"* (Shaw et al. 2010). What we really want is what Shaw et al. (2010) call the *"real demand"* which is what the customer actually wants to achieve from the product. (Barnes, 2011)

The customer centric business then needs to develop products and services based on the *"real demand"*(Shaw, 2010) and *"to do that, you need to segment markets in ways that reflect how customers actually live their lives"* (Christensen et al. 2005)

Focusing on the Right Customer

Driven by marketing, segmentation is often *"trying to understand the need of representative customers in those segments"* but *"the problem is that customers don't conform their desires to match those of the average consumer in their demographic segment"* (Christensen et al. 2005). Customer centricity challenges this strategy and instead *"requires understanding from the demand side, so that the firm knows what each customer segment wants to buy*" and "*being uniquely better [at] giving the consumer what he or she truly always wanted*" (Clemons, 2008).

In an ideal customer centric world, there would be customer segments of one - the individual. However, practically this would be expensive and difficult to manage. There is a cost in being "*better for each of your customers*" (Clemons, 2008). As Fader (2012) argues, "*not all customers are created equal*" and there may be some "*where the economics of delivering superior customer service are not financially viable.*" (Frow and Payne, 2007)

Customer centricity is the approach needed then to meet customers' needs while also ensuring that the company increases in value. It will cost money "*at least in the short term*" (Fader, 2012) but as research by Seldon and Colvin (2003) find "*managers who want to increase the value of their company must understand the true economic profitability of customers.*"

Limitations of Existing Research

Palmer's (2010) concern that "*the term customer experience has been so widely used, and abused, that a potentially important construct is in danger of being dismissed because of the ambiguous manner in which has been applied*" highlights the danger of a lack of agreed definition in the existing literature.

Insufficient agreement on its definition is also the reason for the "*lack in the extant literature of model, interpretation and conceptualization offering a common terminology and a shared mindset*" and the "*lack of structured managerial approaches*" (Gentile et al. 2007)

The existing research is also customer experience dominant and lacks in the topic of customer centricity. There is research into the external facing nature and measurement of customer experience, especially in the marketing context, but there is little available that looks at the internal alignments and constructs needed for its delivery. There has been research on the components of customer experience but "*to date [it] has focused on specific elements…in isolation.*" (Lemke et al. 2011)

There is a research bias towards B2C customer experience, specifically retail environments. Cross-industry research and deeper academic research into customer experience and B2B environments is required.

There is also limited research into the risks of becoming customer centric. Galbraith (2005) argues that it is *"possible to become customer centric to a fault"* and gives the example of Japanese software vendors being *"dominated by their customers"*. He explains *"if a Japanese software company has 200 customers, it will create 200 versions of every software product it creates"* making it very difficult for them to *"scale and expand outside of Japan."*

There is little guidance for organisations on what steps to take to become customer centric. It is difficult to align the organisation without guidance on what *ideal* looks like.

Conclusion

The research into the existing literature looked at definitions of customer experience and customer centricity. It explored the history of customer centricity and looked at how customer centricity evolved from previous dominant logic and management concepts. It looked at the customer centric business and also at the customer and identified key themes for possible measurement and evaluation. Perceived gaps in the existing literature were also identified. The next section, Research Methodology, will explain how the research will build on the findings of the Literature Review to answer the research question and meet the research object

Research Methodology

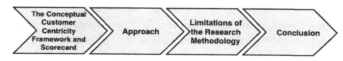

Figure 6 Structure of Research Methodology

Introduction

This section gives an explanation of the methods used for the research. It will discuss the conceptual Customer Centricity Framework and Scorecard, the approach and the limitations of the research (as shown above in Figure 6).

This research aims to provide a practical solution for managers to be able to understand how customer centric their organisation is. The purpose is for its findings to be of *"practical relevance and value to managers"* (Saunders et al. 2016). If as Starkey and Madan (2001) say that *"firms are interested in the application of knowledge rather than knowledge for its own sake"* then this paper's goal is to provide both knowledge of customer centricity and, through the Customer Centricity Framework and Scorecard, provide a tool for its application. This research therefore looks to bridge the *relevance gap* (Starkey and Madan, 2001) and should therefore be considered as *applied research* on Saunders et al.'s (1997) *basic - applied research continuum*. This positioning guided choice in the methods used.

The research questions and the aims of the research propose a theory based upon the variables customer centricity and customer experience. These two variables are related because a change in customer centricity will result in a change in the ability to deliver improved customer experience.

The Literature Review was carried out to explore this theory and with two objectives. The first was to understand key topics and themes related to customer centricity in existing literature. The second was the creation of a conceptual framework and scorecard for measuring it.

Analysis of the literature led to an identification of key topics and themes. These were used to create the Conceptual Customer Centricity Framework and Scorecard. The Framework was then tested through further research. The approach to theory development will therefore be *abductive* (Saunders et al. 2016).

The goal of the abductive approach (Saunders et al. 1997) is to evaluate the design of the Framework and Scorecard, with those involved in customer experience delivery, to seek recommendations on how it could be modified. Were a deductive approach taken the research would have been designed using an existing customer centricity measurement tool. If an inductive approach were taken then interviews would be carried out with customer experience practitioners and a framework induced from the findings. Neither of these approaches was appropriate to the aim of this research paper an abductive approach was taken.

With an abductive approach and because the "*research is concerned not only with knowing what, but goes beyond this to consider questions associated with knowing how*" (Tranfield and Starkey, 1998) it adopts a *critical realist* (Saunders et al. 2016) research philosophy. The discussion of the Research Philosophy can be found Appendix B.

The Conceptual Customer Centricity Framework and Scorecard

This section introduces the *conceptual Customer Centricity Framework and Scorecard*. It will be used as the basis of the qualitative research interview questions. It has been developed from the themes in the Literature Review and designed to address some of the perceived gaps in existing research.

The Framework[2]

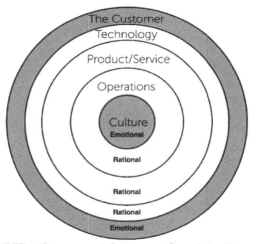

Figure 7 The Conceptual Customer Centricity Framework

The framework shown in Figure 7 is based on the *concentric zone model* (Parks et al. 1925, p.51), which shows a flow from the centre out and a transition at each boundary. In Parks et al.'s (1925) model, there is a suggestion that prices in a city are highest in the centre and lowest in the outer ring. There is no such weighting or implication in this framework.

---

[2] *For the purpose of this framework, operations refers to the processes of an organisation, not specifically an operations department*

27

This model is used here to show customer centricity must start with the business culture. A customer centric *culture* passes out to how a business does its *operations*, which in turn enables delivery of the *product/service* with the customer experience in mind. This is then delivered using *technology* to the end party, which is the *customer*.

As discussed in the Literature Review there are emotional and rational elements to the delivery of customer experience. (Shaw and Ivens, 2002; Mascarenhas et al. 2006; Gentile, Spiller and Noci 2007; Verhoef et al. 2009; Lemke et al. 2011; Manning & Bodine, 2012; Econsultancy, 2015) These elements have been added to the Framework to show that because the business is delivering to an emotional party, the customer, there is also a need for an emotional core, the culture. If there is a purely rational core to the business, for example only focusing on business efficiencies, then it is impossible to be customer centric and deliver improved customer experience.

There is still a need for rationality within the business. As Berry et al. (2002) say, *"companies compete best when they combine functional and emotional benefits in their offerings."* Rational measurements are important for the operational efficiencies required for the *"ticket to entry."* (Shaw and Ivens, 2002) It is of paramount importance, however, that the customer is the focus of these. The *operations*, *product and service* and *technology*, should be built with the customers wants and needs put first.

The Scorecard

A *scorecard* was designed, using the Framework, to provide the measurement of customer centricity. Key themes in the literature, for each layer in the Framework, were used to design statements. The *perceived complexity* and *importance to a customer centric business* were used to assign the statements to levels, with two statements per level. The choice of two was to give consistency in numbers and provide differentiation at each level. Those using the scorecard would give a score of 1 - 10 to each statement for how representative it was of their business.

The scores from the results would give a total *Customer Centricity Score*. This score would be the measurement of customer centricity. Each layer of the Framework would also receive a score, which could then be used as guidance for where improvements should be made. An example of the weighting model and the results dashboard can be seen in Appendix C.

The Levels

Manning and Bodine (2012) cite a *customer experience pyramid* created by Dr Elizabeth Sanders (as shown in Figure 8). The three levels of the *Customer Centricity Scorecard* are an adaptation of this model. The reason for the adaptation was that the pyramid form suggests a peak of *enjoyable* with unequal weighting to the other sections. The top of the pyramid is the domain of *wow* and *delight*. (Oliver et al. 1997; Finn, 2006; Palmer, 2010; Barnes; 2011; Dixon et al. 2013) These are tempting for managers to jump to because they are more fun or interesting to deliver. They are also potentially easier than doing the work to achieve the bottom level of *meets needs* and with more recognition and reward.

The Customer Centricity Scorecard avoids the concept of the peak. It proposes a level based system: levels 1 through 3 with equal weighting given in the visualisation (as shown in Figure 8). Reflecting the need to go through the levels to get to the top and that they are all of importance in the journey to customer centricity.

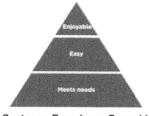

Customer Experience Pyramid

Customer Centricity Scorecard

Figure 8 The Customer Experience Pyramid (Dr E Sanders cited by Manning and Bodine, 2013) and the levels of the Customer Centricity Scorecard

The levels in Figure 8 represent the following:

- Level 1 - Starting requirements for customer centricity
- Level 2 - Mid-level requirements for customer centricity
- Level 3 - Customer Centric

The Statements

The statements in the scorecard are in order of the layers that they represent in the conceptual framework. The statements, the levels and the reasons for each statement are shown in Tables 4, 5, 6, 7 and 8.

Table 4 The Customer Centricity Scorecard statements, levels and the reasons for the statements as related to the culture layer of the Customer Centricity Framework.

Level	Statement number	Statement	Reason for Statement
1	1	Customer Experience is a company value	Customer centricity has to be *"deeply fixed into the convictions and underlying models of enterprises"* (Vandermerwe, 2014).
1	2	A senior person responsible for Customer Experience	*"customer centricity begins at the top"* Loshin and Reifer (2013)
2	3	We have a central customer experience team	*"only by getting cross functional teams together...and design solutions as a group... can companies hope to make fixes that stick"* Duncan et al. (2013)
2	4	We empower to make decisions in the best interest of the customer	Employees need to be empowered to make decisions and trusted to perform (Dixon et al. 2013; Goodman, 2014)
3	5	*"Training, recruitment, and human resources development are guided by the CX strategy"*	Question is direct quote from Klaus, 2015
3	6	Customer Experience is linked to company incentives	*"employee rewards programs"* should *"be revamped to reflect customer centric goals"*. (Fader, 2012)

Table 5 The Customer Centricity Scorecard statements, levels and the reasons for the statements as related to the operation layer of the Customer Centricity Framework

Level	Statement number	Statement	Reason for Statement
1	1	We have a defined customer experience strategy	"Customer Experience strategy is the most important element of CX success" (econsultancy, 2015)
1	2	We measure customer satisfaction	"to satisfy the customer is the mission and purpose of every business" Drucker (cited by Kantrow, 2009)
2	3	We listen to the customer	Voice of the customer programme (Woodruff, 1997; Temkin, 2011; Goodman, 2014)
2	4	We understand the customer experience journey	A "thorough understanding of the journey that your customer takes with your company" is "fundamental piece of knowledge" Richardson (2010)
3	5	We measure customer experience	"The measurement discipline is a set of practices that lets organisation quantify customer experience quality in a consistent manner across the enterprise, and deliver actionable insights to employees and partners" (Manning and Bodine, 2012)
3	6	We continually optimise the customer experience	"continuous concept of customer experience" (Gentile et al. 2007)

Table 6 The Customer Centricity Scorecard statements, levels and the reasons for the statements related to the product/service layer of the Customer Centricity Framework

Level	Statement number	Statement	Reason for Statement
1	1	We understand the expectations of our customers	"To carry out such a [customer] strategy, companies must gain an understanding of the customer's journey — from the expectations they have before the experience occurs to the assessments they are likely to make when it's over." (Berry et al. 2002)
1	2	We simplify a complex product/service offering	"The secret to a good experience isn't the multiplicity of features on offer" (Meyer and Schwager, 2007)
2	3	We are able to serve the customer in the way they want	"We don't just want personalised customer experiences, we want them delivered in the channel that suits us best"(Watkinson, 2013)
2	4	We deliver our service as our customers expect	The fulfilment of expectations as the definition of quality service (Rowley, 1999)
3	5	We are easy to do business with	customer effort score (Dixon et al. 2014)
3	6	We understand the values of our customers	"Reflecting the personal values of the customer through a product or service is fundamental to a great customer experience". (Watkinson, 2013)

Table 7 The Customer Centricity Scorecard statements, levels and the reasons for the statements related to the technology layer of the Customer Centricity Framework

Level	Statement number	Statement	Reason for Statement
1	1	We can track our customers across multiple channels	There should be a "*centralized view of each customer across all business units*" (Peppers and Rogers, 2011)
1	2	We can collect and analyse customer data from all touchpoint	It is on this journey "*across different touchpoints*" that "*customers co-create unique experiences*" (Teixeira et al. 2012)
2	3	We can collect qualitative feedback from our customers	Customer experience is all about "*asking people what they think*" (Underhill, 2009)
2	4	We can deliver a consistent experience across multiple channels	"*Customer-focused retailers coordinate and integrate all channels to support a consistent customer experience*" (Klein and Morrison, 2007)
3	5	Customers can move seamlessly between channels	"*customer experience is generated through a longer process of company–customer interaction across multiple channels*" (Klaus & Maklan, 2013)
3	6	We can offer a personalised customer experience	"*the objective of a customer centric strategy is to deliver the optimal service to each customer on a personalised level*" (Loshin and Reifer, 2013)

Table 8 The Customer Centricity Scorecard statements, levels and the reasons for the statements related to the customer layer of the Customer Centricity Framework

Level	Statement Level	Statement	Reason for Statement
1	1	Our customers understand our values	"Your customer experience strategy [should] match your brand attributes and values" (Manning & Bodine, 2012)
1	2	We understand what customers intend to do	"CEM analysis focuses on developing a multidimensional understanding of customers. This understanding includes...intentions of various customer groups" (Sultana, 2008)
2	3	We measure referrals from existing customers	Advocacy is "is essential for creating referral. retention and profitable growth.". (Wolf, 2006)
2	4	We manage the expectations of our customers	"once you're consistently meeting the expectations of the majority of your customers, you've already done the most economically valuable thing you can do." Dixon et al. (2013)
3	5	Customers enjoy using our service	"The satisfaction and enjoyment that the customer obtains...is important in determining whether a long-term relationship will develop" (Barnes, 2011)
3	6	We measure emotional engagement with our customers	"emotional bonds between companies and customers are difficult for competitors to imitate or sever" (Berry et al. 2002) "emotionally bonded customers tend to invest more in their relationships than do customers lacking affective commitment " (Mattilla, 2007)

Approach

Research Design

This section discusses the methodological choices made and the research strategy chosen to answer the research question and achieve the research objectives. These choices have been made based upon the abductive approach, the ideographic methodology and the pragmatic research philosophy.

The objectives of the research, as previously stated, are:

- To define the competitive advantage of customer centricity that comes from enhanced customer experience
- To identify and explore what elements contribute to customer experience
- To identify and explore common failures in delivering customer experience
- To develop a framework and scorecard which managers can use to evaluate their organisational customer centricity

Methodological Choice

Mingers et al. (2013) say *"critical realism accepts the existence of different types of objects of knowledge - physical. social. and conceptual - which have different ontological and epistemological characteristics"* and *"therefore require a range of different research methods and methodologies to access them."*
Because of this a *mixed method* (Tashakkori and Teddlie, 2010) approach with a *triangulation* (Modell, 2009) model was chosen for the research design.
A multi-method quantitative survey was chosen to research customers' opinions on customer experience and a qualitative study to research business groups responsible for delivering customer experience.

A mixed method approach was chosen because in seeking out *"the real, the actual and the empirical"* (Mingers, 2013) different methods were required

- **The Real (customer centricity)** - Qualitative research with practitioners to understand the "*mechanism and events*"
- **The Actual (customer experience)** - Qualitative research with practitioners and customers and Quantitative Research to understand "*event that occurs*"
- **The Empirical (customer response)** - Quantitative Research to understand the triggered experiences of customers

Quantitative research is needed to answer the questions as to whether customer experience is actually of importance to customers. Qualitative data is needed to answer the why customer experience is important and what it means to customers. It is also needed to understand what customer experience means to producers, consultants and vendors for their input on the design of the Framework and Scorecard.

The triangulation model was chosen because it "*implies that different methods are combined to provide complementary insights into the same empirical phenomenon with the aim of enhancing the validity of representations*" (Modell, 2009). That is, triangulation can be used to bring together the mixed methods to provide deeper insights and to validate the results.

It was also decided that two study types (Saunders et al. 2011) would be used

- "*Exploratory*" - To gain an understanding of what customer centricity means
- "*Evaluative*" - To evaluate the Customer Centricity Framework and Scorecard

Research Strategy

Quantitative/Qualitative Survey

A *survey strategy* (Saunders et al. 2016) was used to question customers about what customer experience means to them. It was important to measure customers as the receiving party in customer experience.

It will be a self-completed online survey and will use *embedded mixed method research* (Saunders et al. 1997) to understand whether customer experience is of importance in purchase decision-making (quantitative method) and what customer experience means to them (qualitative method).

The quantitative questions will take the form of *"closed"* (Martin and Hannington, 2012) questions using a 5-point *Likert scale* (Joshi et al. 2015). The *Likert scale* was chosen because it is an appropriate measurement of attitude. An example of the quantitative questions is shown in Figure 9.

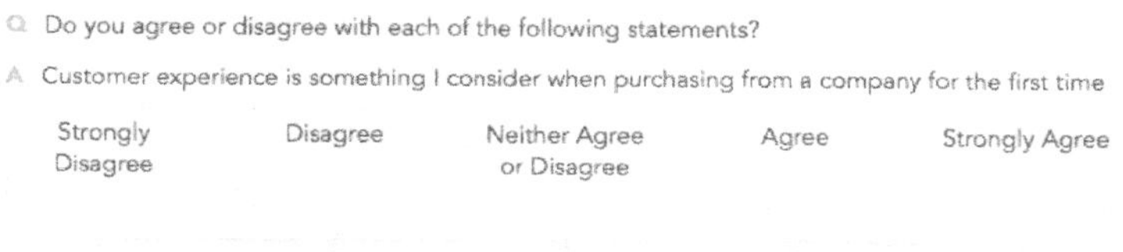

Q   Do you agree or disagree with each of the following statements?

A   Customer experience is something I consider when purchasing from a company for the first time

| Strongly Disagree | Disagree | Neither Agree or Disagree | Agree | Strongly Agree |

Figure 9 Example of quantitative question from the self-completed online customer survey

The qualitative questions will be *"open"* and designed to *"encourage discussion"* (Martin and Hannington, 2012). The answer method for these will be a *text entry box* where any answer can be given.

The survey questions and the reasons for asking are shown in Table 9.

Table 9 The questions, reasons for asking and answer methods for the customer survey

Survey Question	Reason for Asking	Survey type/Answer Method
What does customer experience mean to you?	For triangulation of results with the practitioner interviews and to find out how customer experience was defined by the receiving party	Open/Text entry box
Do you agree or disagree with the statement? *Customer experience is something I consider when purchasing from a company for the first time*	To confirm if customer experience was important to customers when they were purchasing or repeat purchasing. This was to understand if it is a genuine customer consideration or something that businesses are concerned with but customers are not	Closed/Likert Scale
Do you agree or disagree with the statement? *Customer experience is something I consider when repeat purchasing from a company*		
Do you agree or disagree with the statement? *Bad customer experience is something that would stop me purchasing from a company*		
What do you consider to be the key elements of a company delivering good customer experience?	The objectives of the research are to understand the key elements and common failures in customer experience delivery. This question is to investigate these elements as customer understand them	Open/Text entry box
Give examples of good customer experience		
Where do companies fail when delivering customer experience?		

The self-completing online survey for customers was chosen because for the customer group to be interviewed a large sample size was required and an online survey is *"an efficient tool for collecting a lot of data in a short time frame"* (Martin and Hannington, 2012, p.172). It was also chosen because of the advantages of being able to look for trends. Individual interviews with customers would have meant that the sample size would have been too small to see overall trends.

Qualitative Research

The qualitative research will take the form of *semi-structured* interviews with groups involved in the delivery of customer experience (*practitioners*). *Semi-structured* was chosen over *structured* interviews because of the evaluative nature of the research. There was a need for direction but enough space needed to be given for in depth discussion. Unstructured interviews were not chosen because there needed to be common questions, such as the definition of customer experience, in order to achieve the objectives of the research.

The questions of the interviews will be grouped into 3 topics area. The first topic is *background*, to establish the credentials of the person being interviewed. The second topic is *customer experience*, to discuss definitions of customer experience and what its key elements are. The final topic is a discussion of the Customer Centricity Framework and Scorecard. The questions can be found in Appendix D.

Interview questions were the appropriate method for data collection for this exploratory part of the research. The advantage of this method for data collection is that it allowed for a semi-structured discussion about what customer experience meant and to question and evaluate the Framework and scorecard using the experience and expertise of those interviewed. The interview question format also allowed for the research to collect comparable answers from the interviewees. A free form discussion about customer experience would be disadvantageous for the research because it would be difficult to analyse the results. The structured approach allows for more standardised results and therefore easier and more comparable analysis.

The Customer Experience Operating Model

Deloitte (2016) states the primary purpose of an *operating model is* to "*enable the application of a corporate strategy or vision to a business or operation*". For the Customer Strategy the following Customer Experience Operating Model (Figure 10) was created. The purpose of the Operating Model to identify what parties were involved customer experience. This could then be used to identify whom to interview for the research.

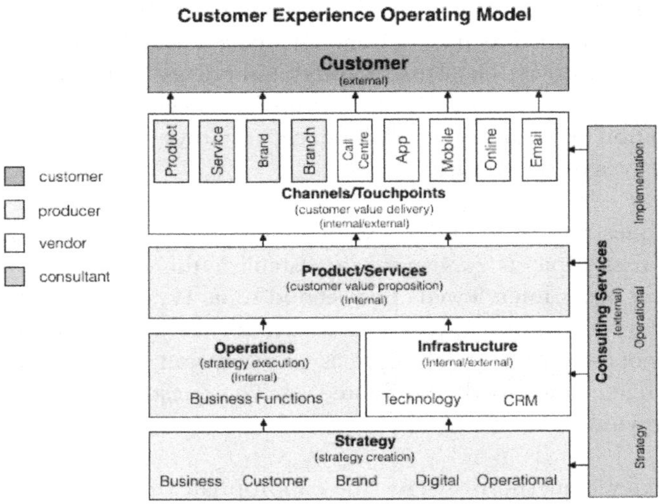

Customer Experience Operating Model

Figure 10 The Customer Experience Operating Model

Validated by Robin Trickett - Director of Business Operations and Strategy at Qubit Digital Ltd
(Trickett, 2016, pers. Comm. 23rd August)

In the Operating Model four groups were identified as being involved in customer experience - Customers, Vendors, Producers and Consultants. The roles that each of these play in customer experience delivery are shown in Table 10.

Table 10 The groups in the Customer Experience Operating Model and their roles in customer experience

Group	Role in Customer Experience
Customers	The receiving party
Vendors	Providing the tools required for delivery
Producers	Responsible for the creation, delivery and management
Consultants	Advising *Producers* on the operations, technology and product or service design required

These groups can be linked to the Conceptual Customer Centricity Framework as shown in Table 11.

Table 11 The layers from the Conceptual Customer Centricity Framework and the corresponding groups from the Customer Experience Operating Model

Framework Layer	Group Involved
Customer	Customer
Technology	Vendor, Consultant
Product / Service	Consultant, Producer
Operations	Consultant, Producer
Culture	Producer

How Interviewees were selected

Representatives were chosen from each of the groups in the Customer Experience Operating Model. Four were chosen to reduce bias. They were chosen across sections of the Conceptual Customer Centricity Framework so that bias was reduced from interviewees only belonging to a single layer of the Framework.

The interviewees were found through LinkedIN, a professional social media networking site, through keyword searches for Customer Experience in job title or job description. They were also selected using *Seniority Level* option so only those of Senior Manager, Director level or higher were interviewed. This was chosen so that interviewees could be deemed to have enough experience and knowledge in the subject to be considered experts and also so that they would have a wide organisational viewpoint. They were also chosen from across departments to give a cross-functional view of customer experience.

The organisations selected were from across a range of industries within each sector in order to reduce industry-based biases

Rationale

The mixed method approach was chosen because by doing quantitative and qualitative research the results could *"be combined to triangulate findings in order that they be mutually corroborated"* (Bryman, 2006). The relevant groups in customer experience (see Operating Model) are involved in different ways. The Producer/Consultant/Vendor groups are involved in the delivery of customer experience. The customer group is the receiving part of the customer experience. This research is looking to define customer experience and its measurement and so it was important that both views could be researched and incorporated.

A single method approach would not have had the *"completeness"* (Bryman, 2006) of a mixed method approach. The customer group is a large, non-homogeneous group and so a self-answering survey was selected in order to provide trends and views across a large group. However this survey method would have missed the depth needed in research into the deliverers group who are smaller and more homogenous in their focus.

The alternative method for the survey would have been to have it as a single method, quantitative or qualitative. Neither option on its own would have been sufficient to answer the research questions.

Sampling

Customer Group

For the customer survey was *probability sampling)* was chosen because this enables estimation statistically of the population. (Saunders et al. 206). The population was defined as anyone in the UK (64.1m) aged 16 or over (81.2%) which was 54.04m people (ONS, 2016). This population was chosen as it represents those of traditional working age or over and could therefore most likely be considered people who make purchasing decisions i.e. customers.

The following were used in the sampling calculation.

- Confidence Interval - 5%
- Confidence level - 95%

With these parameters a minimum target sample size of 384 was required (Creative Research Systems, 2016)

Practitioner Interviews

The practitioners were selected from groups in the Customer Experience Operation Model. They are all directly or indirectly responsible for customer experience and are, therefore, a homogeneous group. Guest at al. (2006, cited in Saunders et al. 2016) says, "within a fairly homogenous group, 12 in-depth interviews should suffice." There are three groups in the Customer Experience Operating model and so four were chosen from each group.

Data Analysis

The data collection methods used for the collection of primary data will be an online survey for the customer survey and manual data collection for the practitioner interviews.

The data collected from the customer survey will be categorical and therefore *"descriptive (nominal) data"* (Saunders et al. 2016). The data will then be coded so that themes can be identified.

The data collected from the interviews will be transcribed and then a *"bottom up"* *"template analysis"* (King, 2012) will be carried out. This thematic analysis will involve the coding of the data for *"identifying, analysing, and reporting patterns (themes) within [the] data"* (Braun and Clarke, 2006).

When coding has been done for both methods, statistical analysis will be carried out for the development of conclusions and recommendations.

Reliability and validation

Laws (2013, cited by Bell and Waters, 2014) say *"the key to triangulation is to see the same thing from different perspectives and thus be able to confirm or challenge the findings of one method with those of another."* This means the findings from the research using the mixed methods (Tashakkori and Teddlie, 2010) should be considered more reliable than through use of a single method.

It also reduces some of the bias that comes from the research approach chosen. There is researcher bias (Saunders et al.), which is the bias that comes from the research being involved in customer experience and its delivery. There is also participation bias because the practitioners chosen are involved in customer experience. The triangulation of these results with the findings from the customer survey, which is to those not involved in customer experience delivery, will increase the reliability and validation of the results.

Generalisation

The data that is obtained through the research methods chosen can be generalised. The selection of the population for the quantitative survey will enable generalisation of the results. The interviewees for the practitioner interviews were chosen across groups from the Customer Experience Operating Model, were from different industries and were cross-functional to ensure *"external validity"* (Saunders et al. 2016) and to ensure the there was adequate representation.

Ethical Considerations

Consent was gained from every person that was interviewed to be interviewed and to be recorded. To respect the confidentiality of the conversations interviewee names have been changed and company names redacted.

An international and well-respected research agency was used to deliver Internet questionnaires. The agency has a privacy policy that covers their ethics and use of their technology. Participants are all willing participants that have agreed to take part.

The reproducibility of this research is discussed in Appendix E.

Limitations of the Research Methodology

There is potential bias in the research methodology chosen for the customer survey. This is because the survey will go to a large sample of *customers* through an online research agency who respondents will be customer of B2C businesses. The practitioner interviews will include people that are B2B customers but the research will not be interviewing them in their capacity as customers but rather practitioners of customer experience. This may present a B2C bias to the findings.

Conclusion

In conclusion, this section looked: at the conceptual Customer Centricity Framework and Scorecard, the research approach and how the research was designed. It also looked at the reliability of the research as well as the limitations and generalisations. These were taken into account during the research, the findings of which are described in the next section.

The Findings and Discussion

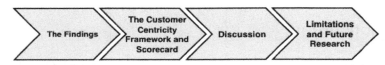

Figure 11 Structure of The Findings and Discussion

Introduction

This section looks at the results of the practitioner interviews and the customer survey. It draws on the findings from the mixed methods (Tashakkori and Teddlie, 2010) for the triangulation of results (Modell, 2009). It will be structured as shown in Figure 11.

In the discussion section, the findings of the practitioner interviews and the customer survey are analysed and discussed. Looking at themes uncovered in the findings and using these to explore the research question.

Practitioner interviews

12 people took part in the interviews. Four belonging to each of the three practitioner groups identified in the Customer Experience Operating Model. The interviewees selected from the groups in the Customer Experience Operating Model are shown in Table 12.

The full transcripts of the practitioner interviews can be found in
Appendix F.

**Table 12 Interviewees selected, the group they belong to, their
position and their relationship to customer experience**

Group	Name	Position	Industry	Relationship to customer experience
Producer	Robert	Head of Digital	Publishing	Responsible for the delivery of customer experience across all digital touchpoints
Producer	Michael	Head of Ecommerce	Mobile|	Responsible for key programs around data driven marketing, personalization and customer experience in the digital channel
Producer	Claire	Director of Customer Experience	Finance	Responsible for the end to end customer journey
Producer	Joseph	Global Director	Information and Research	Responsible for customer engagement, and customer service online
Consultant	Lorne	Managing Director	Management Consulting	Works with clients to understand customer experience challenges and design solutions
Consultant	Patrick	Partner	Management Consulting	Runs the global customer experience practice
Consultant	Matthew	Director	Management Consulting	Responsible for delivery of digital customer experience programs
Consultant	John	Managing Director	Management Consulting	Managing Director of a customer experience consultancy
Vendor	Paul	Director of People Operations	Technology	Responsible for the onboarding and ongoing development of customer experience delivery experts
Vendor	Lucas	Director of Product	Technology	Responsible for a suite of products for delivering improved customer experience
Vendor	Alex	CEO	Technology	Leads an organisation that offers a solution designed to help customers deliver customer experience
Vendor	Edward	VP Marketing	Technology	Responsible for the customer value proposition in a customer experience focused technology vendor

Customer survey

400 people completed the customer survey, which was enough to meet the required sample size. It was carried out to investigate the customer group in the Customer Experience Operating Model. The design of the survey meant every question had to be completed; response rate for each question was therefore 100%.

The respondents were 63% women and 37% male. They were 33% aged 18 - 34, 36% aged 34 - 55 and 31% aged over 55. All respondents were in the UK. These demographics can been seen in Figure 12. Further demographic information can be found in Appendix G.

The complete survey data can be found in Appendix H.

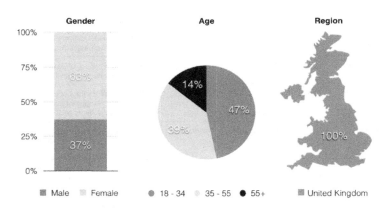

Figure 12 Customer survey respondent demographics for age, gender and location

The Findings

The Relevancy of Customer Centricity

Source: practitioner interview and customer survey

Interview Findings

Interviewees were asked the question *have you seen an increase in customer experience being talked about both internally and externally?*

- 100% of interviewees said that they *had seen an increase in customer experience being talked about internally.*
- 92% also said that they *had seen an increase in it being talked about externally.* The 8% that did not say they had seen an increase externally is a People Operations Director whose responsibility is internally focused rather than on the external end customer.

Interviewees were also asked about their thoughts on a recent Gartner study. The results can be see in Appendix I.

Customer Survey Findings

Participants were asked to respond on a 5 point Likert scale (Joshi et al. 2015) to the question *do you agree or disagree with the following statements?*

1. Customer experience is something I consider when purchasing from a company

2. Customer experience is something I consider when repeat purchasing from a company

3. Bad customer experience is something that would stop me purchasing from a company

Results

- 73% said that they *agreed* (42%) or *strongly agreed* (31%) that customer experience was a consideration when *purchasing* or *repeat purchasing* from a company. There was no significant differentiation across demographics.
- Customer experience was deemed less important in first-time purchases than it was in repeat purchases. While 67% of customers *agreed* or *strongly agreed* that it was important for first time purchase, that went up significantly to 80% when considering its importance in repeat purchasing (a 20% increase). There was a 74% increase in customers answering *strongly agree* between *purchase* (23%) and *repeat purchase* (40%). These results are shown in Figures 13 and 14.
- There was significant agreement (84%) that *a poor customer experience would stop a customer from purchasing from a company* with 38% saying they *agree* and 46% saying they *strongly agree*. The results are shown in Figure 15.

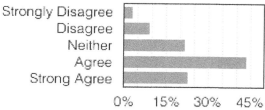

Figure 13 The findings from the questions to you agree or disagree with the statement: customer experience is something I consider when purchasing from a company (above)

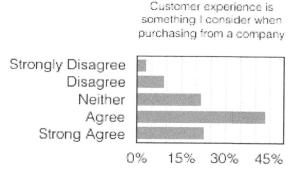

Figure 14 The findings from the question do you agree or disagree with the statement: customer experience is something I consider when repeat purchasing from a company (above)

51

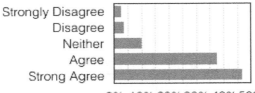

Bad customer experience
is something that would
stop me purchasing from a
company

Figure 15 The findings of the question do you agree or disagree with the statement: bad customer experience is something that would stop me purchasing from a company (above)

Defining Customer Experience

Source: practitioner interviews + customer survey

Interview Findings

Interviewees were asked the question *what does "customer experience" mean to you?*

- 50% defined customer experience as something that is *business created*, 17% defined it as something that the *customer created*, and the remaining 33% of interviewees believe in a *combination creation*.
- Between interviewees, there was a pattern that stood out in that 75% of Producers felt that it was *business created* and 50% of Consultants felt that it was *customer created*. The Consultants group was the only group that gave *customer created* definitions.
- 50% defined customer experience as a *physical interaction* and 17% responded with an emotions based definition. There was no discernible difference between the groups.
- 25% discussed that customer experience is about *on-going relationships with customers*. 33% discussed it as the *complete lifecycle of interactions with a company* and 33% of defined it as *meeting needs and expectations*.

Customer Survey Findings

The question was *what does customer experience mean to you?* The answer method was a *text entry box* chosen to reduce bias from providing predefined options. This approach meant that multiple answers were possible. In this question 405 answers were given.

- 57% of answers defined customer experience as *business created*, 21% as *customer created*, 5% as *combined created* and the remaining 17% of answers did not clearly show any of these (*other*). These results are shown in Figure 13.
- 57% of respondents defined customer experience as a *physical interaction with a company*, compared to 26% who defined it as being *non-physical or emotional.*
- The top 3 answers for physical interaction were *how staff deal with you* (18%); *customer service* (11%) and the *end-to-end journey* (8.40%).
- 18% of answers said customer experience was *how staff dealt with you* and 11% said that it was *customer service.* In the coding of the customer survey responses customer service was defined as any answer given that related to *how companies dealt with customers when there was a problem.*
- Only 3% of responses talked about *meeting needs and expectations.*
- Only 0.26% of answers mentioned *personalised experience* as a definition and no interviewees mentioned it in their definitions.

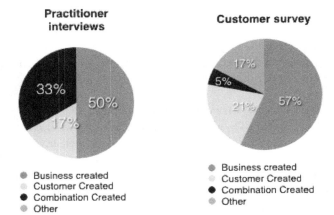

Figure 16 Customer experience creation theme distribution from the practitioner interviews and the customer survey to the question - what does customer experience mean to you?

Key Elements of Customer Experience

Source: practitioner interviews & customer survey

Interview Findings

Interviewees were asked the question *what do you consider to be the key elements of delivering customer experience?*

- The most mentioned element of customer experience was *data and insight* with 58% citing it.
- 25% of respondents said *frictionless buying* was a key element. The respondents that answered with frictionless buying were all Producers, and 75% of Producers gave *frictionless buying* as a key element.
- 16% discussed the importance of *brand*.
- There were no other trends in key elements with single person responses for *product* (8%), *communications* (8%), *employees* (8%), *understanding journeys* (8%) and *culture* (8%).

Interviewees were also asked the question *could you give some examples of companies you think are delivering good customer experience?* The results can be seen in Table 13.

Table 13 Examples of companies delivering good customer experience from the practitioner interviews

Company	Reason for good customer experience	Mentioned by % of respondents
Amazon	Post purchase service Trust Convenience Speed and price Reliability Easy to build	42%
Charles Tyrwhitt	Easy returns	8%
Netflix	Understand customers Cross channel switching	8%
Omelette	Manage the end to end journey Understand my goals Strong communication	8%
Spotify	Cross channel switching	8%
BBC	Cross channel switching	8%
Ocado	Product selection Remembers customers when they return	8%
AO.com	Good online experience	8%
Virgin Atlantic	Issue resolution	8%
Tesla	Buying experience	8%
Boeing Employee Credit Union	Co-creation of value through customer education	8%
Apple	Apple Geniuses (employees)	8%
Direct Line	Cross channel switching	8%
Google	Cross channel switching	8%
GiffGaff	Co-creation of value through customer community	8%

Customer Survey Findings

The question was *what do you consider to be the key elements of a company delivering good experience?* The answer method was a *text entry box.* This approach meant that multiple answers were possible and 427 answers were given.

- The most highly rated key elements of customer experience were *friendly/helpful service* (32%) and *customer service* (9.37%).
- Survey responses could be grouped into two major groups: elements of customer experience that were *in the control of the business* (77%) and elements of customer experience that were *out of control of the business* (11%). The remaining 12% were *other* or *don't know.* These results are shown in Figure 17.

Key Elements of Customer Experience

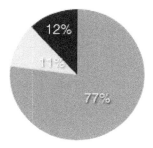

In control of the business
Out of control of the business
Other

Figure 17 Results related to business control from the customer survey to the question - what do you consider to be the key elements of a company delivering customer experience?

- The top 5 elements that were *in the control of the business* were: *friendly/helpful service* (32%); *customer service* (9%);

listening to the customer (5%); *delivery times* (4%); *good quality products* (4%).

- There were 3 elements that were *customer controlled* which were: *feel valued and understood* (6%); *meeting expectations* (4%) and *loyalty* (1%).
- As with the definitions of customer experience, customer service and employees were very highly ranked as key elements of customer experience: *friendly/helpful service (32.08%); customer service (9.37%); efficient service (6.32%); knowledgeable staff (2.58%) and availability to speak (1.64%).*

There was also a section in the survey that asked respondents to *please give examples of good customer experience.* The answer method was a *text entry box.* This approach meant that multiple answers were possible and 411 answers were given.

- 42% of answers were related to employees: *friendly staff* (17%), *helpfulness* (13%) and *knowledgeable staff* (5%).
- 14% of answers were *customer service.*
- 8% of answers were specific businesses. The top 3 of businesses mentioned were *John Lewis* (3%), *Amazon* (1%) and *Marks & Spencers* (1%).

Failing at Customer Experience

Source: practitioner interviews + customer survey

Interview Findings

Interviewees were asked the question *where do you see companies most often failing when delivering customer experience?*

- 25% of the interviewees spoke of *lack of senior vision* for companies failing at customer experience.
- 17% discussing failure as *not delivering on their promise.*
- Mirroring the importance of *data and insight* in the findings for key elements of customer experience, 17% of the interviewees discussed *poor use of data* as a common failure in customer experience.
- Other responses from the interviewees included: *no personalisation* (8%); *culture* (8%); *hygiene factors (8%)* and *being too far removed from the customer (8%).*
- There was no discernible difference between the groups in their answers.

Customer survey findings

The question was *where do companies fail when delivering customer experience?* The answer method was a *text entry box.* This approach meant that multiple answers were possible and 408 answers were given.

- The dominant result was that 69% of answers for failure in customer experience delivery were issues that were *in control of the business.* 17% of answers were for issues that were *out of the control of the business* and 14% were unrelated to either. These results can be seen in Figure 18.

Failure in customer experience delivery

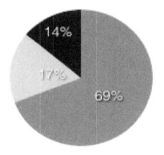

- In control of the business
- Out of control of the business
- Other

Figure 18 Results related to business control from the customer survey to the question - where do companies fail when delivering customer experience?

- The top 3 results for issues that were in control of the business were: *customer service* (14%); *unfriendly staff* (9%) and *rude staff* (7%).
- The results for issue that were out of control of the business were: *not feeling valued* (12%); *not feeling listened to* (5%).

- There was a pattern seen was that employees were the main reason for companies failing at customer experience. 44% of answers were related to *employees*.
- The top 5 employee related answers were: *customer service* (14%); *unfriendly staff* (9%); *rude staff* (7%); *unhelpful staff* (6%) and *unknowledgeable staff* (5%).
- 3% of answers were *breaking promises*.
- An interesting finding, given the level of discussion on expectation management around customer experience was that *not meeting expectations* was only 0.49%.

The Customer Centricity Framework and Scorecard

Interviewees were asked to give their evaluation of the Customer Centricity Framework and Scorecard. The overall evaluation was positive with 33% of interviewees specifically saying that *they liked it* and nobody specifically saying that they *disliked* or *disagreed* with the concept and design of the Customer Centricity Framework and Scorecard.

The Framework

Source: practitioner interviews
The following findings are from discussions on the Customer Centricity Framework

- The most dominant finding was that 75% of the interviewees thought that *feedback loops* needed to be added the framework. They were the key to ensuring that the organisation could listen and then respond to customers.
- 67% of interviewees discussed the importance of the emotional distinction in the Framework.
- 17% suggested that the Framework needed to *include brand* in addition to the 5 current layers.

The Scorecard

For evaluation of the Customer Centricity Scorecard interviewees were asked about the relevancy of the statements and the levels that they were positioned on. If an interviewee thought that the statements were relevant and the level was correct then they *agreed with the level*. If not then they *disagreed with the level*. If an interview did not discuss the level then it resulted in a *did not discuss* for that level.

Culture

Source: practitioner interviews

Interviewees were asked to discuss the *culture* statements of the Customer Centricity Scorecard

- 17% of practitioners *agreed* with statements on *level 1*, 8% *agreed* with the statements on *level 2* and 33% agreed with the statements on *level 3*.
- 33% of practitioners *disagreed* with statements on *level 1*, 50% *disagreed* with the statements on *level 2* and 17% disagreed with the statements on *level 3*.
- 50% of practitioners *did not discuss* statements on *level 1*, 42% did not discuss the statements on *level 2* and 50% *did not discuss* the statements on *level 3*.
- These results can be seen in Figure 19.

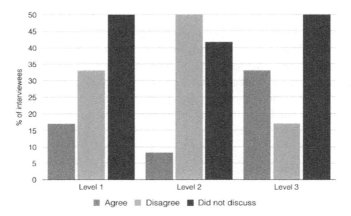

Figure 19 Results on whether practitioners agreed or disagreed with the statements and levels of the culture layer of the Customer Centricity Scorecard

- The most disputed statement in the culture section of survey was the level 2 statement - *We have a central customer experience team.* 50% of interviewees discussed it and 67% of those that discussed it thought that it was a bad idea to have one.

Operations

Source: practitioner interviews

Interviewees were asked to discuss the *operations* statements of the Customer Centricity Scorecard.

- 8% of practitioners *agreed* with statements on *level 1*, 8% *agreed* with the statements on *level 2* and 17% agreed with the statements on *level 3*.
- 59% of practitioners *disagreed* with statements on *level 1*, 33% *disagreed* with the statements on *level 2* and 33% disagreed with the statements on *level 3*.
- 33% of practitioners *did not discuss* statements on *level 1*, 59% did not discuss the statements on *level 2* and 50% *did not discuss* the statements on *level 3*.
- These results can be seen in Figure 20.

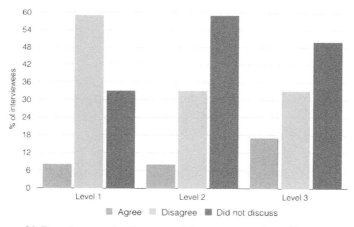

Figure 20 Results on whether practitioners agreed or disagreed with the statements on the levels of the operations layer of the Customer Centricity Scorecard

- The most common theme in the operations discussions is the need for *agile operations* and to be able to use *customer feedback to change operations quickly*. 67% of interviewees discussed this.

- The most disputed level was *level 1* with interviewees feeling that this was too advanced for starting customer centricity and there was a need for a more basic entry point. 8% felt that statement 4 - *we understand the customer journey* - should be moved to level 1 as it seemed more suitable as an entry level inclusion.

Product/Service

Source: practitioner interviews

Interviewees were asked to discuss the *product/service* statements of the Customer Centricity Scorecard.

- 25% of practitioners *agreed* with statements on *level 1*, 25% *agreed* with the statements on *level 2* and 25% agreed with the statements on *level 3*.
- 8% of practitioners *disagreed* with statements on *level 1* and 25% disagreed with the statements on *level 3*. For *level 2* interviewees either agreed or did not discuss, nobody *disagreed* specifically.
- 67% of practitioners *did not discuss* statements on *level 1*, 75% did not discuss the statements on *level 2* and 50% *did not discuss* the statements on *level 3*.
- These results can be seen in Figure 21.

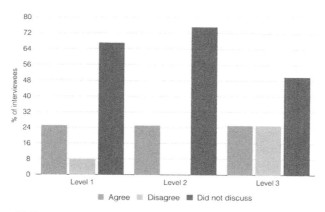

Figure 21 Results on whether practitioners agreed or disagreed with the statements on the levels of the product/service layer of the Customer Centricity Scorecard

- Being *easy to do business with* was seen by 25% of interviewees as a hygiene factor (Herzberg et al. 1959, pp.113 - 119).
- *Apple* was discussed by 25% of people as a good example of keeping products and services simple.
- 17% also discussed simplicity but with the caveat that *simplicity was good but not if it risked the connection with the customer.*
- 17% thought the key to great customer experience was not *meeting expectations* but *expanding expectations* or *creating new expectations.*
- 17% discussed the importance of *feedback loops* in product/service design to ensure the customer was actually part of it.
- Other findings included the *need for a set of competitive benchmarks for your product* (8%).

Technology

Source: practitioner interviews

Interviewees were asked to discuss the *technology* statements of the Customer Centricity Scorecard.

- 8% of practitioners *agreed* with statements on *level 1*, 25% *agreed* with the statements on *level 2*. Interviewees either *disagreed* or *did not discuss* with level 3, nobody agreed with it specifically.
- 42% of practitioners *disagreed* with statements on *level 1*, 42% *disagreed* with the statements on *level 2* and 42% disagreed with the statements on *level 3*.
- 50% of practitioners *did not discuss* statements on *level 1*, 33% did not discuss the statements on *level 2* and 58% agreed *did not discuss* the statements on *level 3*.
- These results can be seen in Figure 22.

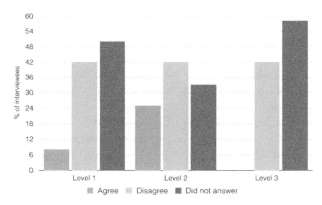

Figure 22 Results on whether practitioners agreed or disagreed with the statements on the levels of the technology layer of the Customer Centricity Scorecard

- 42% of interviewees discussed *qualitative data* being key to improving customer experience.

- 25% discussed the single view of the customer as important and 25% discussed the importance of seamlessly moving across channels.
- 25% also said that segmentation is key to delivering customer experience.
- *Personalisation* was also common discussion with 25% saying it was *essential* and 8% saying it was *powerful*. However 8% also said that personalisation was *expensive*.
- As with the other layers of the Framework, *agility* was described as being key to technology and customer experience delivery (8%).

Customer

Source: practitioner interviews

Interviewees were asked to discuss the *customer* statements of the Customer Centricity Scorecard.

- 8% of practitioners *agreed* with statements on *level 1*, 8% *agreed* with the statements on *level 2* and 33% agreed with the statements on *level 3*.
- 33% of practitioners *disagreed* with statements on *level 1*, 8% *disagreed* with the statements on *level 2* and 25% disagreed with the statements on *level 3*.
- 59% of practitioners *did not discuss* statements on *level 1*, 84% did not discuss the statements on *level 2* and 42% *did not discuss* the statements on *level 3*.
- These results can be seen in Figure 23.

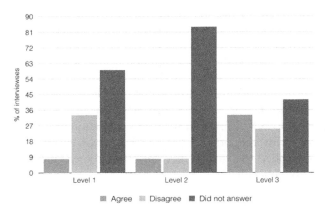

Figure 23 Results on whether practitioners agreed or disagreed with the statements on the levels of the technology layer of the Customer Centricity Scorecard

- 42% of the interviewees discussed the importance of emotional engagement with the customer. 8% discussed branding as being where the emotional connection is made.
- 8% also thought that loyalty was missing from the customer statements.

Evaluation

Source: practitioner interviews

- 58% of the interviews felt 3 levels are not enough to be able to get enough information for giving differentiation in the results of the scorecard. The main suggestions about the levels are:
  - Extra levels
  - Additional statements in each level to give further diagnosis and differentiation
  - More nuance in the statements to give deeper insight
- There was discussion in the interviews as to whether different industries would need different scorecards and models with 42% of those interviewed saying there that would be.
- 33% of interviewees thought that the use of *levels worked well* in the scorecard and that it made sense to use them. 17% of interviewees felt that the *levels do not work*. 17% also suggested that the *ranking system needed changing*.

Discussion

To answer the question and meet the objectives, *exploratory* and *evaluative* research was carried out (Saunders et al. 2011). The *exploratory* research, which included questions in both the practitioner interviews and the customer survey, was to investigate and explore the first three objectives. The *evaluative* research, which was only carried out with the practitioners, was designed to investigate objective for the development of a framework and scorecard. The findings of both types of research were then brought together to answer the research question.

The Relevancy of Customer Centricity

Research type: exploratory

It is important to establish that customer centricity is relevant for practitioners and customers. The findings show that it is. Practitioners say there has *been an increase in customer experience being talked about both internally and externally.* They also largely agreed that *companies expect to compete mostly on the basis of customer experience* (Sorofman, 2013) (as seen in Appendix I). The findings of the customer survey show the importance of customer experience in purchasing decisions.

What is key is the discovery of how much of a consideration customer experience is for repeat purchasing. The findings suggest customer experience is an important part of customer acquisition, but it plays a stronger role in customer retention. Barnes (2011) says *"it is clearly more productive for a business to encourage its customers to come back and do business with it over and over again rather than having to deal with customer churn"* and *"one of the objectives, therefore, in building customer relationships is to reduce customer turnover."* The results of this survey show the importance of customer experience in reducing turnover through repeat purchasing.

Defining Customer Experience

Research type: exploratory

There are 18 definitions of customer experience given by customer survey respondents and 12 different definitions by practitioners. What is clear from the research is there is as much a lack of a *"clear, commonly-held definition"* (Richardson, 2010) from those involved in customer experience as there is in the academic research. (The list of definitions from the customer survey can be seen in Appendix J: Table J1. The list of definitions from practitioner interviews can be seen in Appendix K: Table K1).

What is of interest is that the definitions fall into the same three categories as the literature (*business created, customer created* and *combination created*). There is a stronger emphasis, however, on customer experience being *business created* than seen in the academic research. There is also more weighting given to customer experience being a *physical interaction* than an *emotional experience* for both practitioners and customers.

The importance of the results is the majority of definitions of customer experience for practitioners and customers are *business created* which highlights the need for customer centricity. The organisation should be aligned to create the customer experience and focused on engagement touchpoints with customers.

Despite expectation management being a much-discussed concept in the academic research it does not seem to mean much to customers. Further investigation is needed but the findings from the customer survey would suggest as Barnes (2011) explained, that meeting expectations is a *hygiene factor* (Herzberg et al. 1959, pp.113-119). If expectations are not being met customers will not purchase from a company in the first place. They, therefore, do not see it as part of customer experience. It could also be that meeting expectations is not a natural response to this question if not already familiar with the academic research or management literature on customer experience.

Most interesting is that personalisation is often discussed in the academic research and management texts. It is considered one of the key competencies for the customer focus in delivering customer experience (Klein and Morrison, 2007). It did not, however, register in the definitions of customer experience with practitioners or customers. A *personalised experience* ranked 18th out 18 responses from customers and was not mentioned at all by practitioners. Delivering a personalised experience can be expensive in both time and money, and these results suggest it may not be an essential part of customer experience. There is a counterpoint to these findings, which is customer do not discuss personalisation because they are not aware it is happening to them. A limitation of this research is that personalisation is commonly an online service and the customer survey was limited in its digital discussion.

Key Elements of Customer Experience

Research type: exploratory
To identify what is meant by *enhanced customer experience* it was important to explore what practitioners and customers think the key elements of customer experience are.

For practitioners, *data and insight* are clearly the most important elements of customer experience. They are the most mentioned elements and also the reason 20% of the companies (Netflix, Omelette and Ocado) are given as examples of good customer experience. This matches the findings from the literature review where customer insight is referenced as one of the core requirements of customer centricity (Dougherty, 2009; Ghose 2009; Temkin et al. 2009; Barnes, 2011).

Verhoef et al. (2009) argue there are elements of customer experience organisations can control and elements that are outside of their control. The findings from the customer survey demonstrate that, for customers, most of the key elements of customer experience are *in control of the business*. This closely matches the finding that most customers believe customer experience is *business created*. It is a positive finding for businesses because the majority of elements that make up the customer experience are in their control and so can be improved. It shows, also the importance of customer centricity, to position the customer at the

centre of the organisation to ensure elements that are in control of
the business are being positioned around them.

What is also clear from the findings of the customer survey is the
importance of *customer service* and *employees*. They make up almost
half of the responses to the key elements of customer experience
and good customer experience. This emphasises the findings in the
literature review that engaged employees are essential a successful
customer centric business. (Robert and Alpert, 2010)

Failing at customer experience
Research type: exploratory
"Customer experience is not a technology problem - it's a culture
problem" (Crandell, 2016) was confirmed in both the practitioner
interviews and the customer survey. Almost half of the
respondents in the customer survey give *employees* as the main
reason for failure in customer experience. For interviewees it was a
lack of senior vision that was most responsible for failure, which
suggests that Loshin and Reifer (2013) were correct about the need
for executive involvement.

There an also an interesting finding around *promises* with
practitioners and customer discussing *not delivering on promises* as
being a reason for failure. From these results keeping your brand
promise is something that is key to customer experience success.
Payne et al. (2008) discuss the need for cross-functional alignment
in the creation and delivery of the customer promise and so it
would suggest that customer centricity is essential.

The Customer Centricity Framework and Scorecard

Research type: evaluative

The Framework

The interviewees give the framework an overall positive evaluation. There is some development needed, however, to include key areas that the practitioners feel are missing from the conceptual version.

Included in the positive evaluation are the importance of culture to a customer centric business and the inclusion of the emotional and rational elements. The key areas for development are highlighted as being the inclusion of feedback loops and the inclusion of brand. There is also a question raised by some interviewees about technology being the only touchpoint a customer has with a business.

As discussed previously the customer survey finds that employees are a key element in customer experience and are the main contributor to poor customer experience. The practitioner interviews confirmed this. It is clear a customer centric culture should be the core of a customer centric business. The visualisation of this was the purpose of positioning it at the centre of the framework and this choice was validated by the interviews.

GrØnholdt et al. (2015) citing Balakrishnan (2011, p.222) says, "*economic decision-making is 70 percent emotional and 30 percent rational*" and Berry et al. (2002) say, "*companies compete best when they combine functional and emotional benefits in their offerings.*" This emotional/rational theme was highlighted throughout the academic research and it was important to include this in the framework. This inclusion is well received and reflected on by the practitioners. It was also validated by the inclusion of emotional and rational elements of customer experience by the customer surveys.

Interviewees discuss the importance of including feedback loops in the Framework. Feedback loops are the mechanism for taking the feedback and insight from customers and being able to take action using that feedback. As Bingham (2005) *"customer insight is worthless unless it drives change that increases value"* and feedback loops are for using insight to drive change. The finding is that for the Framework to be more effective it needs to include a visualisation of feedback loops.

Brand was not included in the conceptual Framework and Scorecard and this was a clear limitation. The reason that is was not included is that existing tools and measurements exist for to measure customer experience and marketing and the Conceptual Customer Centricity Framework and Scorecard was designed to be an organisational measurement tool. This was a poor choice and one that is observed by the practitioners. The importance of brand is also highlighted in the customer survey and the interviews with the mention of *keeping promises.*

Technology being the only implied touchpoint with the customer on the framework, is a question raised by the interviewees. The question is raised is the interviews about interactions that are not through technology such retail or professional services engagement. It is not a significant finding from the interviewees. The findings from the customer survey, however, about the importance of employees in customer experience suggest that this should be considered as an addition to the Framework.

In response to the practitioner interviews the Customer Centricity Framework was further developed. It is shown in Figure 24. The *concentric zone model* (Parks et al. 1925) is retained as the basis for visualisation and culture remains at the centre. *Technology* and *product/service* have, however, been moved to *customer touchpoint layer.* The *emotion/rational* elements have been preserved. Additional elements have been added: *feedback* to visualise the customer feeding back into the framework and *brand* to the touchpoint layer.

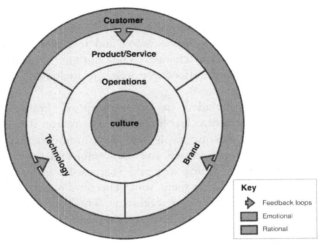

Figure 24 The Customer Centricity Framework

The Scorecard

The Customer Centricity Scorecard is the mechanism for organisations to measure their customer centricity.

The overall evaluation of the Scorecard from the practitioners is there is a need for greater differentiation between levels. If the scorecard is to be of practical use for evaluating and measuring customer centricity, and to be used as a benchmarking tool, then there is a need to have more levels and more depth to the customer centricity requirements. Further development of the Scorecard should include the addition of extra levels or further statements within each level to provide the differentiation.

There is also discussion about the use of the 1 – 10 ranking system for the statements. The findings suggest there needs to be more clarity in the intent of the ranking system so Scorecard users understand what is needed to respond.

Interviewees discussed the risk of having a three level system because level three may represent a customer centric utopia that some companies might not want to, or cannot afford to, reach.

This is linked to Galbraith (2005) concern that is *"possible to become customer centric to a fault."* This research has found that customer centric is a way to find sustainable competitive advantage and to have *"superior revenue growth."* (Manning, 20115) Customer centricity is also a way to "align a company's products with the wants and needs of its most valuable customers" (Fader, 2012) and so the customer centric level should generate a return on investment. This concern should be investigated as part of further research.

Culture

The most discussion on the statements for culture was about having a central customer experience team. This reflected the conflicts found in the academic research. There is very strong agreement that companies *"don't want to have central customer experience"* (Lorne, 2016, 29th April) and Alex (2016, 29th June) went even further in his explanation *"people having central customer experience teams, that's dangerous...if you have a central customer experience team, you're not taken customer experience seriously."* What is put forward is the idea of *a team of teams (McChrystal, Silverman, and Collins, 2015)* in which customer experience experts are placed in every team to ensure a customer focus.

Operations

The findings from the operations discussion validate its place on the scorecard however there is a lot of disagreement with the levels. This is because the level 1 requirement *we have a defined customer experience strategy* is, it was said, more advanced than the level 4 statement *we understand the customer journey.* This is interesting because in the literature the customer strategy is seen as the key to success (Berry et al. 2002; Payne and Frow, 2005; Bingham, 2009; Barnes, 2011; Peppers and Rogers, 2011). The findings from this research suggest however that this is advanced for a customer centric firm and understanding customer touchpoints is a more suitable starting level.

There is academic research that suggests for customer experience to be successful it must be made part of the business model (Thusy and Morris, 2004; Ghose, 2009; Seppanen and Laukkanen, 2015) and this is echoed in the practitioner interviews. John (2016, 23rd June) discussed specifically the need for customer experience to be fully built into the operations and not just done in silos. This suggests that customer centricity in the business model should be included in the scorecard.

Product/Service

Meyer and Schwager (2007) say, *"that the secret to a good experience isn't the multiplicity of features on offer"* and this theme was seen in the practitioner interviews. *Easy to do business* with is seen by many interviewees to be a hygiene factor (Herzberg et al. 1959, pp. 113-119). If a company were not easy to do business with then customers would not work with them. There is also a significant amount of discussion about *Apple* and *simplicity,* which agreed with Meyer and Schwager (2007). The finding is also a simplified product/service offering that is continuously developed around the needs of the customer is key to customer centricity.

The need for feedback loops is highlighted in product/service. Lorne (2016, 29th April) said there is a requirement to *"continually innovate and adapt products and service, based on working with our customer to understand their needs and to under their evolving needs"*

There is a very interesting discussion in product/service about the importance not of *meeting expectations* or *exceeding expectations* (which is delight and therefore expensive and short-lived (Barnes, 2011; Dixon et al. 2013) but *expanding expectations.* This concept links to Joseph (2016, 19th July) defining customer experience as *"providing experience that's so good that customers prefer to use them compared to any other alternative."* A customer centric organisation should not be focused on *wow* but on understanding customer goals so well that is designs product and services that become the new norm. The goal should be to *expand expectations* not just *meet expectations.*

The *need for competitive benchmarks* that is discussed also validates the concept of the Customer Centric Score. The development of the calculations model for benchmarking was beyond the scope of this research and should be an area for future research. The development of the Customer Centric Score as a potential single customer experience metric can be seen in Appendix M.

Technology

Customer centricity *"requires understanding from the demand side, so that the firm knows what each customer segment wants to buy"* (Clemons, 2008). A segmentation strategy is essential because *"not all customers are created equal"* Segmentation was not included in conceptual Customer Centricity Framework and Scorecard and this is a limitation that is discussed by practitioners. Segmentation does, however, have to customer driven and not firm driven. If it is firm driven then is risk, as Christensen et al. 2005, not matching customers desires by only catering to business created *average customers.*

Moving seamlessly between channels is the reason for 33% of companies given as examples of good customer experience and as Thusy and Morris (2004) say *"CEM is the process of managing every step of the customer experience."* With this finding the inclusion of the statement customer can move seamlessly between channels is validated. It also suggests that companies should invest in cross channel switching capabilities, if appropriate for their customers.

Personalised experience is ranked in the scorecard as being the top level 3 statement. There is an interesting finding here. The practitioners think it is *powerful* and *essential* but it is mentioned less than 1% of the time in the customer survey data. The reason for this, which needs further research, is that customers are not aware that personalisation is happening to them and, therefore, do not mention it as important. The other reason is a limitation of this research. The customer survey respondents were bias toward retail and B2C engagements. Digital engagements are not given as answers and therefore personalisation (a usually digital experience) is not mentioned. It is suitable to leave it in the Customer Centricity Scorecard as a high level goal given the importance allocated to it by practitioners.

Customer

Loyalty is a common topic in relation to customer experience. In the conceptual Customer Centricity Framework and Scorecard loyalty was included with the level 2 statement *we measure referrals from existing customers.* This was, however, discussed by the practitioners as not being the right measure for loyalty. The interview findings suggest that there should be two measures of loyalty in the Customer Centricity Scorecard. These are *advocacy* and *rewarding loyalty*. Advocacy is the measure of how much people recommend your business and rewarding loyalty is to encourage repeat business. Both of these are essential for success. This development of the scorecard to include rewarding loyalty is also validated by the results of the customer survey where *loyalty* and *reward of loyalty* were seen as key elements of customer experience.

Scorecard Development

The evaluation has been used to further develop the Customer Centricity Scorecard. Extra levels are added to reflect the need for further differentiation. The scoring mechanism is changed from a 1 – 10 scale to a 5 point Likert scale (Joshi et al. 2015) to provide clarity in the answering requirements. Statements have been moved, combined or removed to reflect the findings of the interviews. Brand is added to reflect the developed Customer Centricity Framework. It is however beyond this initial research to develop the Brand statements and this is an area for future research.

The developed Customer Centricity Scorecard is in Appendix L.

Generalisations

The results from this research are important because it has established, through exploratory research, that customer experience is relevant and its key elements are largely in the control of the business.

It also found through the evaluative research, that the Customer Centricity Framework and Scorecard is both valid and useful. The findings have been used to further develop the Customer Centricity Framework and Scorecard, which is a practical tool for the use of organisations.

Limitations

The limitations in this research are that the customer survey results are skewed towards B2C customers. This was, in part, because of the research method used and part because of the limitations of time and cost for doing the surveys. The online survey was useful for "collecting a lot of data in a short time frame" (Martin and Hannington, 2012, p.172) but there was also a cost involved in doing the survey and a decision had to be taken on types of respondents. To have survey B2C customers and B2B customer would have involved two surveys and the B2B survey would have had costly additional variables.

There is a limitation in the development of the Customer Centric Score. The objective of the research was the development of the Framework and the Scorecard but it was beyond the scope of this research to develop the calculations model to create the score. An example of the model and dashboard is given in Appendix C. Further research should, however, investigate and explore this to develop it further.

A limitation is the research was done with representatives from four industries in the practitioner groups. This was due to time and cost and future research should look to investigate further different industries and their evaluation on the Customer Centricity Framework and Scorecard. The findings showed there was concern about the cross-industry applicability of the Framework and Scorecard and further research is needed to explore this.

Conclusions

In conclusion, this research found through *exploratory* and *evaluative research* (Saunders et al. 2016) customer centricity can be effectively measured. It identified the competitive advantage of customer centricity is the relationships that it builds with customers. It is also the insight it brings, enabling product and services to be built around the needs and wants of the customer. It also found centricity customer centricity is essential for delivering the enhanced customer experience needed to develop those customer relationships.

A review of the academic literature revealed some perceived gaps in existing research. These were that research is heavily focused on customer experience, not customer centricity. It is also weighted towards customer experience as the responsibility of a marketing function. There is limited research on cross-functional alignment for the purpose of enhanced customer experience delivery. While customer experience measurement frameworks are present in the literature, there is little on the measurement of customer centricity. There is also very limited practical guidance available for organisations to use to evaluate and improve customer centricity.

The purpose of the research was to provide a practical solution for the evaluation of organisational customer centricity, and it did this through the development of The Customer Centricity Framework and Scorecard. Using an *abductive approach* (Saunders et al. 2016) existing academic research and management texts were used to develop the Framework and Scorecard and then *evaluative* research was carried out to investigate the framework with customer experience practitioners and customers.

The aim of the research was also to examine common themes in the success and failure of customer experience delivery with the goal of providing practical advice for organisations. Exploratory research was carried out in the form of a self-service online survey with customers and interviews with customer experience practitioners. The choice of mixed methods approach was for the triangulation of results for greater reliability.

The *evaluative* research resulted in 12 practitioners taking part in semi-structured interviews to evaluate the Customer Centricity Framework and Scorecard. The evaluation was positive, but there were additional elements needed for further development. They included the addition of *feedback loops, brand* and *a customer touchpoint layer to the framework*. They also included the addition of extra levels and an improved ranking system for the scorecard. The result was The Customer Centricity Framework and Scorecard, which is in Appendix L.

The *exploratory* research involved 400 people taking part in a survey and exploratory questions asked to practitioners. The findings were customer centricity is a very relevant business topic. Every interviewee has seen an increase in customer experience being discussed both internally and externally. The results of the customer survey showed customer experience is a consideration when purchasing from a company. It showed it was of increased important in repeat purchasing. It should, therefore, play a central role in retention strategy.

The exploratory research identified the key elements of customer experience. For practitioners, representing business, the key element was *data and insight*. For customers, it was *friendly or helpful service*. These findings can be used to show where potential investments should be made for improving customer experience.

Both interviewees and customers identified culture as the main reason companies fail at delivering customer experience. Practitioners cited *a lack of senior vision* as the main failure. Customers cited *employees* as the biggest cause of failure. This highlighted the need to focus on customer centricity and validates culture being at the core of The Customer Centricity Framework and Scorecard.

The *key elements* of customer experience and the *failure* of customer experience were both found to be *in the control of business* by practitioners and by customers. This is a positive finding for business as it means success and failure are in their control. That control is to be found through cross-functional alignment around the customer and through a focus on building customer relationships.

Customer centricity can be effectively measured and it can be improved for enhanced customer experience delivery and for building strong customer relationships. It should be the goal of every organisation looking for sustainable competitive advantage.

Recommendations

The recommendation for senior managers is to use the Customer Centricity Framework and Scorecard to evaluate and measure the business and to use it as a guide for where to invest to make the organisation more customer centric.

The recommendations for researchers are twofold. The first is to continue the research on the Customer Centricity Framework and Scorecard to further refine the calculations model, to explore the additional levels and statements and to investigate its cross industry applicability. The second is to investigate the results of companies using the Customer Centricity Framework and Scorecard. This future research should study if organisations that are measuring and improving their customer centricity are building strong customer relationships and finding sustainable competitive advantage.

Bibliography

Barnes, C.,Blake, H. and Pinder, D. (2009)., *Creating and Delivering Your Value Proposition.* [online].Kogan Page. Available from http://www.myilibrary.com?ID=239559 Accessed: 6 August 2016

Barnes, J.G (2011) *Cultivating the Customer Connection: A Framework for Understanding Customer Relationships* in: Peppers, D. and Rogers, M. (2011) *Managing customer relationships: A strategic framework.* 2nd edn. United Kingdom: Wiley, John & Sons

Bell, J. and Waters, S. (2014) *Doing your research project: A guide for First-Time researchers.* United Kingdom: Open University Press.

Berry, L.L, Carbone, L.P and Haeckel, S.H (2002) (2002). Managing the total customer experience. *MIT Sloan Management Review*, 43(3), pp. 85-89.

Bingham, C.N (2005) 'Hottest new title in the executive suite? Chief customer officer', *Handbook of Business Strategy*, 6(1), pp. 289–296.

Bingham,C.N (2009) "The secret weapon in building customer strategy: the Chief Customer Officer",Business Strategy Series, Vol. 10 Iss: 4, pp.183 - 192

Braun, V. and Clarke, V. (2006) Using thematic analysis in psychology. *Qualitative Research in Psychology*, 3(2), p.77–101.

Bryman, A. (2006) Integrating quantitative and qualitative research: How is it done?. Qualitative Research, 6(1), p.97–113.

Caruana, A., (2002) Service loyalty: The effects of service quality and the mediating role of customer satisfaction. *European Journal of Marketing*, 36(7), pp. 811

Chesterton, G.K in Sutherland, R. (2009, July) Rory Sutherland: Life lessons from an ad man [Video file]. Retrieved from https://www.ted.com/talks/rory_sutherland_life_lessons_from_a n_ad_man?language=en#t-962507 viewed 10th August 2016.

Christensen, C, Cook, S, & Hall, T 2005, 'MARKETING MALPRACTICE: The Cause and the Cure', *Harvard Business Review*, 83, 12, pp. 74-83, Business Source Complete, EBSCO*host*, viewed 6 August 2016.

Clemons, E.K. (2008) 'How Information Changes Consumer Behavior and How Consumer Behavior Determines Corporate Strategy', 25(2), pp. 13–40

Cooperstein, D. M. (2013) Competitive Strategy in The Age of the Customer [Online] Available from: http://solutions.forrester.com/Global/FileLib/Reports/Competiti ve_Strategy_In_The_Age_Of_The_Customer.pdf (Accessed: 11th June 2016)

Crandell, C. (2016) *Customer experience is A culture problem*. Available at: http://www.forbes.com/sites/christinecrandell/2016/05/09/cust omer-experience-is-a-culture-problem/#66b69072137e (Accessed: 26 August 2016).

Creative Research Systems (2012) *Sample size calculator - confidence level, confidence interval, sample size, population size, relevant population - creative research systems.* Available at:

http://www.surveysystem.com/sscalc.htm (Accessed: 30 August 2016).

Deloitte (2016) Target Operating Model - TOM - Elements for a successful growth [online] Deloitte. Available from http://www2.deloitte.com/lu/en/pages/strategy/solutions/target-operating-model.html (Accessed: 22nd June 2016)

Dixon, M., Toman, T., DeLisi, R., 2013. The Effortless Experience: Conquering the New Battleground for Customer Loyalty, (Amazon Kindle) London: Portfolio Penguin

Dougherty, D, & Murthy, A 2009, 'What Service Customers Really Want', *Harvard Business Review*, 87, 9, p. 22, Business Source Complete, EBSCO*host*, viewed 6 August 2016.

Duncan, E., Jones, C. Rawson. A, (2013) The Truth About Customer Experience [Online] Available from: https://hbr.org/2013/09/the-truth-about-customer-experience Accessed: 6th December 2015)

EConsultancy (2015) Customer Experience Statistics Compendium, London 2015. London: Econsultancy

EConsultancy (2016) Customer Experience Excellence Trends Briefing: Key Takeaways from Digital Cream, London 2015. London: Econsultancy
Edigitial Research. (2014) eChannel Retail Benchmark Study. Hedge End: EDigital Research

Fader, P. (2012) *Customer centricity: Focus on the right customers for strategic advantage.* 2nd edn. United States: Perseus Distribution Services.

Finn, A. (2006) 'Generalizability modeling of the foundations of customer delight', *Journal of Modelling in Management*, 1(1), pp. 18–32

Frow, P. and Payne, A., 2007. Towards the 'perfect' customer experience. *Journal of Brand Management*, 15(2), pp. 89-101.

Galbraith, J.R. (2005) *Designing the Customer-Centric Organization: A Guide to Strategy, Structure, and Process:* Available at: https://www.dawsonera.com:443/abstract/9780787979584 Accessed 13th August 2016

Gentile, C., Spiller, N. and Noci, G. (2007) 'How to sustain the customer experience:', *European Management Journal*, 25(5), pp. 395–410.

Gentile, C. Spiller, N. and Noci, G. (2007). How to Sustain the Customer Experience: An Overview of Experience Components that Co-create Value with the Customer *European Management Journal* [Online] **25** (5), pp. 395–410 [Access 18th June 2016] Available from: http://www.academia.edu/574662/How_to_Sustain_the_Custom er_Experience_An_Overview_of_Experience_Components_that_ Co-create_Value_With_the_Customer

Ghose, K. (2009) 'Internal brand equity defines customer experience', *Direct Marketing: An International Journal*, 3(3), pp. 177–185

Golding, I. (2015) *Customer service; Customer experience; Customer Centricity - what is the difference between them?* Available at: http://www.ijgolding.com/2015/11/30/customer-service-customer-experience-customer-centricity-what-is-the-difference-between-them/ (Accessed: 9 August 2016)

Goodman, J., (2014). Customer Experience 3.0. High Profit Strategies in the Age of Techno Service, (Amazon Kindle) New York: American Management Association

Grewal, D., Levy, M. and Kumar, V. (2009) 'Customer experience management in retailing: An organizing framework', *Journal of Retailing*, 85(1), pp. 1–14.

Grønholdt, L., Martensen, A., Jørgensen, S. and Jensen, P., 2015. Customer experience management and business performance. *International Journal of Quality and Service Sciences*, 7(1), pp. 90.

Hashmi, K. (2016) *Introduction and implementation of total quality management (TQM).* Available at: https://www.isixsigma.com/methodology/total-quality-management-tqm/introduction-and-implementation-total-quality-management-tqm/ (Accessed: 15 August 2016).

Herzberg, F., Mausner, B. and Snyderman, B.B. (1959) *The motivation to work.* 2nd edn. New York: John Wiley & Sons (pp.113 - 119)

Hesket, J.L., Jones, T.O., Loveman, G.W., Sasser, W.E., Schlesinger, L.A., (2008) Putting the Service Profit Chain to Work [Online] Available from: https://hbr.org/2008/07/putting-the-service-profit-chain-to-work Accessed: 6th December 2015)

Holbrook, M.B. and Hirschman, E.C. (1982) 'The Experiential Aspects of Consumption: Consumer Fantasies, Feelings, and Fun', 9(2), pp. 132–140

Hunsaker, L. (2013) *Customer-Centricity goes beyond customer experience management.* Available at: https://clearactioncx.com/customer-centricity-beyond-customer-experience-management/ (Accessed: 9 August 2016)

Joshi, A., Kale, S., Chandel, S. and Pal, D. (2015) Likert scale: Explored and explained. *British Journal of Applied Science & Technology,* 7(4), p.396–403.

King, N. (2012) Doing Template Analysis in Symon, G. and Cassell, C. (2012) *Qualitative organizational research: Core methods and current challenges.* Los Angeles: SAGE Publications, pp 426 - 450

Kirsner, S. (1999) The Customer Experience [Online] Fastcompany. Available from: http://www.fastcompany.com/56447/customer-experience (Accessed: 11th June 2016)

Klaus, P., Maklan, S. (2013) Towards a Better Measure of Customer Experience. *International Journal of Market Research*

[Online] **55** (2), pp 227 - 246 [Accessed 18th June 2016] Available
from: https://core.ac.uk/download/files/23/29409439.pdf

Klaus, P. (2015). Measuring Customer Experience: How to
Develop and Execute the Most Profitable Customer Experience
Strategies (Amazon Kindle) Hampshire: Palgrave Macmillan

Kriss, P. (2014) The value of customer experience, quantified
[Online]. Available at: https://hbr.org/2014/08/the-value-of-
customer-experience-quantified/ [Accessed: 3 August 2016].

Heinonen, K., Strandvik, T., Mickelsson, K.J, Edvardsson, B.,
Sundström E., and Andersson, P. (2010) 'A customer-dominant
logic of service', *Journal of Service Management*, 21(4), pp. 531–548.

Heinonen, K., Strandvik, T. (2015) 'Customer-dominant logic:
foundations and implications', *Journal of Services Marketing*, 29(6/7),
pp. 472–484

Laufer, D., Parrish, R. (2015) Predictions 2016: The Spotlight On
CX Helps And Hurts [Online] Forrester. Availble from
https://solutions.forrester.com/Global/FileLib/MPL_Offers/For
rester-Predictions-Spotlight-On-CX-Helps-And-Hurts.pdf
(Accessed: 18th June 2016)

Lemke, F., Clark, M. and Wilson, H. (2011) 'Customer experience
quality: an exploration in business and consumer contexts using
repertory grid technique', 39(6)

Loshin, D. and Reifer, A. (2013) *Using information to develop a culture of
customer Centricity: Customer Centricity, Analytics, and information
utilization*. United States: Morgan Kaufmann Publishers Inc

Manning, H., Bodine, K., (2012). Outside In, The Power of Putting
Customers at the Centre of your Business, Las Vegas: Amazon
Publishing

Manning, H. (2015) Better Customer Experience Correlates With
Higher Revenue Growth In Most Industries [Online]. Available at:
http://blogs.forrester.com/harley_manning/15-07-15-

better_customer_experience_correlates_with_higher_revenue_gro
wth_in_most_industries [Accessed: 3 August 2016].

Martin, B. and Hanington, B. (2012) *Universal methods of design: 100 ways to research complex problems, develop innovative ideas, and design effective solutions*. United States: Rockport Publishers.

Martin, R.L. (2010) *The age of customer capitalism*. Available at: https://hbr.org/2010/01/the-age-of-customer-capitalism (Accessed: 13 August 2016)

Mascarenhas, O.A., Kesavan, R. and Bernacchi, M. (2006) 'Lasting customer loyalty: a total customer experience approach', *Journal of Consumer Marketing*, 23(7), pp. 397–405.

McChrystal, S.A., Silverman, D. and Collins, T. (2015) *Team of teams: New rules of engagement for a complex world*. United Kingdom: Penguin Books.

Meyer, C. and Schwager, A. (2007) Understanding Customer Experience [online] HBR. Available at: https://hbr.org/2007/02/understanding-customer-experience (Accessed 18th June 2016)

Mingers, J., Mutch, A. and Willcocks, L. (2013). Critical Realism in Information Systems Research. MIS Quarterly 37 (3), p. 795 - 802

Modell, S. (2009) In defence of triangulation: A critical realist approach to mixed methods research in management account. *Management Accounting Research*, 20 (3), p. 208 - 221

Oliver, R.L., Rust, R.T. and Varki, S. (1997) 'Customer delight: Foundations, findings, and managerial insight', *Journal of Retailing*, 73(3), pp. 311–336

Osborne, P. and Ballantyne, D. (2012) 'The paradigmatic pitfalls of customer-centric marketing', *Marketing Theory*, 12(2), pp. 155–172.

Parasuraman, A., Zeithaml, V.A. and Berry, L.L. (1985) 'A conceptual model of service quality and its implications for future research', *Journal of Marketing*, 49(4), pp. 41–50.

Palmer, A. (2010) 'Customer experience management: a critical review of an emerging idea', *Journal of Services Marketing*, 24(3), pp. 196–208 http://0-www.emeraldinsight.com.wam.city.ac.uk/doi/full/10.1108/08876041011040604

Park, R.E, Burgess, E.W., (1925) *The City* London: The University of Chicago Press (p. 51)

Payne, A., Storbacka, K., Frow, P. and Knox, S. (2009) 'Co-creating brands: Diagnosing and designing the relationship experience', *Journal of Business Research*, 62(3), pp. 379–389.

Payne, A. and Frow, P. (2005) 'A Strategic Framework for Customer Relationship Management', 69(4), pp. 167–176.

Payne, A.F., Storbacka, K. and Frow, P. (2008) 'Managing the co-creation of value', 36(1), pp. 83–96.

Peelen, E., van Montfort, K., Beltman, R. and Klerkx, A. (2009) 'An empirical study into the foundations of CRM success', *Journal of Strategic Marketing*, 17(6), pp. 453–471.

Peppers, D. and Rogers, M. (2011) *Managing customer relationships: A strategic framework*. 2nd edn. United Kingdom: Wiley, John & Sons

Pine, B.J. and Gilmore, J.H. (1998) *Welcome to the experience economy*. Available at: https://hbr.org/1998/07/welcome-to-the-experience-economy (Accessed: 9 August 2016).

Prahalad, C.K. and Bettis, R.A. (1986) 'The dominant logic: A new linkage between diversity and performance', *Strategic Management Journal*, 7(6), pp. 485–501.

Ramirez, J. (2011) *7 reasons why it's never been easier to start A business*. Available at: http://www.businessinsider.com/7-reasons-why-its-never-been-easier-to-start-a-business-2011-6?IR=T (Accessed: 24 August 2016)

Reichheld, F. (2011). The Ultimate Question 2.0 (Revised and Expanded Edition): How Net Promoter Companies Thrive in a Customer-Driven World (Amazon Kindle) Boston: Harvard Business Review Press

Richardson, A. (2010) *Understanding customer experience.* Available at: https://hbr.org/2010/10/understanding-customer-experie (Accessed: 18th June 2016)

Roberts, C. and Alpert, F. (2010) 'Total customer engagement: designing and aligning key strategic elements to achieve growth', *Journal of Product & Brand Management*, 19(3), pp. 198–209.

Rowley, J. (1999) 'Measuring total customer experience in museums', *International Journal of Contemporary Hospitality Management*, 11(6), pp. 303–308

Saunders, M.N.K., Lewis P. and Thornhill, A. (2016) Research Methods for business students. 7th Edition United Kingdom: Pearson Education.

Saunders, M.N.K and Lewis, P. (2011) Doing research in business and management: An essential guide to planning your project. Harlow: FInancial Times Prentice Hall.

Schmitt, B (1999), 'Experiential Marketing', *Journal Of Marketing Management*, 15, 1-3, pp. 53-67, Business Source Complete, EBSCO*host*, viewed 14 August 2016.

Schmitt, B.H. (2003) *The customer experience management: A revolutionary approach to connecting with your customers.* New York: Wiley, John & Sons.

Schunck, O., Quiring, K., Wollan, R. (2015) 2015 B2B Customer Experience Research Findings. [Online]. Accenture. Available from: https://www.accenture.com/t00010101T000000__w__/gb-en/_acnmedia/Accenture/Conversion-

Assets/DotCom/Documents/Global/PDF/Industries_18/Accent
ure-Strategy-B2B-Customer-Experience-2015-Research-
Report.pdf#zoom=50 (Accessed 18th June 2016)

Seldon,L. and Colvin, G. (2003) *M&A Needn't be a loser's game.*
Available at: https://hbr.org/2003/06/ma-neednt-be-a-losers-
game (Accessed: 16 August 2016)

Seppanen, M. and Laukkanen, I. (2015) 'Business model
innovation: Focus on customer experience', *2015 IEEE
International Conference on Engineering, Technology and Innovation/
International Technology Management Conference (ICE/ITMC)*

Shah, D., Rust, R.T., Parasuraman, A., Staelin, R. and Day, G.S.
(2006) 'The path to customer Centricity', *Journal of Service Research*,
9(2), pp. 113–124.

Shaw, C. and Ivens, J. (2002) *Building great customer experiences.*
Houndmills, Basingstoke, Hampshire: Palgrave Macmillan.
Available   at:
http://www.palgraveconnect.com/pc/doifinder/view/10.1057/97
80230554719 (Accessed: 9 August 2016)

Shaw, C. and Ivens, J. (2004) *Building great customer experiences.*
Basingstoke: Palgrave Macmillan (p. xix)

Shaw, C., Dibeehi, Q. and Walden S. (September 2010). *Customer
Experience.* [Online] Available at: http://0-
www.palgraveconnect.com.wam.city.ac.uk/pc/doifinder/10.1057/
9780230291775. (Accessed: 8 August 2016)

Sorofman, J. (2014) Gartner Survey confirms customer experience
is the new battleground) [Online] Gartner. Available at
http://blogs.gartner.com/jake-sorofman/gartner-surveys-confirm-
customer-experience-new-battlefield (Accessed: 18th June 2016)

Starkey, K. and Madan, P. (2001) Bridging the relevance gap.:
Aligning stakeholders in the future of management
research. British Journal of Management, 12 (s1), p. S3 - S26

Sultana, N. (2008) 'Achieving Customer Satisfaction through Customer Experience Management', *CMRD JOURNAL OF MANAGEMENT RESEARCH*, 7(1), pp. 59–63

Tashakkori, A., Teddlie, C. (2010) Putting the human touch back in human research methodology: The researcher in mixed methods research. Journal of Mixed Methods Research, 4 (4), p.271 - 277

Teixeira, J. Patrício, L., Nunes, N.J, Nóbrega, L., Fisk, R.P. and Constantine, L. (2012) 'Customer experience modeling: from customer experience to service design', *Journal of Service Management*, 23(3), pp. 362–376.

Temkin, B., (2009). 7 Keys to Customer Experience. *Customer Relationship Management*, 13(12), pp. 12.

Sorofman, J. and Thompson, E., (2015) Customer Experience is the new competitive battleground [Online] Gartner. Available at https://www.gartner.com/doc/3069817?refval=&pcp=mpe (Accessed: 18th June 2016)

Thusy, A. and Morris, L. (2004) *From CRM to Customer Experience: A new realm for innovation.* Available at: http://innovationlabs.com/CRM_to_CEM.pdf (Accessed: 9 August 2016)

Tranfield, D. and Starkey, K. (1998) The nature, social organisation and promotion of management research: Towards policy. British Journal of Management, 9 (4), p.341 - 353)

Trickett, R. (2016) Interview on the Customer Experience Operating Model with G. Evans, 23rd August.

Underhill, P., 2009. Why We Buy: The Science of Shopping, New York: Simon and Schuster Paperbacks

Vandermerwe, S. (March 2014). *Introduction in Breaking Through*, 2nd Edition pp.1–14. [Online] Available at: http://0-www.palgraveconnect.com.wam.city.ac.uk/pc/doifinder/10.1057/9781137395511.0006. (Accessed: 9 August 2016).

Vargo, S.L. and Lusch, R.F. (2004) 'Evolving to a New Dominant Logic for Marketing', 68(1), pp. 1–17.

Verhoef, P.C., Lemon, K.N., Parasuraman, A., Roggeveen, A., Tsiros, M., Schlesinger, L.A., (2009) Customer Experience Creation: Determinants, Dynamics and Management Strategies. *Journal of Retailing* [Online] **85** (1), pp.31-41 [Access 18th June 2016] Available   from https://www.rug.nl/staff/p.c.verhoef/jr_customer_experience.pdf

Watkinson, M., 2013. The Ten Principles Behind Great Customer Experiences, (Amazon Kindle) Harlow: Pearson Education

Woodruff, R.B. (1997) 'Customer value: The next source for competitive advantage', 25(2), pp. 139–153. http://0-link.springer.com.wam.city.ac.uk/article/10.1007/BF02894350

Zink, K.J. (2007) 'From total quality management to corporate sustainability based on a stakeholder management', *Journal of Management History*, 13(4), pp. 394–401.

Appendix A - Definitions of Customer Experience from the Literature research

Table A1: Definitions, sources and key quotes from the literature research

Definition of Customer Experience	Sources	Key Quotes
Customer experience is all moments of direct contact between a business and a customer	(Barnes, 2011) (Grewal et al, 2009) (Kirsner, 1999) (Thompson, 2015) (Watkinson, 2013)	"every interaction with a company or brand is an experience, whether it involves face-to-face contact with employees, telephone interaction with a call center, visits to the Web site, or actual use of the product" (Barnes, 2011) "Customer experience includes every point of contact at which the customer interacts with the business, product, or service" (Grewal et al, 2009) "the sum total of the interactions that a

		customer has with a company's products, people, and processes" (Kirsner, 1999) "In other words, the customer experience is the sum of all branded interactions, pre- and post-sale" (Thompson, 2015) "The customer experience is the qualitative aspect of any interaction that an individual has with a business, its products or services, at any point in time" (Watkinson, 2013)
Customer experience is all moments of direct contact AND indirect contact	(Verhoef et al, 2009) (Meyer and Schwager, 2007) (Lemke et al, 2011) (Klaus & Maklan, 2013)	the customer experience construct is holistic in nature and involves the customer's cognitive, affective, emotional, social and physical responses to the retailer. This experience is created not only by those elements which the retailer can control (e.g., service interface, retail atmosphere, assortment, price), but also by elements that are outside of

		the retailer's control (e.g., influence of others, purpose of shopping). Additionally, we submit that the customer experience encompasses the total experience, including the search, purchase, consumption, and after-sale phases of the experience, and may involve multiple retail channels (Verhoef et al, 2009) Customer experience is the internal and subjective response customers have to any direct or indirect contact with a company. (Meyer and Schwager, 2007) the customer's subjective response to the holistic direct and indirect encounter with the firm, and customer experience quality as its perceived excellence or superiority (Lemke et al, 2011) Customer experience, unlike customer

		satisfaction, measures a more holistic consumer construct by taking into account the sum of all direct and indirect interactions with a service provider providing both better explanatory power and identification of priority areas for managerial attention (Klaus & Maklan, 2013)
Customer experience is an emotional response	(Shaw et al, 2010) (Payne et al, 2008)	A Customer Experience is an interaction between an organization and a customer as perceived through a customer's conscious and subconscious mind. It is a blend of an organization's rational performance, the senses stimulated and emotions evoked, and intuitively measured against customer expectations across all moments of contact (Shaw et al, 2010)

		The customer's experience of a supplier and its products is a culmination of the customer's cognitions, emotions and behavior during the relationship (Payne et al, 2008)
Customer experience is not just the physical interaction the product, service or brand but also the customer's emotional response to the interaction	(Shaw and Ivens, 2002) (Verhoef et al, 2009) (Mascarenhas et al, 2006) (Econsultancy, 2015) Gentile, Spiller and Noci (2007, p397) (Manning & Bodine, 2012, p.7) (Lemke et al, 2011)	"The customer experience is a blend of a company's physical performance and the emotions evoked" (Shaw and Ivens, 2002) "the customer experience construct is holistic in nature and involves the customer's cognitive, affective, emotional, social and physical responses" (Verhoef et al, 2009) "the customer experience process as a blend of the physical, emotional and value aspects of the search, purchase, use and post-use stages" (Mascarenhas et al, 2006) "the sum of all the experiences a customer has with a business during their

		entire lifetime relationship, taking in not just the key touchpoints (product awareness, social contact, the transaction itself, post purchase feedback) but also how personal and memorable these experiences are" (Econsultancy, 2015) "This experience is strictly personal and implies the customer's involvement at different levels (rational, emotional, sensorial, physical, and spiritual)" Gentile, Spiller and Noci (2007, p397) "what products and services your company offers, how you managing your business, and what your brand stands for. It's what your customers think happened when they tried to learn about and evaluate your product, tried to buy it, tried to use it, and maybe tried to get help with a problem. What's more, it's how they felt about

		those interactions: excited, happy, and reassured, or nervous, disappointed and frustrated" Manning & Bodine (2012, p.7) the customer's subjective response to the holistic direct and indirect encounter with the firm, and customer experience quality as its perceived excellence or superiority (Lemke et al, 2011)
Customer experience every touchpoint a customer has with an organisation	(Meyer and Schwager, 2007)	Customer experience encompasses every aspect of a company's offering—the quality of customer care, of course, but also advertising, packaging, product and service features, ease of use, and reliability. (Meyer and Schwager, 2007)
Customer experience is whether expectations are met (or not)	(Shaw and Ivens, 2002) (Shaw et al, 2010)	"intuitively measured against customer expectations across all moments of contact" (Shaw and Ivens, 2002)

Customer experience is not just transactional. It is over the lifetime of being a customer	(Richardson, 2010) Econsultancy (2015)	"the sum-totality of how customers engage with your company and brand, not just in a snapshot in time, but throughout the entire arc of being a customer" Richardson (2010) "the sum of all the experiences a customer has with a business during their entire lifetime relationship, taking in not just the key touchpoints (product awareness, social contact, the transaction itself, post purchase feedback) but also how personal and memorable these experiences are" Econsultancy (2015)
Customer experience is the engagement between customer and brand at each stage of the sales - pre, during and post	(Verhoef et al, 2009) (GrØnholdt et al, 2015) (Thompson, 2015)	Additionally, we submit that the customer experience encompasses the total experience, including the search, purchase, consumption, and after-sale phases of the experience, and may involve multiple retail channels (Verhoef et al, 2009)

		experiences include product and service experiences during the customer's product search in the pre-purchase phase (decision process), purchase phase, use and post-use phase. (GrØnholdt et al 2015) In other words, the customer experience is the sum of all branded interactions, pre- and post-sale (Thompson, 2015)
Customer experience is what it is like to be a customer	(Weill and Woerner, 2013)	"The customer experience embodies what it's like to be a digital customer of your organization, whether buying digital or physical products." (Weill and Woerner, 2013)
Customer experience includes external influences on the customer, it is not all brand driven.	(Verhoef et al, 2009)	the customer experience construct is holistic in nature and involves the customer's cognitive, affective, emotional, social and physical responses to the retailer. This experience is created not only by those elements which the

		retailer can control (e.g., service interface, retail atmosphere, assortment, price), but also by elements that are outside of the retailer's control (e.g., influence of others, purpose of shopping). Additionally, we submit that the customer experience encompasses the total experience, including the search, purchase, consumption, and after-sale phases of the experience, and may involve multiple retail channels (Verhoef et al, 2009)
Customer Experience is a memorable event (*experience economy - Pine and Gilmore*)	(Pine and Gilmore, 1998) (Econsultancy, 2015)	An experience occurs when a company intentionally uses services as the stage, and goods as props, to engage individual customers in a way that creates a memorable event (Pine and Gilmore, 1998) "the sum of all the experiences a customer has with a

		business during their entire lifetime relationship, taking in not just the key touchpoints (product awareness, social contact, the transaction itself, post purchase feedback) but also how personal and memorable these experiences are" (Econsultancy, 2015)
Customer Experience is how the customer *perceives* the interaction	(Shaw et al, 2010) (Meyer and Schwager, 2007) (Ghose, 2009) (Lemke et al, 2011)	A Customer Experience is an interaction between an organization and a customer as perceived through a customer's conscious and subconscious mind. It is a blend of an organization's rational performance, the senses stimulated and emotions evoked, and intuitively measured against customer expectations across all moments of contact (Shaw et al, 2010) Customer experience is the internal and subjective response customers have to any direct or indirect contact with a

		company. (Meyer and Schwager, 2007) "the user's interpretation of his or her total interaction with the brand' <Ghose, 2009> the customer's subjective response to the holistic direct and indirect encounter with the firm, and customer experience quality as its perceived excellence or superiority (Lemke et al, 2011)
Customer experience is inside out - it is the company designing an engagement/product/service with the individual	(Pine and Gilmore, 1998)	An experience occurs when a company intentionally uses services as the stage, and goods as props, to engage individual customers in a way that creates a memorable event (Pine and Gilmore, 1998)
Customer experience is holistic	(Verhoef et al, 2009) (Lemke et al, 2011) (Klaus & Maklan, 2013)	the customer experience construct is holistic in nature and involves the customer's cognitive, affective, emotional,

		social and physical responses to the retailer. This experience is created not only by those elements which the retailer can control (e.g., service interface, retail atmosphere, assortment, price), but also by elements that are outside of the retailer's control (e.g., influence of others, purpose of shopping). Additionally, we submit that the customer experience encompasses the total experience, including the search, purchase, consumption, and after-sale phases of the experience, and may involve multiple retail channels (Verhoef et al, 2009)

the customer's subjective response to the holistic direct and indirect encounter with the firm, and customer experience quality as its perceived excellence or superiority (Lemke et al, 2011) |

		Customer experience, unlike customer satisfaction, measures a more holistic consumer construct by taking into account the sum of all direct and indirect interactions with a service provider providing both better explanatory power and identification of priority areas for managerial attention (Klaus & Maklan, 2013)
Customer experience is your product and service as well as how you manage the organisation	(Kirsner, 1999) (Manning & Bodine, 2012, p.7)	"the sum total of the interactions that a customer has with a company's products, people, and processes"(Kirsner, 1999) "what products and services your company offers, how you managing your business, and what your brand stands for. It's what your customers think happened when they tried to learn about and evaluate your product, tried to buy it, tried to use it, and

		maybe tried to get help with a problem. What's more, it's how they felt about those interactions: excited, happy, and reassured, or nervous, disappointed and frustrated" Manning & Bodine (2012, p.7)
Customer Experience is defined as the next level development of customer relationships	(Gentile et al, 2007)	an evolution of the concept of relationship between the company and the customer (Gentile et al, 2007)

Table A2: - Summary of customer experience definitions and the creation themes

Definition of Customer Experience	Sources	Theme
All moments of direct contact between a business and a customer	Kirsner, 1999; Grewal et al. 2009; Barnes, 2011; Watkinson, 2013;	Business created
All moments of direct contact AND indirect contact	Meyer and Schwager, 2007; Verhoef et al. 2009; Lemke et al. 2011; Klaus & Maklan, 2013	Combination
An emotional response	Payne et al. 2008; Shaw et al. 2010	Customer created
The physical interaction with the product, service or brand and the customer's emotional response to the interaction	Shaw and Ivens, 2002; Mascarenhas et al. 2006; Gentile, Spiller and Noci 2007; Verhoef et al. 2009; Lemke et al. 2011; Manning & Bodine, 2012; Econsultancy, 2015	Combination
Every touchpoint a customer has with an organisation	Meyer and Schwager, 2007	Business created
Whether expectations are met (or not)	Shaw and Ivens, 2002; Shaw et al. 2010; Thompson, 2015	Combination
Not just transactional. It is over the lifetime of being a customer	Richardson, 2010; Econsultancy 2015	Combination
The engagement between customer	Verhoef et al. 2009; GrØnholdt et al. 2015;	Combination

and brand at each stage of the sales - pre, during and post	Thompson, 2015	
Is what it is like to be a customer	Weill and Woerner, 2013	Customer created
Includes external influences on the customer, it is not all brand driven.	Verhoef et al. 2009	Combination
How the customer perceives the interaction	Meyer and Schwager, 2007; Ghose, 2009; Shaw et al. 2010; Lemke et al. 2011	Customer created
Holistic	Verhoef et al. 2009; Lemke et al. 2011; Klaus & Maklan, 2013	Combination
A company's product, service and organisational management	Kirsner, 1999; Manning & Bodine, 2012;	Business created

Appendix B - Research Philosophy

Table B1 Summary of research philosophies used

Research Philosophy	View
Ontology	Realist (Mingers, 2013)
Epistemology	Interpretivist (Easton, 2007)
Axiology	Subjectivist (Saunders et al. 1997)
Human Nature	Mixed (Burrell and Morgan ,1979)
Methodology	Ideographic (Burrell and Morgan, 1979)
Research Paradigm	Functionalist (Burrell and Morgan 1979)
Research Philosophy	Critical Realist (Saunder et al. 1997)

The above summary table shows why a critical realist (Saunders et al. 1997) philosophy is the most appropriate philosophy for this paper and for understanding the choices of research methods and design.

With an abductive approach and because the *"research is concerned not only with knowing what, but goes beyond this to consider questions associated with knowing how"* (Tranfield and Starkey, 1998) it adopts a *critical realist* (Saunders et al. 1997) research philosophy.

This was chosen because customer experience is not *"one true social reality experienced by all social actors"* (Saunders et al. 1997) which is an objectivist view but neither is there *"no underlying reality to the social world beyond what people attribute to it"*, which is an extreme subjectivist view. Critical realism *"begins with some accepted phenomenon and asks what the world must be like for this to occur"* (Mingers, 2013). In this research customer experience is the accepted phenomenon and research objectives are to understand what must be in place for it to occur.

"Critical realists propose an ontology that assumes that there exists a reality 'out there' independent of observers" (Easton, 2007) and this *realist* (Mingers, 2013) stance is adopted in this research. Customer

experience can be considered real. not because it has a physical form but because it *"makes a difference to people's actions"* (Fleetwood, 2005) and *"for critical realists, an entity is said to be real if it has causal efficacy: has an effect on behaviour, makes a difference"* (Fleetwood, 2005).

With this understanding of customer experience it would then be appropriate to use Bhaskar's (1978) *"structured and layered ontology"* (as cited in Saunder et al. 1997) and what Easton (1997) refers to as a *"world [that] is differentiated and stratified, consisting not only of events, but objects, including structures, which have powers and liabilities capable of generating events."*

In this there are *"the domains of the real. the actual. and the empirical. The real contains mechanisms, events, and experiences; the actual consists of events that do (or perhaps do not) occur and includes the empirical. those events that are observed or experienced."* (Mingers 2013)

The layers can be ascribed to customer experience.

- The Real - Is customer centricity
- The Actual - Is customer experience
- The Empirical - Is the customer's response to customer experience

These can then be used in the research design as the layers with which to explore and measure to answer the research question.

The epistemology of critical realism is also one that is in neither the objectivist or subjectivist extreme but one that rather one of *interpretivism* (Easton, 2007) and *relativism* (Saunder et al. 1997). This research looks to define customer experience and customer centricity and then create a measurement of these and therfore the interpretivist epistemological stance is appropriate for this as *"interpretive researchers assume that access to reality...is only through social constructions such as language, consciousness, shared meanings, and instruments "* (Myers, 2008).

Saunders et al. (1997) say that *"epistemological relativism recognises the knowledge is historically situated (in other words, it is a product of its time and specific to it)"* and they cite Reed (2005) saying *"this implies that critical realist of causality cannot be reduced to statistical correlation and quantitative methods, and that a range of methods is acceptable"* (Saunders et al. 1997)

The *axiological* position of this paper is *subjectivist* because as a researcher that is experienced in customer experience design and delivery it is to an extent unavoidable that the choice of methodologies and philosophies are *"a reflection of [the researcher's] values"*. (Saunder et al. 1997).

According to Burrell and Morgan (1979) there exists two notions, that of the *"sociology of regulation"* (regulation) and that of the *"sociology of radical change"* (radical change) . Regulation is concerned with providing *"explanations of society in terms which emphasise its underlying unity and cohesiveness"* whereas radical change concern is *"to find explanations for the radical change, deep-seated structural conflict, modes of domination and structural contradiction"*. Because this paper seeks to find measurement of customer centricity and a framework with which to measure it, it therefore suggests a regulatory approach.

Whilst the critical realist philosophy that underpins the research is neither fully objectivist or subjectivist in an extreme it does *"assume that there is a real world out there"* (Easton, 2007) which itself sites closer to an objectivist view of the world than the fully subjective. Therefore, and because of the aims of this research, the research paradigm that will be adopted will be that of functionalist (Burrell and Morgan,1979). Functionalism *"is characterised by a concern for providing explanations of the status quo, social order. consensus. social interaction, solidarity, need satisfaction and actuality"* and *"its overall approach it seeks to provide essentially rational explanations of social affairs"* (Burrell and Morgan, 1979) and this paradigm is a good description of the aim of this research which is understand measurement (rational) of customer experience (social/emotional).

The views *human-nature* are mixed and this paper takes an *"intermediate standpoint which allows for the influence of both situational and voluntary factors in accounting for the activities of human beings"* (Burrell and Morgan, 1979)

The methodology appropriate for this study is a *ideographic* approach (Burrell and Morgan, 1979). Given the researcher's experience in customer experience *"the generalisations derived from experience are dependent, upon the researcher, his or her methods and the interactions with the subject of study"* (Myers, 2008).

Appendix C - Customer Centricity Scorecard - Model and Dashboard

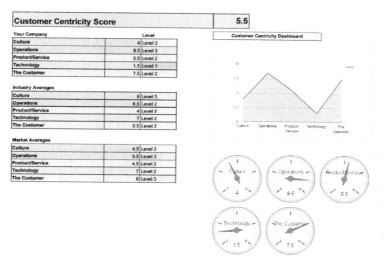

Figure C1: The customer centricity scorecard results dashboard

Questionaire

Score	1	2	3	4	5	6	7	8	9	10
Culture										
Customer Experience is a company value										10
A Senior Person is responsible for Customer Experience									9	
We have a central customer experience team				4						
We empower staff to make decisions in the best interest of the customer		2								
Training, recruitment, and human resources development are guided by the CX strategy			3							
Customer Experience is linked to company incentives		3								
Operations										
We have a defined customer experience strategy			3							
We measure customer satisfaction		2					7			
We listen to the customer								8		
We understand the customer experience journey							7			
We measure customer experience									9	
We are easy to do business with										10
Product/Service										
We understand the expectations of our customers	1									
We have a complex product/service offering		2								
We are able to the serve the customer in the way they want			3							
We deliver our service as our customers expect				4						
We are interested in the well being of our customers							7			
We understand the value of our customers									9	
Technology										
We can track our customers across multiple channels						5				
We can collect and analyse customer data from all touchpoints				4						
We can collect qualitative feedback from our customers		2								
We can deliver a consistent experience across multiple channels										
Customers can move seamlessly between channels	1									
We can offer a personalised customer experience	1									
The Customer										
Our customers understand our values	1									
We understand what our customers intend to do			3							
We measure referrals from existing customers							7			
We manage the expectations of our customers							7			
Customers enjoy using our service									9	
We measure emotional engagement with our customer										10

Figure C2: An example results sheet from the Customer Centricity Scorecard

Weightings

Culture	Level	Score
Customer Exper	Level 1	2
A Senior Perso	Level 1	4
We have a cent	Level 2	6
We empower st	Level 2	8
Training, recruit	Level 3	10
Customer Exper	Level 3	12

Operations	Level	Score
We have a defin	Level 1	2
We measure cu	Level 1	4
We listen to the	Level 2	6
We understand	Level 2	8
We measure cu	Level 3	10
We are easy to	Level 3	12

Product/Servic	Level	Score
We understand	Level 1	2
We have a com	Level 1	4
We are able to t	Level 2	6
We deliver our s	Level 2	8
We are interest	Level 3	10
We understand	Level 3	12

Technology	Level	Score
We can track ou	Level 1	2
We can collect	Level 1	4
We can collect	Level 2	6
We can deliver	Level 2	8
Customers can	Level 3	10
We can offer a	Level 3	12

The Customer	Level	Score
Our customers	Level 1	2
We understand	Level 1	4
We measure refe	Level 2	6
We manage the	Level 2	8
Customers enjo	Level 3	10
We measure e	Level 3	12

Figure C3: Examples level weightings from the Customer Centricity Scorecard weightings model

Points by Level

Culture	Level	Score	Weighted Score
Customer Exper	Level 1	10	20
A Senior Persu	Level 1	9	36
We have a cens	Level 2	4	24
We empower st	Level 2	2	16
Training, recrui	Level 3	3	30
Customer Exper	Level 3	3	36

Operations	Level	Score	Weighted Scor
We have a defin	Level 1	3	6
We measure cu	Level 1	9	36
We listen to the	Level 2	8	48
We understand	Level 2	7	56
We measure cu	Level 3	9	90
We are easy to	Level 3	10	120

Product/Servic	Level	Score	Weighted Score
We understand	Level 1	1	2
We have a core	Level 1	2	8
We are able to	Level 2	3	18
We deliver our s	Level 2	4	32
We are interest	Level 3	7	70
We understand	Level 3	9	108

Technology	Level	Score	Weighted Score
We can track cu	Level 1	5	10
We can collect	Level 1	4	16
We can collect	Level 2	2	12
We can deliver	Level 2	0	0
Customers can	Level 3	1	10
We can offer a	Level 3	1	12

The Customer	Level	Score	Weighted Score
Our customers	Level 1	1	2
We understand	Level 1	3	12
We measure rele	Level 2	7	42
We manage the	Level 2	7	56
Customers enjo	Level 3	9	90
We measure e	Level 3	10	120

Total Points by Level

Culture	
Level 1	56
Level 2	40
Level 3	66
Total	162
Operations	
Level 1	42
Level 2	104
Level 3	210
Total	356
Product/Service	
Level 1	10
Level 2	50
Level 3	178
Total	238
Technology	
Level 1	26
Level 2	12
Level 3	22
Total	60
The Customer	
Level 1	14
Level 2	98
Level 3	210
Total	322

Total Available Points 2080

Culture	
Level 1	60
Level 2	140
Level 3	220
Total	420
Operations	
Level 1	60
Level 2	140
Level 3	220
Total	420
Product/Service	
Level 1	60
Level 2	140
Level 3	220
Total	420
Technology	
Level 1	60
Level 2	140
Level 3	220
Total	420
The Customer	
Level 1	100
Level 2	180
Level 3	120
Total	400

			Overall %	To Numbers
Culture	162	14%	38.57%	3.86
Operations	356	31%	84.76%	8.48
Product/Servic	238	21%	56.67%	5.67
Technology	60	5%	14.29%	1.43
The Customer	322	28%	76.67%	7.67
Total	1138	100%	55%	5.47

Culture		
Level 1	56	35%
Level 2	40	25%
Level 3	66	41%

Operations		
Level 1	42	12%
Level 2	104	29%
Level 3	210	59%

Product/Service		
Level 1	10	4%
Level 2	50	21%
Level 3	178	75%

Technology		
Level 1	26	43%
Level 2	12	20%
Level 3	22	37%

The Customer		
Level 1	14	4%
Level 2	98	30%
Level 3	210	65%

Figure C4: Example calculations for the Customer Centricity Scorecard

Appendix D - Practitioner Interview Questions

Question Topic: Background

- *Question 1:* What is your name?
- *Question 2:* What company do you work for?
- *Question 3:* What is your job title?
- *Question 4:* What are you responsible for?

Question Topic: Customer Experience

- *Question 5:* What does "customer experience" mean to you?
- *Question 6:* Have you seen an increase in customer experience being discussed both internally and with your customers?
- *Question 7:* What do you consider to be the key elements of delivering customer experience?
- *Question 8:* Could you give some examples of companies you think are delivering good customer experience?
- *Question 9:* Where do you see companies most often failing when delivering customer experience?
- *Question 10:* A recent Gartner survey on the role of marketing in customer experience found that, by 2016, 89% of companies expect to compete mostly on the basis of customer experience, versus 36% four years ago - What are your thoughts on this?
- *Question 11:* According to the same Gartner research, fewer than half of companies see their customer experience capabilities as superior to their peers—but two-thirds expect these capabilities to be industry leading or much more successful than their peers within five years - How do you feel about this?
-

Question Topic: The Customer Centricity Framework and Scorecard

- *Question 12:* Could you please give me your feedback on this framework
- *Question 13:* How useful is the framework ?
- *Question 14:* What would you change?
- *Question 15:* What was missing?
- *Question 16:* Any other thoughts or recommendations?

Appendix E - Reproducibility

The interpretative nature of the results from the qualitative methods could make the exact results harder to reproduce. However, this study could be reproduced using the following steps.

1. Use groups identified in the Customer Experience Operating Model and select senior level interviewees responsible for Customer Experience.
2. Carry out the qualitative interviews to a similar sized group of practitioners using the chosen groups from the Customer Experience Operating Model and the Customer Centricity Framework and Scorecard
3. Send customer survey out to same size sample group (384) with same demographics and same questions
4. Code the results of the practitioner interviews and customer survey for results

Appendix F - Practitioner Interview Qualitative Research Transcripts

Interview 1 - Robert

Interviewee: Robert
Interviewer: Gareth
Date and Time: 5th/March/2016
Location: London
Customer Experience Group: Producer

Robert: My name is Robert. I am head of digital for <a publishing company> where I am responsible for enabling and driving digital products services and strategy across our eleven businesses. That includes websites, ebooks, apps, audio books, games and video.

Gareth: What does customer experience mean to you in your role?

Robert: Two part answer to that. Historically, we had a poor understanding of consumer experience because it was mediated through a reseller, a bookshop generally. Over time, we've developed a new understanding of customer experience which is that there ought to be a feedback loop. We produce a product or service, it is made available to someone, they interact with it. The difference that digital brings is that they can respond to us in many ways. Whether it's actually using the service, whether it's giving us feedback on a service and we can then use that information either to retain them, for the customer in the context of software as a service, or to see them an alternative product, in the case of our consumer business. For us, good consumer experience is an experience that causes them to have that ongoing relationship with us.

Gareth: Have you seen an increase in customer experience being discussed both internally and with your customers?

Robert: Yes we have. The first thing I would say is that digital has enabled direct contact with consumers in a way that we never had before. A simple measure like, for example, quality problems on products. On print books you've got very, very few reports of quality problems even when they existed. On digital, even very trivial things are raised because it's a very easy thing to tweet or to send a Facebook message or to email or whatever other means of communication. Consumers are much more vocal. We're also increasingly aware that consumers being vocal about product online have an effect on other consumers purchasing habits. A negative consumer experience is related on, Amazon or another review site may actually hold back the sales of the product. We're very focused about getting things right first time but very importantly if something has gone wrong, which it inevitably will, remedying it as quickly as possible so we turn a poor experience into what we hope is a positive one.

Gareth: What do you consider to be the key elements of delivering customer experience?

Robert: Using consumer insight at a planning stage of the product, understanding a customer's needs, understanding a customer's lifestyle as a conceptual stage, using consumer information panels et cetera to help iterate and develop the product through its lifecycle. Then post release being able to use digital channels to gather feedback and then feed that back in. What we're ultimately trying to move to is a sort of constant improvement loop. We build something, we need to measure it, we need to learn from that data and we need to do it better than next time round. What depends on all of this is data and communication.

Gareth: Do you have any examples of companies that you think are delivering good customer experience where you've had a personal good experience with customer experience?

Robert: Yes. I would say for my world particularly Amazon is a really good example of this. The fact is, you order something, the parcel goes missing, they replace it no questions asked. They don't make you jump through hoops. The assumption is that you're an honest person and that your experience really matters. I also think in slightly different worlds, companies like Charles Tyrwhitt, the clothing manufacturer, are very focused. The fact is in the old world, you could buy something and it wouldn't quite be right and you were stuck with it. With them, you've got three months of washing and wearing and you can return something at the end of three months having worn it all of that time, if you're genuinely not happy with it.

These are companies which are really going out of their way to do it. The other one that I think is really interesting is Netflix. It feels to me that Netflix really understands my lifestyle as a consumer they understand that I'm highly mobile, that I'm not in the same place a lot. That at different times of the day, my primary device for using the Netflix might be the media center at home or a phone on the go or a tablet at the office. The same product is available across all those and when I load up a program on it, it's queued to wherever I left off on any other device. It really feels like thought has gone into the lifestyle that I have and how to create a product that's fit for it.

Gareth: The examples you've given have been very much, I guess, your experience at the end point. Do you think that there is a culture behind that in the organization that is leading to delivering that experience to you?

Robert: Absolutely. I think that there is absolutely a customer centric culture in those companies. I would say that my own company historically, did not have a customer centric culture. What we had was an intermediary centric culture. We cared a lot about the shops that we sold product to. We didn't really care who they sold product on to. That's very different from actually putting the customer first in all of these. Companies that are genuinely customer centric, are borderline obsessive about their customer. Their borderline obsessive about collected data, about analyzing it and about learning from it.

I think, there is that underlying culture of curiosity. I think most of all the management buy on you will act on what you learn. There are lots of companies where you get poor data. I think McDonalds would be a really good example of this. They get very good data and historically what they used to do was become defensive with it and not actually to iterate and improve. What they're doing now is getting hostile data and they're using it to change menus, change their positioning to the customer and that I think is an example of how a 20th century business, becomes a 21st century business.

Gareth: Where to do you see companies most failing in delivering customer experience?

Robert: I think really, there are three ... I would say three interesting points of failure. The first point of failure is, as I articulated in my company being focused on your intermediary or your trade customer. Not really understanding where the value is in the relationship. The second point of failure is either not using data or almost as bad, using data unintelligibly. We see a lot of people who collect a lot of data but they don't analyze the correct data points, or they analyze but then they don't act on it. Sitting behind all of these I think is the third point of failure, which is you can have a consumer insight on an option but actually what I think the prerequisite is an organization that acts. I think what that really requires is a strong senior level buy into it.

This doesn't work if you don't have a CEO who is obsessive about the consumer. This doesn't work if you don't have a CMO, who is empowered to act on that vision. It's very interesting that if you think of those really big consumer friendly businesses that I talked about, Charles Tyrwhitt, Amazon, Netflix, even to a lesser extent, businesses, like in food, like say, Leon or Aarons, the common denominator in all of them is they very public CEO is very focused on consumer relationships.

Gareth: Okay. I'm now going to take you through my customer experience maturity framework, and take you through steps on how I got the framework looks like and what the questionnaire looks like. I would greatly appreciate at the end of that, or even during it, give me feedback on what you're thoughts are, your changes and if it matches what you experience and see in your role.

Robert: Sure.

Gareth: I'm going to take you through my findings on the research and what that customer experience maturity index model would look like. The research that I've been doing is really been a study of customer experience. That's been through textbooks, readings, whatever about the literally part that's been out there. For now, I've identified key themes within customer experience, I've identified key topics and I've classified the topics against themes. That's created a series of questions.

Robert: Sure.

Gareth: Forrester have a customer experience permit that they have created which says that, in customer experience, you basically have three steps: meets needs, is easy and then it's enjoyable. So I come for my goal, I didn't work too hard and then I felt good about that. My argument and the reason that I've created the levels that I have is that I believe too often that companies don't particularly have a pyramid on the top and piece, which is a small section that, actually, if you look at the customer experience, it becomes unsustainable.

Too often, you hear companies saying, "We want to wow our customer. We want to be the best at customer experience. We empower our people to make any decisions to keep our customers happy." Now I would argue that that's not sustainable. It would take a call center or do anything to keep the customer and it's logical enter point is you're virtually saying, "Give them a Porsche if you keep a customer." You are saying, "Do anything."

What I'm arguing is actually consider it being based around a pyramid, it needs to be based around levels. Where level one is you are the doing the basics towards delivering customer experience, level two is that you are able to articulate and deliver a good customer experience that really the customer ... the point that you're delivering outstanding customer service is level three. Getting enough of customer experience is level three. So, if you're doing the things within this, then that's the level that you want to be aiming for.

Robert: Yeah. In lay person's terms, level one is effectively survival. Level two is transacting well and level three is actually having a relationship.

Gareth: Yeah and that's a really good way of putting it. When we talk about delivering customer experience, quite often we focus on people, process and the technology but I think that neglects the importance of an inside part of the business and the outside part which is the culture of the customer. If you weren't paying attention to your culture and making it customer centric, and your understanding your customer, the whole thing falls apart and it goes from being an emotional need to the very rational. I'll show you what that means in the framework.

I realized that the culture needs to be customer centric. That then heeds your operations that need to be focused around the customer. That then the operations allow you to deliver a customer centric product which then allows you to have a customer to place in technology, that then you deliver out to the customer. Now there is ... there should be within this model although there is now, a feedback what the customer wants and then feeding back into the culture and so on and so on.

Now, you have that emotional harp, then you go through your rational steps and you deliver to an emotional being. If you get that wrong, then you have a rational call, then you end up with a thing like a call center, where all they're doing is focused on is getting your phone as quickly as possible, not about giving you a good customer experience. From a business optimization point of view, it's a very rational focus. There's an emotional focus which would be actually understanding the human side and the things that I need to achieve.

Robert: I think what's very interesting about this is, I hate coming back to me again and again, that they're such a good example of this. If you think about Amazon, Amazon is a company has a reputation of being hyper rational, hyper data driven very much about organizing systems and doing everything as efficiently as possible. But actually, culture is never expressed in terms of that Jeff Bezos, never says in an interview, something about rationality. He frames everything in very emotional things. Kindle is not about targets for conversion.

Kindle is about any book any book ever published available in 60 seconds, anywhere in the world. That's a very emotional call for the consumer. That's something that I respond to personally as a reader. Similarly, you should think about making things easy. The Amazon actor is all about just making things really really easy. Making your life a little bit easier. It will be really for them to talk about in the hyper rational terms but actually, I think what you really care for is because there is the emotional call at the heart of a very rational business.

Gareth: Absolutely. I think as well if you look at Apple who always gets over their customer experience, so much to the point where it becomes irrelevant talking about they always want to [inaudible 00:15:06] up and you hope that there are a lot of companies that can do it better. But Apple at its core is staying different as an emotional call for action and their culture surrounds ... at least the culture that injects externally is around that I think. Something like the Samsung, actually, it's all about the makeup excellence of the latest or the edge technology and that is a very rational product.

Robert: Yeah. The fact if any consumers genuinely make purchasing decisions on rational grounds, we'd all be using Samsung kits and I can see three pieces of technology on this table and not one of them has been made by Samsung.

Gareth: It's very much the Simon Sinek selling for the wine or the bottle of the ...

Robert: Yeah. It's quite interesting. There's a great advertising case study about this. First generation console was Nintendo versus Sony PlayStation. In many respects, there was better kit than the PlayStation available. The 3DO was technically superior, some of the Nintendo kit was. What did PlayStation do? They came up with a superb advert. Do you remember the concurred worlds advert?

Gareth: No.

Robert: I sent you a link to it but it was the single most emotional piece of film making you can imagine and actually nothing else matters, that was what shifted product.

Gareth: Even now, with PlayStation 4 it's for the players. It's that whole, 'it's the emotional [inaudible 00:16:28]'.

Robert: Yeah, totally.

Gareth: Looking at this framework then, is then a series of questions that would lead to you to be able to diagnose your organization as to what is, each of these layers, what stage are you at. We've got a goal of being at level three on all of them, you should be delivering outstanding customer experience.

Robert: Got it.

Gareth: Then culture, the key things within culture are expectations setting, employee engagement, trusting your employee to meeting expectations but not relating that triangle piece, having an incentive for employees based around customer experience, customer experience being part of your company values and having CXO and management control. We can ignore the quotes, this is for a different part of the presentation, there's far too many of them. The questions in here for culture would be, customer experience has become a value as senior person's response of a customer's experience. Level two, we have a central customer experience team and we empower them to make decisions in the best interests of the customer, question point training including human resources development and is guided by strategy. Customer experience is linked to company and standards.

Robert: That feels broadly right. At level one, yeah, no disagreement whatsoever. At level three, I think I agree completely there as well. I think my question is with level two. Empowering people to make decisions in the best interest of the customer, I think does feel right, my question is whether a centric customer experience team is a prerequisite for that? Actually I think you could find examples of organizations where customer experience is proudly decentralized, but is very good. I think Timpson ... I think we did a case on Timpson, is a very good example of this. Store managers have a considerable about of autonomy in this. Actually, if you think about that business, if you're Amazon, and you can reduce all of your business down to a cent fourteen quite easily because it's 100% digital. A central team makes complete sense.

If you have 600 retail locations around the UK, and you centralize the consumer experience function, you create a bottle neck and you frustrate the customer. It's actually what I need on Saturday morning in Salisbury town center is the problem to be sorted out instantly not for it to be sent to a [inaudible 00:19:13]. I wonder whether actually, you need to reframe question three as, we have a customer experience team that is situational appropriate for our business and our business model. I think physically retail, hospitality would be hugely different to econ there, for example.

Gareth: Yeah I guess there's almost an argument there that if you have a central customer experience team you are suggesting that not everybody is responsible for customer experience, it is that customer experience team and ...

Robert: I think it's completely situational. If you think about banks, mobile phone networks, other institutions that typically interact with their consumer through a call center, the fact is that if your inquiry is sufficiently non-trivial or sufficiently serious, you get escalated very quickly, out of the call center and into a specialties retention group. Those people have better training, better initiative, and that's absolutely right. The fact is that 95% of the cases that the business addresses, the call center can handle it. For the 5%, you do need a special group. It makes complete sense for their business.

For Amazon, where everything can be done centrally, it makes complete sense to have a customer service function. Say in hospitality or retail or other sectors, I think it has to be devolved. I do feel quite strongly that that is situational dependent on your business but what I think you could do is say, from a framework point of view, is look at different sectors or different use cases and say level two in this sector means this, level two in that sector means something quite different and set some sectoral norms that you can use for bench marking. Does that make sense?

Gareth: Yeah. Thank you. Then operations. These and when I think you're moving into I guess more rational piece of strategy and measurement, outcome metrics, voice to the customer, customer journey mapping, simplification of the product, customer effort, channel switching, all of these more operational pieces. For this, you're looking at ... we have a defined customer experience strategy, we measure customer satisfaction, we listen to the customer, we understand the customer experience journey, we measure customer experience and we continue optimizing customer experience.

Robert: Yeah. I think all of those make complete sense to me. It's quite interesting. Something that I suspect you could do, and this would actually be an empirical piece of research, is to take a site like the Internet Archive Wayback machine preserves early versions of websites over time and take something like the amazon.com homepage. You'd be able to ascertain very precisely how many times per year the design or structure iterates and you could actually have an empirical calculation of how often consumer experience changes. I'm sure you would find econ sites that actually change relatively little, one change or two changes a year and you look at a site like Amazon and I suspect you'd see thirty or forty changes a year. I think if you looked at most Google products you'd see a similar level of iteration.

Gareth: I wonder if you would find that those companies that don't change very often are the ones that are actually lagging behind in both not just customer experience measures but in revenue.

Robert: It would be extremely interesting. I don't know the answer but I would intuit that that would be the case. Have you seen by the way, the Google analytics video about the e-commerce they made?

Gareth: The one with L'Oreal?

Robert: A guy walking up to the super**mark**et checkout and the cashier behaves as though it was an e-com checkout rather than a physical world checkout.

Gareth: I'll have to check it out.

Robert: I'll send you the link. It's very funny. I think all of those make complete sense and I think for five and six particularly ... and one of the key things there is not just e-measure customer experience and that you continually optimize but there is a constant feedback loop between those two. I think you can see businesses that probably measure experience and then optimize but do that separately. There isn't the loop between the two. I actually know someone and I'll have to ask his permission to introduce him to you who works for business where actually there were siloed functions, one measuring customer experience and one iterating product and the two weren't talking to one another. Actually, I think, you could almost say that a link between those two is a prerequisite.

Gareth: In product and service so ... I'm really interested in the idea of customer effort. How easy is it to use your product? How easy is it to buy your product or your service? Do you understand the expectations of a customer? Are you making it easy for them to use? Are you meeting expectations? We understand the expectations of our customers. We have a complex product service. We're offering to serve our customers in the way they want. We deliver our services our customers expect. We're easy to do business with and we understand value to our customers.

Robert: I think two observations on that. First of all I think the point about e-use is quite fundamental. Amazon patented one click ordering and that's pretty transformational. Look at Amazon dash. You've seen Amazon dash? It's a great piece of customer experience. It just works. All of that I think is absolutely right. On product and service and it actually probably relates a little to the previous area as well. I think there's a very interesting question around who are your benchmarks so for example, if you are in my world and you're a book publisher, are your benchmarks, Harper Collins and Random House and Faber & Faber or actually point at my CEO [inaudible 00:25:35] which I thought was very astute but actually know those are the three wrong benchmarks to be using.

The benchmarks we use are Netflix and Bing and YouTube because they're three successful businesses who are competing fundamentally for the same thing as us. Consumer attention. They are not only doing that really well and absolutely killing it but they're also sufficiently large and sufficiently influential that they set a consumer expectation around what good looks like. Actually if you are in content delivery, if you're in retail banking, if you're in delivering take away food online, Netflix is a really good example of what you ought to look at in all sorts of areas so I would say having a broad set of competitive bench**mark**s and taking a broad definition of what good looks like is quite a good positive indicator of excellence.

Gareth: Interesting. How would you phrase that as a question for [inaudible 00:26:34]? Do you compare?

Robert: I don't know the exact structure of your survey so you'll have to tinker with this. I think my first question would be, do you regularly and systematically bench**mark** your experience versus third parties? Follow up question, are those third parties primarily in your immediate competitive set or peer group or are they the best of the best of online services that people use? Something along those lines.

Gareth: Interesting. Technology, say, this is all around segmentation, self service, different touch points, multichannel, MPS measurements, using surveys, voice of the customer so we can track all our customers across multiple channels, we can collect and analyze customer data from touch points. We can collect qualitative feedback from our customers, we can deliver a consistent experience across multiple channels, customers can move seamlessly between channels and we can offer personalized customer experience.

Robert: Yeah, absolutely. Interesting within my own business one of the key things this year is a strategic theme is the single customer view. The idea that we can take disparate data sources and identify use and individual across all of them and respond to it so I think that's absolutely right. It's interesting that in question three you specifically say qualitative feedback as well as quantitative. I think actually the financial times are really good about this, because they have a quite fragmented product base. They're maintaining different platforms, different sorts of services and actually as a consumer, I relatively often will get a survey from them, which generally comes in a very sensitive way. It's "We've got three questions that will take two minutes. Would you be prepared to answer them?" Which actually I feel quite inclined to respond to and actually being able to say something qualitative about it feels much better than them just mining my data and trying to get insight from me.

Consistent experience is an interesting one, to a certain point. I actually don't want a consistent experience across multiple channels. All I want is an appropriate experience across multiple channels. That is to say, on an Amazon product page on a desktop device at home, I'm probably more in a browsing frame of mind. I'm prepared to see the reviews; I'm prepared for them to be featured more prominently on the page. I'd be more interested in having an appropriate video surf alongside it. All of those extras are fine. On a mobile, where I am probably more task-focused, consistency experience doesn't matter to me as long as it's got an A at the top and I'm on the right site and it's got an image and it's got a buy button. That's actually all I need in that use case so I'm not sure how highly I rank consistency.

I think customization is in, you imply here, is in two levels. The personalized experience alters the experience depending on whether I'm **Gareth** or **Robert** depending on our buying histories and that is super, super powerful. I think even below that, I suspect that both of us buy very different books, say, but we behave in a consistently similar way when on mobile versus on desktop, so I think I would perhaps ... I don't know if I would consider situationally appropriate rather than consistent across multiple channels there.

MEASURING CUSTOMER CENTRICITY FOR COMPETITIVE ADVANTAGE

Gareth: Finally, the customer. Just around customer perceptions, again emotional engagement, loyalty, expectation setting, the simplification being brought up again and say, our customers understand our values, we understand what our customers intend to do, we measure referrals of existing customers, we manage the expectations of our customers, customers enjoy using our survey and we measure emotional engagement of our customers.

Robert: I changed the order of questions one and two around personally because I think it's quite possible for a business to understand what its customers intend to do even if those customers don't understand its values. This implies a certain hierarchy and I think those go the other way around. Question three, yup, you can absolutely measure referrals but I think that you also ... there's a sort of level beyond that which is, we feel sufficiently confident that we base the growth of the business around customer recommendation. The fact is if you are top box and you ask people to refer others for a bonus if you are ... what other businesses have done this well that I've seen recently. It's called Top Cash Back, I think, that does this really well.

It's quite a ballsy thing to base your growth on the idea that people will like you that much that they'll tell all of their friends. Actually that's an expression of their confidence in you and your confidence in what you're doing so I think it's not just the measuring of the referral but just making referral available is a measure itself. Could you just expand we manage the expectations of our customers? I just want to unpack that because I don't quite ...

Gareth: Yeah, I think it is the ... how do I explain manage the expectations of our customers? It comes back to understanding what your customers expectations are and then saying, "Right. This is what we are going to deliver for you. We're not going to do more and we're not going to do less. Don't expect more or less from us." If you are in a utilities company you are here to pay your bill, "We're going to do this in this way. Don't expect us to solve [inaudible 00:33:30]" or something along those lines. It's all of understanding customer expectations and then giving them the messaging that they know what to expect and achieve on the site.

Robert: I would say and by the way if at any point we get too far away from the interview to the discussion just tell me to stop because I could talk about this for hours but to me, I would say Dell feels like a business that manages the expectations of its customers. You get a perfectly functional machine built to your specification in a reasonable period of time for a reasonable price and the genius of Steve Jobs as opposed to Michael Dell was the idea of surprise and delight but actually I think really genuinely, it's right at this level because an adequate business does that but surprise and delight are hall**mark**s of an exceptional business.

Gareth: Interesting and I agree but do you think that surprise and delight is a very difficult or unsustainable model to approach when approaching customer experience because then it's very hard, given the speed at which things evolve in innovation, to continually surprise and delight. You need to make the expectations met and then if you get it right every now and then, it's the same delight. Otherwise what happens is surprise and delight becomes your mantra and Apple is seeing this now. We've gone through seven generations of iPhone and people are getting bored of it and iPhone sales have just gone, not off the cliff, but they've reduced. Do you think while surprise and delight is a good strategy, can be a useful strategy, if we're measuring capability delivering customer experience actually and expectation but as a stronger measure?

Robert: Yap, that's valid.

Gareth: A very complicated way of explaining that, if you get what I mean.

Robert: No, I do. I think it's really interesting. I suppose part of it is what surprise and delight comes from. If anything, if it's a product based surprise and delight then yes, you're in that Apple trap. You're trying to sustain the unsustainable but actually ... and I don't know I haven't really thought about this, is a service base surprise and delight an easier thing to achieve? It's not about doing something new and fundamentally different; it's just about consistently doing the right things well.

Gareth: Yeah, which is an interesting thought but is it because the state of most service industries could be considered so low that actually just meeting expectations would be surprise and delight?

Robert: That's certainly true. I suspect if you looked at utility companies or phone companies that would absolutely be the case.

Gareth: Maybe instead of managing expectations in here, what we do is move back down to a lower level and then maybe have something like, we can meet the expectations of our customers and surprise and delight when required or something along those lines. I don't know.

Robert: Yeah, I think that makes sense. Five and six make complete sense to me. There's almost a sort of a level four here which is, what happens when you get to the point where people are using your company name as a verb? That's almost the proxy for having won this completely.

Gareth: Yeah, I agree. The basis for my model is to get everybody to a level where if you are going to compete on customer experience this is what you need to get there. I think shooting for the moon every time on, [inaudible 00:37:33] to take my company, to cubit it, it's such a difficult thing to do and such a ... you need a revolutionary product that's first in its category or is so mind-blowing in its category that it happens. I wonder whether putting my extra level four ... and I'm not against putting extra levels into the survey but I think as a ...

Robert: It was a procedious observation. It wasn't a criticism of the model.

Gareth: No. Actually an extra level might be worthwhile because between levels ... having one, two, three doesn't give you and lot of variations in companies either but ... so that's it. Overall, your thoughts on the model if there's any constructural changes, anything ...

Robert: Structurally, it makes sense. Tell me about the waiting and how the scoring worked because I'm a data nerd and I'd just like to understand that. Is there a waiting applied to the various levels of the model in terms of culture versus operations, technology versus customer and then secondly, what level of waiting is applied to the three tiers within each of those?

Gareth: Every one of the survey questions we've looked at is based on a one to ten scale so that would be your survey,, like a slide of one to ten.

Robert: Keeping a total score of what, 360 or so.

Gareth: Five times six. 300?

Robert: 300. Okay, yeah. I think it's six categories.

Gareth: I do have six categories.

Robert: Six questions per category. Six categories. Thirty six.

Gareth: We've got six categories or five categories? One, two, three, four, five.

Robert: Five, so 300?

Gareth: 300 and then the idea would be that within the level one would be acquainted just as an example on level two, two level three, three so if you are scoring very highly on level one questions but very low on level ... no in fact, sorry, would it be the other way round? You'd weigh higher levels ... yeah, I've got it. You would wager so that if you're scoring higher in level three questions you are scoring higher overall in that category.

Robert: Do you score higher on a score ...Let's suppose you've got a level three question and you got a five in culture and you got a level three question and you got a five in customer, is there any weighting between those two? Is there any value judgment that actually ... it's harder to get that because they're all the prerequisites and so you weigh that higher?

Gareth: Sure. On the current model, no, they are all given 20% of the overall score, purely on the basis that I was trying not to take a value judgment on each one because you need all five to be performing top of your game. in order to be delivering it. My concern about weighting is that you say, "We understand that the customer's the most important thing," but then that then gets away from the point of the model which is that everything needs to be working in unison.

Robert: Yeah, got it.

Gareth: Any other final thoughts?

Robert: No. That makes total sense. It's very structured. It's simple enough for a very busy person to understand which is always a helpful thing. I think being able to say ... being able to sort of quantify ... I can say, my company is historically bad at customer experience and getting better at it, which is fine. Being able to say, "We score X, the sectoral average for our business is Y, our main competitor is Z," and being able to compare those three numbers immediately makes it a very real thing which I think is good.

Gareth: Excellent. Well thank you very much.

Robert: Not at all.

Interview 2 - Lorne

Interviewee: Lorne
Interviewer: Gareth
Date and Time: 29th/April/2016
Location: London
Customer Experience Group: Consultant

Gareth : Wonderful. I hope it's recording. What's your name?

Lorne: **Lorne**.

Gareth : What company do you work for?

Lorne: I work for <digital consultancy>, which is the digital agency part of [Accenture 00:00:14].

Gareth : What's your job title?

Lorne: I am managing director with <digital consultancy>. I look after the resources [inaudible 00:00:22] that covers oil and gas and utilities and chemicals and mining, mainly.

Gareth : What are you responsible for? What's your day to day responsibilities?

Lorne: My day to day responsibilities are to work with our key clients and to understand the challenges they have [inaudible 00:00:43] the challenges they have and think about how digital [inaudible 00:00:48] solutions, so interactive solutions, experience, **mark**eting content and comments, can be applied to those business [inaudible 00:00:58] that add value and [inaudible 00:01:01].

Gareth : When you talk about customer experience, what does that mean to you?

Lorne: I think it's quite self-explanatory. I think it does mean how individuals experience your brand and your products and your services in a holistic manner across all channels, across all periods of time, and it means ... I think it's as simple as that. That's all it is really. That is it. Then you can talk about what's good customer experience versus bad customer experience, but I think it is long ... I think we're keeping it holistic across channel, and it's long term experience with customers.

Gareth : Have you seen an increase in customer experience being discussed both internally at Accenture and when you're out talking to your customers?

Lorne: Yes. I think in some ways it's a little bit of a fad, and that doesn't mean it's not very, very important, it's just people tend to latch onto the next word that falls out there and people have gone through information after [inaudible 00:02:14] customer experience, and people who want customer centricity. When I say it's a fad, I don't think that it's actually [inaudible 00:02:21] businesses, but I think at the moment it's a bit of a buzz word, so lots of people say it who don't actually know what it means. But it's good, because at least there's the call [from clients 00:02:32] to ask the question about it. They may not understand what they're really asking about, but it opens up conversations.

Gareth : Interesting. Just on that, then what do you consider to be the key elements of delivering customer experience? People don't really understand what it is. It's a buzz word, but what should people be talking about?

Lorne: Firstly, you've got to understand your customers and understand what their experience is, which sounds really, really obvious, but it's absolutely not obvious. I see lots of organizations try and redesign their customer experience having never interacted with their customers and never asked them what they wanted, never really understood the experience they're currently having. They're redesigning the customer experience by reorganizing the organization or restructure the organization on the basis the they have, in a way that they think might be better for their customers. Whereas I think, if you're going to be successful, it's about turning around and saying, "What is my ability to understand what customers really go through, their points of pain, their points of delight, know their underlying motivation, and then your ability to take that insight and return to that by [providing 00:03:39] better experiences.

MEASURING CUSTOMER CENTRICITY FOR COMPETITIVE ADVANTAGE

Gareth : Do you have any examples of the companies that you think are delivering good customer experience?

Lorne: Yeah. You'll find this very bizarre. I spent most of my time in the last weeks talking about chickens. I became an accidental farmer the other week, through very good customer experience. I'll explain why. I was talking a bit to my wife about whether we got a dog or not, and the answer was no because she's already got two kids to look after and I'll bugger off traveling. She then ... It's just the cat. I was like, "There's no way the cat's happening, because that loses my argument for a dog for ten years, so that's not happening." She said, "How about chickens?" I was like, "Well, that would work. The kids want to [inaudible 00:04:22] something. We could do that." Logged online, searched on chicken hatch, because apparently they're not [inaudible 00:04:26] hatched, but I didn't know that. Up pops this company called Omelette. Firstly, they understand exactly what I'm trying to do at the end of it. Went online. Really great website. Really easy to understand. They really understood my motivation and what I was really trying to achieve, because this was ... Omelette is a ... They're a design company who's designed a modern coop essentially.

What they had done is they had realized that most people don't buy a coop if they never get the chickens. Most people browse around, which is what I was essentially doing, and there you have, I wouldn't know how to get the chickens. It's all too hard. They went through and the said, "How many eggs do you want a week?" I moved the styler, and they said, "Do you want friendly chickens or do you want good looking chickens?" And I was like, "I want friendly, hardy ones for kids." Then it showed me ... It told me that I needed X number of chickens, and it showed me the right coop for those number of chickens. Then, just in case I was worried ... Then it said, "I can deliver this to you in 24 hours time with a picker to pick it and install the coop, and it has free training on how to [start 00:05:33] the chickens, and we'll deliver chickens live to you, and we'll show you how to clip their wings, etc," and I thought, "This is really good."

They then showed me a business case that showed me that it was cost [inaudible 00:05:43] over three years, and there was no brains I was going to buy, so we moved that projection. Then they said, "Would you like to buy our food and bedding subscription service for hens?" I'm like ... I hadn't even thought about feeding them yet. That's really quite an idea. So I bought that. Then they contacted me afterward and said, "What are you going to do when you're on summer holidays?" And I was like, that was the one thing that was kind of ... I'd already ordered it, but it was the thing that I was a bit worried about. They said, "We have a hen hotel, and six pounds a day, we can look after your hen whilst on holiday."

Then they followed through. They delivered them. They personally came out to do what they promised. The communication throughout was excellent. I think, how is it that if I can accidentally become a farmer in 24 hours, and that I find it so hard to switch to a new provider, or I find it so hard to do multiple things that should be far easier than becoming a farmer by accident.

I think that there are firms that do it, but that's where someone has thought about that their point in the process was selling me a hatch, but that they realized that in order to effectively build brand loyalty and to actually get me to buy that, they had to go about not just their part of the business, but the whole of my experience, and then craft experiences that work for that, and more importantly, that generated much greater business for them than if they had just [inaudible 00:07:06]. It's now turned them clearly into an [inaudible 00:07:10]. Now I regularly talk of them and talk about chickens, and I spoke at [inaudible 00:07:17] last week, and started with [inaudible 00:07:20] got tweeted all over the place, Omelette re-tweeted it. Brand advocacy, which is what we're all after. Fantastic.

Gareth :   Where do you see companies, and this is what I'm interested in [inaudible 00:07:30], where do you see companies most often failing in delivering that customer experience?

Lorne: Lack of insight. They don't actually know what their customers think. They have very, very basic metrics on that. They have very poor use of data. Like that. In terms of where that then lends failings, I'd say marketing and sales tend to be better, because they tend to be more focused on that. I think customer service part is, they'll often want the struggle, particularly businesses that have large call centers. I think one of the problems is that they think there's a way out of interacting with the customer, which it shouldn't be. There's a huge amount of focus on them, but self-serve. They actually, if I asked you about anything, banking, booking a holiday, I would say, "Do you want to self serve?" Your answer probably wouldn't be yes. What you would say is, "I want to get it done, and I want to do it as easily and quickly as I can." The business has been taken out and leading into that what you want to do is self serve, because that's what they want.

Gareth :   Do you think that's driven as well by the likes of Amazon and Facebook, who hide away their contact centers and make them so successful in doing things self serve, and people look at them as the leaders and say, "Well actually, if they can hide everything away, so can we?"

Lorne: Yes. I think that's true. I think what you want to do is what you want to achieve something quickly, differently, as fast as you can in your daily life, not even necessarily digitally. If that is self serve, then great. But the trap people fall into is that therefore that's what the customer's nirvana is, whereas the customer's nirvana is getting sh*t done. If they can do it self service, fantastic. Most stuff on Amazon, they've got patterns of understanding the customers, they've built a process, they've learned very clearly what communication to put in at what times, the amount of tracking data you get, information about when your products need to start, is directly related to the fact that without that it generates customers' queries. They've had to think about, all the way along the line, if they're going to self serve, how do I make sure that they are fully informed all the way through?

That's fine if you're dealing with selling [inaudible 00:09:53] products, product sale, but when you get things more nuanced, you may be able to self serve, but at the same time, someone should be able to start something, and then start ... If you recognize that a customer is about, for example, going back to chickens ... If you recognize the customer was at the last point in the process and then bailed out, and if you think, "Well, I want to run a best self serve business," that would be insane, because the value of that sale [inaudible 00:10:17] pretty close to buying, why wouldn't you stay and offer a chat? Why wouldn't you offer a video chat? You know what I've added to my basket. You can get tons of data about who I am. If you think I'm a valuable customer, why would you force a self service experience?

It's about the idea of progressive service, rather than self service. You want to build a situation where customers can self serve if they need to, but they also can escalate through the same channel effectively, whereas often the solution is self serve, if that doesn't work for you, start my process again in the old fashioned way, and good luck to you, start again.

Gareth : A recent [Gardner 00:10:58] survey on the role of marketing customer experience said that by 2016, 89% of companies expect to compete mostly on the basis of customer experience, versus 36% four years ago. What are your thoughts on that?

Lorne: Rubbish. That's what they would say, because that's what they would then like to do. But, if you think about this inter-mediation of brands ... Let's take Amazon. Or let's take [Cardo 00:11:26] for example. Cardo, you get your weekly shop, it used data analytics to discover what you shop every week, put it in your [inaudible 00:11:33] shop, that generates a shop for you. Already, if they haven't got products in stock, they'll just put something else instead. They'll use the data on what other people have bought, how much it costs, and how star rated it is, to just replace that in your bucket.

If you think about that for a moment, it's not far to say, "Well actually, I'm not going to bother with the brand or your customer experience. I would just find, what is the product is that is good enough, at the right price," and you distance maybe as a brand, and as a company, completely, if that makes sense. Doesn't matter what advertising you do, doesn't matter what experience you provide, because we have these intermediates that deal with it for you.

Take [Uswitch 00:12:17]. Uswitch is an energy provider. [inaudible 00:12:20] is buying any longer on the experience they're given by [inaudible 00:12:24] in that market, which is millennials particularly, because they just say, "Uswitch, you just deal with it for me." If you fail dreadfully in customer experience, then obviously you're going to hit the headlines, or you're going to find that you're not rated well, and you're going to quickly drop out of those kind of [inaudible 00:12:46]. You don't have to have outstanding customer experience to succeed. You just need to have good enough. I think it's understanding, if you're providing a really great service experience to your customers, then you need to compete on it, but you also need to think about ... I don't think that 70% of companies are going to compete on that. I think a lot of people are going to become completely dis-intermediated, become just [inaudible 00:13:13] function, operates well enough, and it [inaudible 00:13:16]. The people who become the disintermediators are the people who really understand customer experience, but I think the idea that every company is going to be in that space is not likely.

Gareth : Actually, according to that same research, they said fewer than half of the companies see their customer experience capabilities as superior to their peers, but two thirds expect these capabilities to be industry leading, or more successful within the next five years.

Lorne: Which isn't realistic. If you look at the level of brand loyalty you have to the brand that gives great customer experience, you trust them more than most other providers who provide that experience, so you're going to get winners and losers. You're going to get, whether it's the Amazons of this world, whether it's Uber. I'm sure you've heard of the fact that they're delivering [inaudible 00:14:02] in New York. People trust that because they've got a good experience already. Suddenly you have [inaudible 00:14:09] by that company. I think the companies that really, really succeed ... No. Some companies who really, really succeed in being deliberate about planning customer experience, and that would be the [USP 00:14:20], and they would be better than anybody's ever been. They would focus on it more obsessively, and they would be very successful. For others, they have to think, well, do I play that game and become one of the loved brands that ends up on the front page of your app screen, etc, or do I think about how I work in the ecosystem with those people, in which case, they don't need to have industry leading customer experience.

Gareth :   Fantastic. Okay. I'm now going to take you through the customer experience framework that I've built. As I said, it will be giving you framework. At the end, tell me how you think it is. Is there anything you think you'd change, that's missing, thoughts, recommendations? That would be greatly appreciated. This is the customer experience maturity framework. I'm just going to briefly take you through my research and my findings, and then look at how we've developed that into this framework.

I've been doing a lot of study around customer experience, a lot of reading academic papers. As someone's who's done the [BMP 00:15:22] before, you're probably familiar with what [crosstalk 00:15:24] do. I've then identified key themes. I've taken out of these, identified key topics, classified them against each other, and I've created a series of questions, and a survey, that, what I would like people to have to do is to take that survey to give themselves a rating, so that we can then index where you are against the **mark**et and against People within your industry, and the greater **mark**et as a whole.

[First 00:15:47] we'll have a customer experience period, which is sort of similar to [inaudible 00:15:51] hierarchy. I met my needs, it was easy, I felt good about that. My proposal is actually that too many companies take this to mean that they need to focus on this top bit and this wow, and it sort of goes back to what you were saying, whereas actually it's very few companies that can deliver absolutely outstanding customer experience, and it's not sustainable a lot of the time anyway. If you are saying to your call center reps, "Save this customer at any cost," that's the wow. They might give away a Porsche.

Lorne: If everybody were to delight their customer.

Gareth : Yes. If you're going to become ... Your key asset is going to be customer experience. But for many others, as you say, meeting the needs is probably plenty. What I'm suggesting actually is that we get equal weighting, and we move it into levels one, two, and three. How are you delivering this, up to having a maturity that is delivering ... I'm not going to stay outstanding customer experience, because that nullifies my point, but delivering customer experience that is enjoyable and recognized and the like.

The key themes that I have pulled out of this, it goes back to, we usually talk about people, process, and technology, but I think this misses out two key points, which are culture internally and the customer on the outside, as you said at the beginning, too many people forget the customer when they're talking about customer experience. Do you actually understand it? What I'm suggesting is that culture then feeds out into operations, then feeds out into your products and service, then feeds out to your technology, which then feeds out to your customers. What you need to get to get it balanced is to remember that you have an emotional core to your business that then go through these very rational steps to deliver to an emotional being, a customer. I think too many companies forget this emotional culture bit, and make everything around things like, for example, the call center. Let's make it all about how quickly we can get the customer off the phone. Let's make all of our key about the metrics. Rather than actually what do these people need, and what are they looking to achieve. What I've proposed is that we take these five key areas as what you would measure to be whether you are ready to deliver customer experience.

The key themes around culture are things like expectation setting, voice of the customer, culture, empowered employees, are you meeting expectations rather than delighting, a customer quotient, incentives for employees on customer experience, are you tied to it, is there CXO in management control at the board level? I won't bore you with the key quotes around that. What you would use to measure your culture will then be on a scale of one to ten, basic levels, customer experience, company value, a senior person is responsible for customer experience, we have a sense of customer experience team, we empower it, this is starting to get more ... You are becoming more customer centric if you're doing this in a cultural point, and finally, training the crew in human resources that are then guided by this [inaudible 00:18:49] strategy, and we actually have company incentives that relate to customer experience.

In operations, you're then looking for customer experience strategy measurement, outcome metrics, [exception 00:19:00] metrics, all the way through to, again, company values, your MPS score ... Something I'm really interested in is the customer effort score, rather than just MPS, how easy are you to do business with? Again, quotes. The questions in there. We have a defined customer experience strategy. We measure customer satisfaction, we listen to the customer, we understand the customer experience journey, we measure customer experience, and we continue to optimize customer experience. I think when the company is doing continuous optimization in customer experience they're probably in a pretty good place to obtain they're delivering from operations point of view.

Product and service. How easy it is to do business with, [inaudible 00:19:38] key words. How simple is the product to understand? Is it meeting expectations? Again, we understand the expectations of the customers. We have a complex product. We're able to serve the customers in the way that they want, so not which channel we serve them through, but which channel they come to get us in. We deliver service customers expect. We're easy to do business with, and we understand the values of our customers.

From the technology point of view, it's then we track our customers across multiple channels, we collect and analyze customer data from all touch points, we can collect quality feedback from customers, we can deliver a consistent experience, customers can move seamlessly between channels, and we offer a personalized customer experience. Then the customers, as you were talking about, actually analyzing customer. Do you understand what the customer actually wants? Our customers understand our values. We understand what our customers intend to do. We measure referrals from existing customers. We manage it [inaudible 00:20:36] our customers. Customers enjoy using our service, and we measure emotional engagement with out customers.

That would then give you, if you answer all of those, against a different weighting, then gives you a customer experience which is your index score, and then each one of those would have their own score as well. [inaudible 00:20:52] there's a model of [inaudible 00:20:55].

Lorne: Okay. Let's get to it. There's a lot of really good stuff in there. I think this all makes sense. Just from a visual perspective of your story telling it, my concern there is it feels like the culture of the organization is dis-intermediated from the customer by all these pieces of the puzzle. It's more visual representation issue to me. It's not really a fundamental issue, but it's like the implication is that those potentially ... To me those things connect, and are supported by all of those. Does that make any sense?

Gareth : Yeah, absolutely.

Lorne: It's more a visual representation than anything else.

Gareth : How would you change that visually to represent that?

Lorne: One of my thoughts was to put a feedback loop around the outside if you like, the customer then feeds back into the culture. But you are right, then that doesn't get rid of this step issue. I'd be tempted to put culture ... The customer and your culture as one big spot, and then these three sit inside it as enablers.

Gareth : Okay.

Lorne: If that makes ... I fully agree that culture is at the heart of it. But it's almost like you've got your customer on the outside, then you've just got one big circle, which is culture, and inside that ... I also think that there's no logic to me in why you're stacking it up in that particular order. Why is operations, product and service ... Why is technology [inaudible 00:22:33] customer? Whereas if you'd say, the customer experience, the whole of our organization is driven by culture, and there are three key parts sitting inside that, almost like a Venn diagram type approach, that feels ... It says to me ... Is there a logic to how they stack up there particularly?

Gareth : It's your culture being the heart. Culture is your people. Your people, the way that they work, are the operations in the organization. The way that your processes operate effectively are what deliver your product or your service, because that's what ultimately produces them. Then the product and service is, the way that you usually get that to your customer is through your technology stack, which then the technology is the bit that the customer usually [crosstalk 00:23:22]

Lorne: Are we talking about digital customer experience only?

Gareth : No.

Lorne: You may not be delivering it through technology.

Gareth : True. In fact, maybe actually it's the product and the service.

Lorne: It feels to me like, yeah, if you want to put anything close to the customer, it would be product and service. I think whatever you do, whatever you set it up, is to be quite hard, whereas if you just say, there are three fundamental things that drive this, they're all wrapped around by culture, and culture is what connects through to the customer, that feels -

Gareth : Interesting. I see what you mean.

Lorne: The three wheels in the middle. I haven't got any paper. Those are basically, you've got your customer around the outside, and I would say you'd almost, I'd argue, put customers, because [inaudible 00:24:07], and then I would have the culture, which doesn't matter which segment you're working with, but yes, you might be working [BBC 00:24:16]. Ultimately your culture is the same. The how you deliver customer experience through culture. Then inside that, you have a Venn diagram of three things, which are product and all integrations, all of which are important, and that actually they all sit on top of culture. Does that make sense?

Gareth : Yeah.

Lorne: [inaudible 00:24:33]

Gareth : Does the emotional rational story make sense?

Lorne: Yes.

Gareth : I guess we can build that into the whole thing as well.

Lorne: I just didn't risk it, just suggests there's this big divide between internal emotional culture that's then there are barriers of operations, products, technology, then the customer.

This one, I think this makes sense. I'm not convinced about this, because you're saying that you have a central customer experience that is one solution to how you do it.

Gareth : You could have customer [inaudible 00:25:13].

Lorne: This question potentially points to what I'm actually suggesting is not what you should do in order to achieve it. You don't want to have the central customer experience.

Lorne: I think it's kind of saying, [inaudible 00:25:27] person makes sense, but here it's ... We know we have a framework or community of people within our organization who we clearly understand are accountable for customer experience, and work together in a holistic or collaborative way. That's almost like, you're just defining an organization. Someone could say, actually I've got 20 amazing people, they come together once a month and meet with the CX, so they sit in their own teams, and there's geocentric customer experience you all know. Are you good at customer experience? Yeah, absolutely core. I think that probably ... Then this one. I'd say it's ... I think the only question that I'd have in here around culture, is it one of your ... Whether it's ... Maybe it's in the top one, or maybe it's at level one actually. I think it probably is actually probably down here, is customer experience. Oh, you've got it at core company value. Yeah. That makes sense. Yeah. It all makes sense.

Gareth : I had to go and get internal buy in on this, which is where all the quotes came from.

Lorne: Yeah, I know. [inaudible 00:26:49] with all sorts of educational crap.

You see, the only thing at this rate is that, in order to delight, you've got to do more than optimize. If this is like the nirvana, I'd almost say optimizing customer experience sits at this level.

Gareth : The mid level?

Lorne: Mid level. So does measuring. I'm just thinking about, if you use an operational level, we are outstanding because we continue our customer experience and measure customer experience, it's like, really? Nah. I would say level one is almost like, we measure customer satisfaction and listen to our customers. I think those, to me, is basics.

Gareth : Actually, it looks, from in this one, what one, two, three, and four can also almost compress down the the basics. Five and six [crosstalk 00:27:59].

Lorne: I'd challenge, what's up here?

Gareth : What's nirvana?

Lorne: I think it's ... We continually innovate to deliver a better customer experience. That's the right thing. The problem, optimize. I've got a contact center. I improve the script. Yeah, I optimize and I measure. So what? Actually, I'd be saying ... My question to CX is, what have you tried that's completely new? What have you tried? What have you tried and failed, and what have you tried that you've learned from that is now core to your business, that was not there? Ultimately, that's what everybody else is ... The people who are leading, they're going, you know what? What about ... Let's do some video chat online. Let's deliver a bunch of flowers with the engineer. Whatever it is, they're constantly thinking and doing. That's not just optimizing. That's not taking it to the next level. If you really want to ... If you want to be a leading brand, who is, as I said, your asset, or one of your key assets of your business, is customer experience, you've got to do way more than optimize to re-continually innovate the customer experience.

We continue to innovate. I would also probably put ... I'm not sure whether it sits in here, but co-create with your customers. We measure experience, we listen, we understand, we optimize, then there's one where we innovate, and we co-create with our customers. Actually, if you look at the best companies, they're talking to the customers. They're not just talking about the customer, saying, "Give us some data and we'll go off and figure the problem out." They'll be genuinely engaging with them in one way or another to actually figure out what the next thing is, whether they have a customer board, whether they do innovation hack-a-thons with their customers, whatever it is they do. They'll be figuring out something that's really different and innovative to push their [inaudible 00:29:49].

Gareth : I imagine your chicken example, they didn't come out, for want of a better way, fully hatched. No pun intended, but they don't come out delivering that. They probably went, "Oh actually, these are the things that we're ... We do this one thing," and actually then the next bit, and the next bit.

Lorne: Things like the hen hotel, they probably just ... That was not [inaudible 00:30:09] in the current experiences going ... They've got chickens. Chicken. That's the first one. They were just selling hatches. Coops. Got to get this right now. Someone just said, "F**k it. If they're going to buy a coop, they must want to put some chickens in it. Why the hell aren't we selling chickens?" But that's not optimizing.

Gareth : How many chickens did you buy?

Lorne: Only four. At the moment.

Gareth : How many eggs does that give you?

Lorne: About four a day.

Gareth : Wow.

Lorne: About one a day per chicken. The neighbors are very happy.

Gareth : Are they tastier eggs?

Lorne: I haven't actually eaten any of them yet. I've been away most ... I'm going to try some this weekend and see what they're like. They've got a field taste. You just go out and pick them out.

Gareth : [inaudible 00:30:51] product and service.

Lorne: I guess [going back to 00:31:00] last one. The operations one. I guess the only question I'd have is, does the innovative piece, whether that's it. I

146

think it does fit, because to add to the chicken example, [inaudible 00:31:16], let's sell them chickens as well. That's, what would they need? Operations piece would more be, that they probably didn't channel the communications at the start, being able to do the engineering updates by what's up, because that's not really product and service, that's the operations. I think it's the same two. I would actually, again, I would squash this. To me, if your premise was that ... You go back to ... Meets needs, easy. Easy is middle, but then you've got a level three item there. Easy to do business with. Hang on. You've just said that's a middle tier. How can that be -

Gareth :   Again, squishing these down, and then discovering what the nirvana piece is.

Lorne: Yeah. I think so. Yeah. I think that's ... It's got to be more ... If you're saying [inaudible 00:32:23], and you don't have to be there, everybody has to be easy to do business with, everybody has to understand the values of their customers. That is the middle ground. That's kind of like, if you're not there, you're not going to be successful and be able to operate.

Gareth :   Baseline.

Lorne: That's your baseline. If it's around products and service, again I would say it's more about if you continually innovate, and adapt our products and services, based on working with our customers to understand their needs and to understand their evolving needs. That's got to be there at the top. I'd actually question, too, we have a complex product, and question five, reasons to do business with, are pretty much the same thing, because if you have a complex product, you're probably not ... Actually, saying that, you can have a complex product and still be easy to do business with, but I don't think [crosstalk 00:33:13]. It's the same kind of thing really. I think squeeze them down. Something that's more challenging.

Gareth :   Then the technology piece.

Lorne: Only question is, you could squish down. The other option you could ask is, do you not need four levels? Is there just a baseline? Is there, if you're not doing this, is there a baseline, then ... Rather than try and squeeze them down, it's almost like baseline, level one, level two, and then -

Gareth :   Nirvana.

Lorne: Nirvana. Might be better.

Gareth :   Yeah.

Lorne: Otherwise you might find you'll ... You could argue not many people are going to do this, so this gets ... Now you've just suddenly boxed this three into two. You're not getting a very differentiated ... You might find that you look at it and score 30 companies, and none of them reach this, so they all ... There's not ... You squeeze the ratings into two, therefore you haven't really got as much insight, because you're not being able to look at ... They're all going to look more similar. That makes sense?

Gareth :   Yeah, I wonder. Absolutely. I wonder actually if we have baseline, levels one, two, three, and nirvana. That could be five states of being, and your journey between them, based on the top. Interesting. Okay.

Lorne: I think the top one should be something around ... Nirvana is fine, but I think it's more like you are going to specifically win, on the basis of customer experience. None of these ... if you do all this, if someone comes out with something that's incredible, you are [missed out 00:34:55]. Whereas if you've got that, then you're saying, "No, I'm going to actively compete to be that," that

147

whole point about, people say they want to have the leading experience. Unless you're doing that one, you're not doing that, in which case that's fine, but you just need to accept that you're not going to be [inaudible 00:35:11], and you're not going to be driving a business fundamentally through customer experience. You're just not going to piss people off by doing what they say. Make sense?

Gareth :   On that, do you think certain industries don't need to reach that level? Do you think that just getting the baseline right is enough? For example, within [inaudible 00:35:33], do people really want that innovation, incredible -

Lorne: Yeah, I think they do. Does everybody want it? No. Does everybody know they want it until they see it? No. You look at [inaudible 00:35:46] Not really. But then someone comes out with it. There will be a category leader who figures that out. Will that drive everybody to them? Absolutely not. A lot of people just buy on price. Most people are inherently lazy. Most people stay with ... This is the thing. If you're with one of the big six, and it's okay, you're probably not going to bother to change. The vast majority [inaudible 00:36:12] public, even when there's a better energy price, don't change. The reason they'll change is that experience. That's why ... I don't need to pave the way. I just need to keep them happy enough that it doesn't enter their thinking to move. Once someone has made the decision to move, where are they going to go? They're going to go to the person who is ... Most brands probably operate perfectly well in that space, and particularly if their price ... If you outspend your competitors, and therefore you can't effectively price at the same level as your competitors, because you've delivered the best customer experience, how much premium is someone prepared to pay for that? Utilities argue, not a lot.

How much are you prepared to pay for service of a standard? Quite a lot, because it's bloody irritating to sit in [inaudible 00:37:01]. I'll pay a bit for that. If it's because you're going to get this amazing app and information and someone's going to ring you and you're going to get flowers on your birthday, is that going to make you ... Are you going to pay a price premium for that? Probably not. I think, again, it's starting whether that's the space you want to compete for. Then whether you want to compete for the customers who give enough of a sh*t in your category to pay a premium, and to select you on that basis.

Gareth :   Interesting. Last one then is the customer ... That was technology. Last one is the customer themselves.

Lorne: I think this is a bit too specific. I'd say we measure advocacy. There's lots of ways of doing advocacy, of which one is referrals. Another one could be people shouting about your brand out there. It doesn't have to be ... Referrals is quite specific advocacy. That makes sense to me. Yeah.

Gareth :   Wonderful.

Lorne: Cool.

Gareth :   That's good. Thanks a lot.

Lorne: That's it? Fantastic.

Gareth :   Thank you.

Lorne: No, thank you. Looking forward to reading the final product.

Interview 3 - Matthew

Interviewee: Matthew
Interviewer: Gareth
Date and Time: 19th/May/2016
Location: London
Customer Experience Group: Consultant

Gareth: What's your name?

Matthew: Matthew

Gareth: What company do you work for?

Matthew: <consultancy> . I'm a director in their digital practice.

Gareth: Okay. What are you responsible for?

Matthew: Good question. I would say 50/50 as far as business development and delivery. If we're delivering digital programs around customer experience or analytics or cloud implementation it would be making sure that we're delivering to scope but also selling it through the new services in those areas, all to media and entertainment company.

Gareth: What does customer experience mean to you?

Matthew: When we talk about it it's really the end customer. Is the product or service that they're using meeting their needs? And down to a personalized level so for media are they reading the news or experiencing the news in a way that's convenient for them whether that's through an app or the website or audio or video. Whatever is appropriate.

Or entertainment, same thing. Can they view something on all their devices at the time they want to at the pace they want to. It's a rather broad definition from that standpoint.

Gareth: Have you seen an increase in customer experience being discussed both internally cap Gemini and with customers? Has it become a hot topic?

Matthew: Yes. Arguably in the last 12 months our entire engagement model with clients has slipped and we've been a technology company for 20 years and normally we would lead with our technology capability. I can implement the sales force or I can integrate your CRM to your ERP, whatever.

Now it's been the customer experience. How does this technology changed the way your end customer or your internal customers are experiencing the service or product or the company itself? It's completely changed.

Gareth: What do you consider to be the key elements in delivering customer experience?

Matthew: I'm not sure I understand completely but there are a couple things. Data and information. Customer experience relies on, in my opinion, feedback loops and if you're really personalizing things to a customer do you understand that either through their behavior or through what they're actively telling you?

Either in a survey, your survey is the customer experience good? Or through some clicks or likes or whatever. Therefore their comments on social media?

I think in the past customer service was sort of one directional for customer experience. I'm delivering this to the customer and we're sort of done there. But now it's, "Am I measuring in any number of ways how they thought of the experience and am I speaking my products and services based on that?"

Gareth: Have you got any examples of companies that you think are delivering good customer experience?

Matthew: That's a good question. I do but they're probably not ... I mean I can't give any specific client examples.

Gareth: Any personal examples, though?

Matthew: Yeah, the services that I use? I mean Spotify continues to exceed my expectations all the time and it's the little things as far as if I turn it off getting off the train and then turn it back on at work, it continues where I was. If I turn it off for 24 hours then when I come back in it assumes that I want to listen to something different. It's very subtle things that they don't even let you know about.

I think the BBC though is also increasingly interesting. They're linking up all their services so if I watch something on iPlayer and then something on the radio or something on one of their other channels is a similar theme to that they would notify me so I think they're increasingly using data and behavioral analysis to let me know what's going on across their whole portfolio which I think is interesting.

Gareth: Wow, that seems pretty advanced for basically a government licensed organization. You talk about some people at the forefront of things you wouldn't expect the BBC necessarily to be there.

Matthew: True and maybe they're not as advanced but I think the way they're funded also gives them the right to explore some different things where they don't have to worry necessarily about the revenue on that side of things and they can really do something to focus on the experience and is it enhancing and, you know, the experience when people touch the service.

Gareth: [inaudible 00:04:51] companies who most often failing when they're delivering customer experience?

Matthew: That's a good question. Okay. Two things. Maybe number one is, and I keep going back to this personalization because I think at least all of our clients, it's the same thing. Customer experience equals a personalized experience and they're not interested in implementing something now that will give all of their customers with the same experience because it's fundamentally different.

For that it's making generalizations. We call it the light bulb problem. If I buy light bulbs am I just recommending light bulbs to you in the future? It's the way Amazon's experience used to work. But no, it's I bought light bulbs, what do I want next time? What does a person who bought light bulbs this week want next week. Maybe they want more books because they can see better in their house now with more light bulbs but it's anticipating those things.

But then also I don't think these things get translated well in companies down to the rank and file people. If I have some sort of live chat experience or a bot experience in customer service but that didn't fulfill me and I have to call in now, is the process joined up? Are they saying, "Well I know you were just on live chat. Sorry we couldn't answer the question. Let's work through this." Just from a customer service side of things.

It's easy at the levels we work at. At the CXO level because they know the strategies but are they just implementing technology or are they really changing the organization, the culture throughout the organization to be more customer experience?

Gareth: Now I recent got in a survey on the role of marketing customer service found that by 2016 89% of companies expect to compete mostly based on the basis of customer experience. that was 36% three years ago. What are your thoughts on this?

Matthew: I think all of our clients, 100% of my clients are talking about customer experience. In an RFP that I get, in some proposal that they want us to do they will say be customer experience focused. Keep the customer at the heart of whatever technology or whatever consulting proposal.

Are they saying that just because [Dartner 00:07:20] is saying that and they got advice from Dartner is here's the way you have to write an RFP? Or is it truly that they're understanding the value that they can drive through the organization by being customer focused? I don't know. But 100 of our clients who we're talking about are using that language now.

Gareth: Okay, now according to that same research fewer than half the companies see their customer experience capabilities as superior to their peers but two thirds expect these capabilities to be industry leading or more successful that their peers within five years. How do you feel about this?

Matthew: That just means everybody's investing in a program that will deliver in five years and that they are acknowledging some deficiencies today. Five years, that's a long time to turn around the customer experience. You could lose a lot of customers in that time frame.

It seems like customers and clients should be a little bit more focused on shorter term value delivery to customers. I would agree with that.

Gareth: The interesting thing I take away from a lot of these things is that industry leading and customer experience, by what measurement? There isn't a unified customer experience metric. MPS is pretty close.

Matthew: I think it's also just the way business is going that people expect this. People expect a good experience now. When I started in consulting or technology you never heard this word. You did not care, fundamentally on the UI or the UX that you were delivering for a website or an application. You didn't care. It was all about the business rules and the work flow sort of under the covers.

Again I started in the late 90's and I remember UX stuff was always saved til the end because it didn't matter. The whole thing has shifted and now people expect personalization. People expect recommendations because there's so much content out there. There's so much stuff out there they expect a company to hold their hand to curate their experience through whatever's product or service. It's kind of just the new norm to some extent.

Gareth: Okay, now I'm going to take you through the framework that I designed and I set. I had a [inaudible 00:09:41] free to tear it to pieces. Whatever feedback you have to go through would be greatly appreciated. We're going to look at my research, my findings and let them [chersy 00:09:50] next.

What I've done from research is I've done a lot of literature study around customer experience. I've identified what I think key themes are, what the key topics and then I classified the topics against those themes. That's led to the creation of a set of questions that are all one to ten scale.

On to one to ten, now they run through a model that spits out your score at the end of it so you can then measure that against the industry, your market, however you want to chop and change that.

Matthew: Yeah. Good.

Gareth: Now what I've created is a level one, two, three where everyone is the base level to be delivered in customer experience. They would [do easy 00:10:24] doing pretty well in level three as you get to go. This is slightly different to the usual model which is almost like a Maslow pyramid, it's a forest model.

The reason I moved away from this is in this sort of pyramid, I always get the feeling like people like CEO's and people that say [we are centric 00:10:39] want to jump straight to this small bit at the top and where this resides is in the we'd wow our customers statement which to me is not a sustainable business practice.

I think we talked about this last time, actually. You can't continually wow your customer because if you take that to it's logical conclusion in order to keep a subscriber for a newspaper you could give him a Porsche to keep him because that would keep him happy and that wow's him but you've just given away the farm rent and so that's why I'm trying in this model to move away from this pyramid idea.

The questions that I've developed are mentally base-level, mid-level and [crosstalk 00:11:18] you doing not nirvana because I don't know [inaudible 00:11:22] but that sort of idea.

What I've done is based it around, it's kind of like this onion model where actually culture is at the heart. That then, if your culture is customer-centric and customer experience focused it feeds into operations which then feeds into the way that you deliver your product and your service which then is delivered to the customer through a technology most of the time these days and that then is the customer on the outside.

Now usually we talk about product, people, technology. Product process [inaudible 00:11:51]. Process [did I start 00:11:53]?

Matthew: Yeah, yeah, yeah.

Gareth: The reason I've added in culture and customers is I think they're often forgotten when we talk about these things. At the heart you have an emotional, people are the culture of your business and you have this emotional people, this customer you're delivering to and too often when we focus on this rational piece the operation, product and technology where you're trying to [geek 00:12:13] out efficiencies but you don't necessarily talk about the experience we talked about so the model is trying to convey that you have a heart, a customer-centric heart that feeds out through the customers delivering it.

Any initial thoughts on the ...

Matthew: It makes sense. I guess the first thing is I don't think that you have to have a culture of customer experience or whatever, customer service. I think maybe a willingness to change is more important and a culture that people aren't stuck to their ways of doing things because you could argue that if a company thinks that they're customer focused but the operations, the way you deliver a customer experience changes a person but a person is not willing to change or think, "Well a customer still wants me to deliver the service this way."

Then everybody can still be customer focused but not in the right way that the organization is so if a CEO delivers a new strategy, says, "This is the way our customers are behaving now so we have to change our operations or our products."

Are people willing to say, "Okay, I acknowledge that. Based on the data you're giving me I'm willing to change my approach to being customer-centric."

Gareth: Yeah. Okay. Introducing that level of flexibility and agility to it ...

Matthew: Yes. Yes.

Gareth: Okay.

Matthew: Still the culture of the organization is key it's just what is that culture?

Gareth: That's actually really interesting because I think if you went to most companies they would tell you that they have that customer-centric but no one goes, "Ah, it should be done care about customers.

Matthew: Exactly.

Gareth: But they're locked in their ways.

Matthew: Exactly. Operations, definitely that follows on and do people, I guess, following on. Are people willing to change the operations because so many times technology is not the reason most of our projects fail even though they're technology projects. It's are people willing to change their operations? Are they willing to change the business process that is delivering to the customers? So many times it's that.

Whoever our primary stakeholder is saying, "We want to implement technology that's simple so we want to take Q-bit or whatever other standards of technology. We don't want to change it. We want to adapt our business processes to that technology because it will allow us to be more efficient in the future and the technology companies are changing the software all the time anyway so we can get those skills."

But then inevitably you get down to a lower level that says, "No we need the software to do this because that's the way we do our business." Then budgets balloon and things just take much longer and you get something that [mispoke 00:15:02] and now it costs more to operate going forward and you can't change or be as agile as you want.

That goes culture of people, are they willing change the operations? Are the operations flexible and agile? And then the technology. Are you using sort of standard modular things or are you just creating something that's only applicable to you?

Gareth: I think that really rings true for me as a sales manager so this is brilliant. As a salesperson [inaudible 00:15:29]. Because one is my processes and I get to measure everything and the other is actually I hate using it.

I [inaudible 00:15:39] go through these questions so that they were key kind of things that came out within my research around culture and how to create that to be more customer [service 00:15:47] focused. Things like voice of the employee and empowering employees to make decisions.

The layers in this are customer experience as a company value, seeing if a person is responsible for customer experience, we have a central customer experience team, we empower to make decisions in the best interest of the customers, training material in human resources development are guided by the CX strategy and customer experience is linked to company incentives.

GARETH EVANS

Matthew: Yeah. This is your level three. This is the top of the pyramid, right?

Gareth: [inaudible 00:16:19] yeah. It may be that actually we want to move that lower down and there might be something beyond there or ...

Matthew: All of those things are good. Do you have [paithy 00:16:34] eyes? Are you managing through the whole organization? How do you measure customer experience? Is it just surveys? Is there a customer qualitative number coming back from the customers? Or are you tying it somehow to product usage or a more tangible API? That would be a good thing.

I don't know if that's level three or if that's just sort of goes to here. Almost tied to it's a company value and it's more than lip service. It's we're trying to measure this thing.

Gareth: Yeah.

Matthew: I look at us <consultancy> as a company as well. We're trying to transform as well because all our clients are saying it and we're trying to push it down. It's not just the team. It's not just like a practice that's a customer experience practice. It's a different skill or it's a different [flexibility 00:17:33] that everybody has to have. Internally in somebody's tool set it has to sit alongside all their traditional consulting or technology skills of how do you stay customer focused.

Gareth: Interesting. I was listening to a talk by those saying that data analysis and business intelligence was really important but by having a separate function you almost [answers 00:17:56] responsibility of different answers to that function.

A better way to do it is to put somebody responsible for [VI 00:18:01] into every [different 00:18:03] team and therefore each team becomes, they're based around that and they have to make [them loyal 00:18:08]. I wonder whether that's a better way of doing customer instead of a central customer experience team you actually say ...

Matthew: Somehow everybody is ...

Gareth: Somehow we disburse this and ...

Matthew: The Guardian has an analytics tool that they're journalists use [inaudible 00:18:22]. It's not the best analytics tool out there but when they were designing it they designed it for journalists so they didn't design it for IT or for managers like an executive dashboard or for a VI team who sort of knows what data means and lookup.

They designed it for reporters so that reporters can easily look at it and say, "My article is doing this so this worked and this didn't." That type of thing. They have adoption of 90% or 99% of their journalists use this and it's changed the culture of how they're ...

Because before journalists would say, "I'm the expert on this. Screw the customer. I'm the journalist. I know where the story is and I know how to tell a story." But now it's changed so that journalists are more analytics driven. They're looking at comments. They're seeing what is spiking and what is not and that feeds back into the way they write the next story or the way editors commission the next story. It's not the best tool but the adoption of it exceeds most of their peers.

Gareth: This is slightly off topic or it is in my head. Does that not lead to a almost self filling or homogenization of news? If an article's around, I don't know, Beirut or things that could be constantly shared then we're only going

154

to write things about that and you therefore ... [seeded an 00:19:49] interesting question.

Matthew: Yeah. Throw everything to the wolves.

Gareth: Popularity which I guess is [blood 00:19:54] street model. Lists.

Matthew: It is, true, but our clients are talking about that as well and the BBC is very, very concerned about that in their personalization program because they have a charter to expose people to a lot of different things to educate and entertain and inform I think are their three objectives.

If somebody clicks on something on one specific crime drama, am I only going to serve them crime dramas? Or do I know enough about that type of person to know that yes they like crime dramas from 9:00 to 10:00 pm during the week but on the weekends they like sports or whatever. It's driving down your segments and you're into a lot more.

I forget which client this is but just take personalization segments and customer segmentation whereas I think a year ago, two years, in the not too distant past you would have been looking at a dozen or something being a lot of customer segments and it would be the urban whatever, I don't know.

Gareth: [crosstalk 00:21:01] yeah.

Matthew: And these segments and you'd deliver recommendations to them. Now you're looking at hundreds of segments. I mean the BBC would be looking at hundreds of segments of people to say where they are, how old they are, the types of things that they do, and they serve them a whole bunch of different things across their portfolio because they don't want to get to that of just serving Scandinavian crime dramas to you because you watched it once.

Gareth: And also part of the enjoyment is is discovering new things and learning which actually I think to go to your earlier example is what Spotify is very good at. Give me my discover weekly because it's going to ...

Matthew: But that is pure automation.

Gareth: It is based around, based on what I listened to already in there. Although doesn't it go and listen to ... It works out what other people within their playlists have around songs that are similar to the stuff I listen to.

Matthew: It does but I guess it's missing the curated, the human curated aspect which some people, I don't know. There's all different things. Some people take it pure algorithmic. Other people have a mix and like Apple just took it on radio or whatever. They took a purely human curated experience so there's different ways to think about it.

Gareth: Okay.

Matthew: Off topic.

Gareth: And that's how the interview lasted four hours.

Matthew: Sorry, this is [coffee 00:22:18] more expense drive.

Gareth: Then operations, so this is a lot more I guess [quantalytics 00:22:25], it's measurement [extrapalates 00:22:25] perception and metrics. It's resolution times [et cetra 00:22:29].

This is then, we have a defined customer experience strategy, we measure customer satisfaction, we listen to the customer, we understand the customer experience journey, we measure customer experience and we continue to optimize the customer experience.

Matthew: This one's interesting because you don't have anything here about how agile the organization is to change operations to adapt to customer experience or changes to customer experience.

I would have thought, "Yes, absolutely all of this applies."

Gareth: I do wonder whether question four is almost a level one question, though. If you don't understand your customer experience journey you are potentially ...

Matthew: We continually ... okay. That's a question but how long does it take to do that is another question. Again, all my examples are media and entertainment focused but take Snapshots for example. That's only been around a year and three months, excuse me, Snapshot Discover. The content delivery engine for them then.

You have a bunch of media companies that wanted to get on that to get in front of millennials but it's completely different format of content. It's vertical video, it's very short clips. You have to curate it daily.

How do you set up an operation to do that to create stuff for that? If I have my content supply chain that's delivering to a channel or YouTube or any of these other digital channels to my app or my OTT platform. How do I add Snapchat into that? How do I plug in an operation in the operation for that.

A lot of our clients have struggled with that and they just end up creating their own team that creates their own content, that manages their own content, that delivers their own content. That's not really efficient. You're not leveraging the rest of the organization.

Maybe their taking clips from other areas in the organization but it's not scalable. If the next Snapchat comes what are you going to do? You add 12 more people? We're seeing that now with bots. Now I want a bot that delivers to messenger or a bot that delivers to Whatsapp.

Is it completely automated? Is there some human curation behind that? Okay, the next channel and the next channel and the next channel.

What we try to consult our clients on is how agile is your operation to really add the next channel, add the next ten channels. How long would it take you to do that? Can you do that, scale that up in a quarter? Will it take you a year? And by then you've maybe missed out on a lot of these opportunities.

Maybe what I'm thinking is all of these things you have here should be condensed down here. Are our operations agile? That's the basis. That's the basic. Are we responding to all this information that we're getting. And then how agile are my operations to plug in new things? To change the business props?

That's potentially where the technology comes in as well is if I have Salesforce for some of these things, how quickly can I change a process in Salesforce? Are my content delivery, my content managements or content delivery pieces? How agile is that really? Or my algorithms on my dashboard? Can I change those in a week to two weeks and two sprints to adopt this new channel [I've got 00:25:59]. That's really where the operations comes in.

Gareth: And then products, what I'm really [casing in 00:26:07] products and service is I think MPS is an amazing school but [AGIE 3 00:26:11] Customer [Equa 00:26:12] is something that people don't measure enough.

How easy are you to do business with? If you say you're customer-centric for them when it comes to invoicing I have to fill out an enormous thing. I have to write the PO numbers. All this from my experience [is destroyed 00:26:26]. That's this is where it is [really excited 00:26:28].

We understand the expectations of our customers. We have a complex product service operating. We are able to serve the customers in a way that they want. We deliver our services that our customers expect. We're easy to do business with and we understand the values of our customers.

Matthew: All of those are valid. I think question four is interesting. When you talk about customer experience and surveys and you get feedback from the customer. That's one way to look at it but then there's other companies that say, "Well my customer only knows what they've experienced so far. If I can give them a completely different experience, something they're not expecting maybe that's what I should be doing? Do I know better than my customer?" I think that was Apple's thing, right?

Gareth: Yeah.

Matthew: It's understanding what type of company you are.

Gareth: That you passed the horse from.

Matthew: Yeah, yeah.

Gareth: Yeah, but the interesting thing around expectations to me is let's take your utility company and we're going to become [custom expense00:27:30] I don't know why I want customers. I don't really want to be wowed by British Gas. I want to get on the page, pay my bill and leave. I don't need [billeting and dancing 00:27:39]. Say do you understand what I actually want to achieve?

Matthew: Yeah, yeah.

Gareth: And then the technology piece. This is around, well we've been talking about surveys and listening, voice of the customer, segmentation, understanding the different channels that people are coming through.

We can track our customers across multiple channels, we can collect and analyze customer data from the touch points, we can collect quality feedback from our customers, we can deliver a consistent experience across multiple channels, customers can move seamlessly between channels and we can offer a personalized customer experience.

Matthew: Yeah. All of these are valid. Question three. Talking about customer experience design from a product standpoint is, again, that thing of am I just asking them or am I designing the product in a way where they're telling me through their actions? I think that's something I'm not even qualified for but it's kind of how are you collecting data and how are you creating interactions that allow you to collect data?

Maybe it could be passive. Maybe it could be that iPlayer, the OTT thing tracks where you are. Are you thinking about that as well? The underlying data which may not be exactly customer experience, like the customer isn't experiencing anything but it's giving you the data to change the customer experience if that makes any sense.

Gareth: Yeah. Yeah it does. I think it's like if you go and ask people what they want they're not always able to tell you quite what they want but if you try and get them to maybe describe what they're doing which is the data points that you can watch that just sort of ask them to describe what they're future experience they would like and you design back, [I enter that 00:29:28] ...

Matthew: Yeah, no. I think these are very relevant.

Gareth: Do you think they're layered right? Is that a sort of top end question or is that actually a lower thing and then there's something beyond it?

Matthew: Six is increasingly in layer two or one. It's if people are expecting it. If I'm not being told here's my daily digest of things that are applicable to me. That's odd for people now or potentially in the future but it's hard to get there at the same time.

It depends upon the company internally saying, "This is my end goal." But customers sort of, "Well that's just what I expect. Does everybody else?" Everybody else does that.

Gareth: Do you think, again this is off topic, but do you think the majority of customers who are out [with all wells 00:30:23] actually know they're getting a personalized experience?

Matthew: No, but that's the goal. That's the goal. That's a good point but I guess if it's relevant to them. That's a good point.

Gareth: We took [credit 00:30:40] the same way. Our customers expect the personalized experience. Do they or do they not know that it's happening and we know that we're giving it to them?

Matthew: Maybe it's framing. Maybe it's saying it wrong. They expect the service or product to be relevant to them and if it's not relevant then maybe it's because you're not personalizing. I take the point.

Gareth: Yeah, that's quite a nice way of framing it because I'm not always sure that people are aware it's happening. The easiest way for me to explain personalization is always the Amazon bit. They think about, oh yeah they do do that don't they? It is different. And you're like, "Oh you have no idea what [inaudible 00:31:12] do to me.

Matthew: Yeah, exactly. No, that's a good point.

Gareth: All right, and then the customer, I think we often forget the customer when we're talking about customer experience. It's all the business and so here is, our customers understand our values. We understand what the customer intends to do. We measure referrals from existing customers, we manage the expectations of our customers, customers enjoy using our service and we measure emotional engagement with our customers.

Matthew: Yeah, the emotional piece is interesting. We've done some work just around content of what emotions does content illicit in individuals and that's a whole other sort of analytical piece of really understanding, but a much deeper level than before and requires different skillsets. I mean really more academic, psychological skillsets than I think [these olfinger 00:32:10] technology companies normally would have had so absolutely. Absolutely.

Gareth: Anything you'd move around?

Matthew: That's an interesting one. That seems like it should almost be at a higher level. I mean if you're anticipating people's needs, that's a pretty mature capability.

Gareth: How about question two, we'd understand what customer's intend to do, maybe move that higher, okay.

Matthew: Yeah, because maybe swapping that one, for example. People should enjoy it no matter what.

Gareth: Maybe swapping question two for question five.?

Matthew: Yeah.

Gareth: Wonderful. Then at the end [and then space 00:32:54] how you're saying can I over your overall score?

Matthew: Mm-hmm (affirmative)-

Gareth: And then that would then break down into a dashboards. Back to dashboards.

Matthew: Yeah.

Gareth: But then say I didn't want to apply in technology but you didn't score very high in culture therefore you should potentially allocate in your resources. You should potentially being doing some projects here just to kind of give you a road map into what you should be doing.

Matthew: If you're delivering this to a board or somebody, absolutely, but this blends together. The overall score blends things together so it's almost more interesting why, like if it's culture that's dragging you down, your technology investment, your agile operations is fine but it's something cultural, then it's okay, so tell me what to do on that. What does that number mean?

Gareth: I think that's where the frame work hits its endpoint and what [ever sends 00:33:44] from there would be then, "Okay, then at this point you probably then need to know who to speak to."

Matthew: If it's a culture [sheet 00:33:50]

Gareth: Maybe you go to McKenzie. If it's a product offering maybe or a marketing thing maybe you go to WPP. If it's technology you go to <consultancy>. It's, "All right I understand where I should be going now let's go to find department that can hand deliver."

Matthew: That's not necessarily giving a solution. That's pointing to different partners who can tell you what the solution is.

Gareth: Yeah, I wondered that. That's the limitation of the framework I think.

Matthew: But you're still asking a lot of good, valid questions in there. It's maybe that under each one of the questions you have in there there's another set of five questions to further diagnose. Sort of a choose your own venture. If you say the answer is yes or if the answer is no. Maybe if it's no then you're exploring further.

Gareth: Well I'm wondering whether you could taking it further actually, okay you scored under five on this question and the action to take.

Matthew: Yeah.

Gareth: Go and do this, have a look at this project. Here's a case study on someone that fixes this project and build out from there. Adds to your interest. Any other final thoughts and pieces?

Matthew: Maybe one way to sell this to board levels is do they really understand their organization. So many times you have a board or CXO's viewing the organization one way and they think that their operations are agile or whatever. But really at the lower levels the story is just considerably different.

Using this as sort of a discovery tool for them to say really what is our capability at the lowest levels. I think that goes down to who are you asking these questions of and is it a blend of everybody in the pyramid or is it talking to managers who they want their bosses to think that they've implemented good things and done good programs as well.

Gareth: Yeah it would be interesting as a cross company survey to then compare the scores. Managers thought that you were great at culture but you were terrible at technology before things were amazing in technology.

Matthew: Exactly.

Matthew: Thank you very much.

Gareth: My pleasure.

Interview 4 - Lucas

Interviewee: Lucas
Interviewer: Gareth
Date and Time: 16th/May/2016
Location: London
Customer Experience Group: Vendor

Gareth: What's your name?

Lucas: **Lucas**.

Gareth: What company do you work for?

Lucas: I work for <technology vendor>.

Gareth: What's your job title?

Lucas: I am the Director of Product Management.

Gareth: What are you responsible for in that role?

Lucas: As Director for Product Management, I look after all our product testing, which way we're taking the product. I work across all of the product managers, tech leads and product design, making sure we're all going in the right direction together. Importantly that means collaborating with our sales team and client sales team to understand what it is they want from a customer experience platform, which is what [inaudible 00:34].

Gareth: What does customer experience mean to you?

Lucas: I'll answer this in two ways. To me it means every single person is a consumer, a customer. It's the experience you have when you're interacting with a brand as you're going through a decision making process to interact with that brand. As an example, I often go out and want to buy a pair of trainers and the customer experience I have is, I haven't experienced every single digital or more digital brands are going on that journey to try and find out what it is I'm looking for. Find that down all the way through to as you make that first decision, that customer experience then continues with the brand that I've chosen. After actually making that final decision, all the way through the lifecycle of actually having and owning that product, until you get to the point where actually that product is no longer in your possession.

How that brand and business deal with that entire life cycle is the full end to end customer experience from the consumer point of things. In terms of my role at [inaudible 00:01:50] and how I see customer experience, it's much more around helping the businesses that we work with to provide a platform to their customers, how a platform obviously can give the best customer experience to their potential customers. In that instance, it's very much around messaging and giving people communications ultimately to help support that customer experience, but that's only 1 angle of customer experience in the grand journey.

MEASURING CUSTOMER CENTRICITY FOR COMPETITIVE ADVANTAGE

Gareth: Have you seen an increase in customer experience being discussed both internally and also with customers?

Lucas: Customer experience is actually definitely on the rise. From our own company's journey, we've managed to build a product which has very much been working with the market, working with our customers or people in the market who are after our type of technology. The journey has gone from people have data and don't know what to do with the data, they have a vision of improving their website as a result of that. What they really meant by improving the website is to improve customer experience, but they haven't yet put that into works. Then that turns into this runs some tests, this runs version A versus version B to figure out which one of these pages is better. Again, what they're really trying to understand there is which of those pages best gives the customer a better customer experience, and then where the platform is today is actually how do you provide that customer experience end to end from a buying position process.

What we've seen in the market is many of technology providers, including Google and Adobe, Oracle as well as IBM, are all trying to get on the customer experience bandwagon as it were, as it's increased in problems across the technology industry from a marketing perspective.

Gareth: What do you consider to be the key elements of delivering customer experience?

Lucas: They key elements of customer experience? From a [inaudible 00:03:55] perspective, that's very much around communication. How do you communicate with that customer in the [inaudible 00:04:00] getting the information you need? It's more than that. It's more around, it also goes as far as what's in the product itself. Ultimately someone's only going to buy a product if it's got all of the attributes that someone's looking for. It also is the brand. People buy into a brand as well. For example, people want to be associated with Nike for example, and if they wear Nike it gives them association of being sporty and aspirational to be like Usaine Bolt.

There's also implicit in that is the interaction with someone with a brand employees, or the people who are representing them. Say, for example, I've got an issue with an Apple product, I phone up Apple support or go into an Apple store. The experience that employee gives me represents directly on what I think and associate about that brand as well. You've got the product, you've got the communications, you've got the brand, and you've got the employee. I'm trying to think if there's anything else.

You've also got an outside influence to this as well. How good that experience is is based on what your previous experiences have been with any other brands. Say for instance all you've ever done in your life is bought an Apple computer where the experience is very high. The moment you go and try to buy broadband where the experience may be perceived to be less high, or a completely alternative industry, that's also going to impact your perception of industries. The perception of course is very important in here as well. You've got across industry, but you've also got across brand as well. [inaudible 00:06:03] cross brand, let's say for example that I'm used to buying Adidas trainers and then buy Nike. That experience might be very different, so that perception is going to affect me.

Then the 3rd way [inaudible 00:06:12] affects you is if you're used to buying, go back to the Apple example, an Apple laptop, and then you buy an iPhone, there's different products there within the same brand, so that's another way in which the experienced perception can be different.

Gareth: A recent [inaudible 00:06:29] survey on the role of marketing customer experience found that by 2016, 89% of companies expect to compete mostly on the basis of customer experience, versus 36% 4 years ago. What are your thoughts on this?

Lucas: Say again? 89% on customer experience versus 36 4 years ago?

Gareth: Yeah.

Lucas: Customer experience in itself, it very much depends on how customer experience is defined within that framework. Customer experience is a very broad attribute. If you're basically, if in customer experience you're saying customer satisfaction, I'd say customer satisfaction goes a long ways towards retention. Customer satisfaction to a group of people who have never even heard of your brand before, it's kind of like 0% of a startup. Or 100% of a startup when the startup is worth 0. You have an acquisition problem in there.

Competing on customer experience alone, if I was the CEO of a company that would be troubling, but at the same time, I would also say it's actually very valuable as a metric. Once you do have those customers, you want to keep them, and therefore that's a very powerful proposition.

Gareth: According to that same research, fewer than half the companies see their customer experience capabilities as superior to their peers, but two thirds expect these capabilities to be industry leading or more successful to their peers with 5 years. How do you feel about that?

Lucas: Then you have to ask the question of how many of them have a good measurement framework in place. They see it as being industry leading at, what are they actually comparing that against? They're comparing it against probably internal reporting, but if there's no industry framework, then it actually becomes very difficult to be able to put that in place. That's why I mentioned earlier, in an industry framework, it's very difficult to compare across different sectors where actually someone who's buying petrol from a petrol station, their expectation of what customer experience is would be very different from someone who's going out and buying a luxury holiday. They're completely different product offerings, so you need to have some sort of understanding of actually who are you benchmarking yourself against, and how do you grow a universal understanding.

Gareth: Okay. I'm now going to take you through the presentation on the customer experience maturity framework that I've created. If you could give me your feedback on the framework, how useful do you think it is, what would you change, what's missing, what do you think of the questions that are in there, any other thoughts or recommendations, we can go through it sector by section.

Lucas: Did you want feedback as you go through?

Gareth: Yeah, just as thoughts come in, give me your thoughts, give me your feedback. Especially around the framework and around the questions and the layers that we're going to talk about.

This is a look at the research, the findings, and the customer experience maturity index, branded Q at customer experience for the moment because this an internal one. Basically, I've gone through and done my research, I've been doing a lot of literature research on customer experience, MPS, the various different perceptions of customer experience. Identified key things, identified key topics, classified those topics against those things, and that's created a series of questions which will be a survey where you answer from 1-10 on each of the different levels. That will then spit out a score that you should be able to then use to say, "We're strong in this area, we're not in this area," and it should give you a way to give focus on your change for delivering outstanding customer experience.

Lucas: All of those literatures are based on ... You've got Zappos for example as one example industry there. They're all legitimate businesses and that kind of stuff. One thing I wanted to raise that actually I was reading over the weekend that even illegitimate business such as drugs industry, there's even drug dealers now who are providing a loyalty cost savings. When you buy your 5th gram of whatever it is you buy, you get 1 free. Which is interesting aspects on customer experience in the illegitimate industry, which I imagine has never been documented properly before.

Gareth: I have not gone into the illegitimate industry for this framework. This is largely around legitimate businesses. It's things like looking at [inaudible 00:11:02] looking at Zappos. Zappos are a market leader or considered the gold standard, what do they do? Looking at the Forester Books on Outside In, looking at MPS and how that's measured it. Really, all of the different components of customer experience, and then I've tried to tie all that together and seen what the common themes are.

The Forester design one which was around this pyramid of meets needs, easy, and enjoyable. I actually don't really like that it's a pyramid because what tends to happen is that it forces you into a point where you think this enjoyable bit is smaller and it is this idea of ... Companies seem to take this to mean that I have to wow my customers all the time, we have to aim for this enjoyable bit. We have the pyramid. This is where we need to go. Actually, it's unsustainable. "I felt good about that and it's enjoyable," for me it's that should be part of the experience, it shouldn't be this tiny bit of it, and it also shouldn't be ... The wowing part of customer experience is the bit that I think people get wrong because they tell people, "We wow our customers," but actually if you're just giving free reign to your sales team or to your retention team to do whatever they need to retain a customer, then by and large they could just give away a Porsche in order to stop a 299 turn, if you take it to its logical extreme.

Lucas: This works in the basis of if you're selling a commodity which is highly competitive and everyone has one, where I also think I agree with you, this fall down on if you're in any kind of disruptor mindset, and if you've read Clayton Christensen's Innovative Dilemma, you don't need to feel any kind of optimal foundation need. You can go straight to the top level and you can come at it from a different angle. You can completely wow someone with one narrow feature set which doesn't help 70% of the population accomplish their goal, but the 30% of people who are absolutely wowed by that one feature set, they were switched to you by the fact that you have that attribute in much better than your [inaudible 00:13:18]

Gareth: Interesting. What I suggest is we get away from a pyramid and we move actually to a level 1, 2, 3 and give every level equal weight. Say, "Right, this is the basics of delivering customer experience, this is what a decent customer experience capability would look like," then if you want to provide solid good customer experience across everything, you need to be level 3 in every one of the pieces. Those layers that I have suggested, it's moving beyond just people, process, and technology, and actually moving into a 5 stage process which includes culture and the customer, which I think is a very important part that we often leave out of the customer experience. It goes with what you were just talking about with your brand, going across brands interactions piece you were talking about.

What I've suggested is that we have culture at the heart, which then feeds operations, which then feeds your product and service, which feeds your technology, which then feeds the customer. Then there should be a feedback mechanism by which the customer feeds back into the customer. You have an emotional core, because if you have a rational core at the heart of your company, you're focusing too much on numbers, and forgetting that ultimately you're dealing with an emotional being at the end, which is a customer. Therefore, if you don't have an emotional customer experienced culture, you can't serve the customer properly. Then leading out into these rational pieces, operations, product, technology, and then dealing with an emotional piece with the customer at the end. You need to have these different layers all focused around the customer, the end person, before you can actually stop delivering the outside [inaudible 00:14:51] experience.

Lucas: Where would the interests of an employee fit into this?

Gareth: Within culture and operations. Employees is largely culture. They are the people at the heart of the business. It's why I think quite often people fall down is they're like, "We can buy this new technology, and it will completely revolutionize our customer experience." It's like, "Well that's brilliant, but have you trained your core center staff, have you trained your delivery staff on the last mile?" If I order a bottle of wine from Virgin Wines, and have an amazing experience on the website, and then some dude turns up and smashes the bottle on my front doorstep, that's a pretty bad experience.

Lucas: For me, employee interaction is a really powerful one. Previous job I was working [inaudible 00:15:41] the ski result. The onboarding training for me as an employee was such that I felt very passionate and I was a big advocate of the brand that I was representing. It didn't matter whether or not I was working in finance or I was a ski instructor. Every single person who went to work for the mountain back home was proud to be there. As a result, the feeling that they had was that if every employee every since in goes to work for the mountain is absolutely loving it, then the tourists who also come and are serviced by those employees, they're more likely to have a better experience that comes with it. That's very much a cultural employee interaction piece. I think culture is one aspect of it. I definitely would say that employee interaction and the operational part for me was probably a bit louder.

Gareth: One interesting thing that I've had some feedback here is that actually within this model it seems like culture and the customer are almost separated by you have to fight through these layers to get to it, and actually you're saying the same thing, that really it's where culture and the customer touch, which is employee interaction is a key piece.

Lucas: That's really good. Operations is very much around how the business operates, so I guess in that operational part you've got frameworks around the example you gave around giving someone a Porsche in order to satisfy a 299 purchase. There's some sort of guidelines within those operations which enable you to say, "This is the maximum which one can provide financial support in order to satisfy the customer." That has to be clearly documented and understood by people. That makes sense that that's rational. Products and service, that's more around I'm buying a pair of Nike [inaudible 00:17:42] boots.

Gareth: Actually, if we go through these separate sections, you'll see where I'm going with these. If we look at culture, some of the key things in the research around culture is that you are setting the right expectations, you're engaging your employees in the right way. You're looking for decent customer quotient, they call it. Are you able to deal with customers in the right way? You have a customer experience that's integrated into the mission and the values of the company. The way that then spits out the survey questions would be level 1, customer experience in the company value and a senior person is responsible for customer experience. Level 2, we have a central customer experience team, we're empowered to make decisions in the best interest of the customer. The 3rd level would be customer experience is linked to company incentives; training, recruitment, and other human resources development are guided by the CX strategy.

Lucas: What would a [inaudible 00:18:39] results from customer experience? What would that look like?

Gareth: That would be, for example, the CMO has a customer experience metric that he's measuring and it's his responsibility. Or, you have a CXO where the X is experience. It's not just, "Okay, there's a manager down in some team somewhere that's measuring MPS score," but rather an actual senior stakeholder saying, "This is what the company is. This is the value, and we're going to drive this."

Lucas: The way I see the world perhaps simplistically in some ways making a household of our customers, look at their world. [inaudible 00:19:21] people who are responsible for acquisition, which goes into a marketing budget. Then you have other people who are responsible for customer service, customer support, all these kinds of things which all fall under the customer, which is fundamentally driven around trying to drive retention of those customers. In that sphere, customer experience could come under just the latter half of that, which is around retention.

Gareth: This is already suggesting that you need to elevate beyond traditional job roles and beyond metrics and say actually it needs to be a company wide initiative. If you're going to make it that, then you need to have somebody who's given his backing to it at a senior level.

Lucas: That can be at the senior level. Why isn't it just a case of everybody? Why does it have to be a single individual person who's responsible for that? I'm more inclined to agree with the notion that there should be people throughout representing different departments at that senior level should be able to understand the satisfaction that they are leaving either their customers or prospects or whoever it is, the people they are engaging with, with some kind of measurement as opposed to being an individual. Otherwise that role could end up being fluffy.

Gareth: Yeah, okay. Customer experience as a company value, you would agree with?

Lucas: Yes.

Gareth: Then this senior person responsible for customer experience and potentially that central customer experience team, actually no. It ought to be there ought to be customer experience function within each team, something like that, right?

Lucas: Yeah. In the same way that I guess many teams would probably have some sort of specialist in BI or accessing data, and that becomes a core fundamental skill that is woven into every single department.

Gareth: Then the training, recruitment, and human resources are guided by the CX strategy and customer experience is linked to company incentives? That's actually making sure that when you're out hiring people you're looking at can they deal with customers? Is the employee engagement there? Are they capable of interacting? Is it something that you can hire on, and actually then are you linking it to company incentives? Did we raise our MPS score? Then we link that, or whatever it may be.

Lucas: Training, recruitment and human resources are guided by CX strategy. Yeah, I think I agree with that being an important part of it. Customer experience linked to company incentives, well again it comes down to how tangible that metric is to incentivize someone by. It's much easier to just talk about retention or a number of sales or revenue of sales.

Gareth: Interesting. I wonder whether in here you would have almost we have a basket of metrics by which we define our customer experience. If we're going to measure customer experience, what metrics are we using to contribute to that score?

Lucas: Interestingly, within our platform we've been looking at how do we score each experience which goes live on a customer's digital properties. At the moment we leave it down to each individual customer to define what their goal is, to say, "This experience is here to drive increased conversions. This thing here is to increase engagement." I can [inaudible 00:23:04] science team where actually is there a single guiding CX metric which we could use to some kind of composite of these things.

Where we ended up actually, every experience that we put live to impact the customer is going to have a different flavor experience. What is right for someone who is brand new to the site or the brand who's never interacted with Far Fetched is going to have a different goal to someone who's on their 12th purchase. Actually, what might be great for one might be terrible for the other. You wouldn't want to show your most loyal customer a message you'd give to someone you'd want to get to purchase for the first time. It would need to come from a different geography, or whatever else it is.

That's at the very micro level. Then if you have enough of these in place, you need to basically have an overriding strategy so that all the different aspects of the entire customer experience are filled out. If you map out an entire journey from end to end, as I described from the first time I ever interact with the brand, made a buying decision, that entire journey should have almost a score across it where you want to be above a certain threshold or benchmark. For example, as soon as you fall below 7 in any of those categories of let's say post purchase satisfaction, then that becomes a red flag. Then that relevant team who deal with that function are aware of that, that they are failing below that on that goal, and could then come back to this point around company incentives.

Gareth: Yeah, so actually I wonder whether we put a question within here around that. Do you have a measurement system? Do you have a ... I'm wondering where that would come in. I might have a look at that and say, "Okay, is there a metric ... Do you understand what metrics you're actually measuring customer experience by?" Is quite powerful. Okay.

Looking at operations, here you're looking at more tangible qualitative stuff: strategy measurement, outcome metrics, perception metrics, channel switching. Here we are looking at we have a defined customer experience strategy. We measure customer satisfaction. We listen to the customer. We understand the customer experience journey. We measure customer experience and we continue to optimize that experience.

Lucas: Is there one more page?

Gareth: Sorry, it hasn't [inaudible 00:25:40] there we go.

Lucas: Interestingly, based on what I said before, this step would come before the previous one because you always need to map out that journey in order to put in place any kind of recruiting or hiring or incentivization program, because that would be intrinsically linked to what the operational structure of the business is.

Gareth: In which case here what would be saying is that on that onion framework, operations is almost feeding culture because you have to define any number of things before you can go and do a lot of the things around hiring. Which goes back to my I wonder if the onion [inaudible 00:26:20] is not the best depiction of what we're trying to get across.

Lucas: Yeah. That's an interesting point.

Gareth: They all feed each other right? It's almost a Venn diagram.

Lucas: Let's talk about cube it a second. One of the challenges we have, and I [inaudible 00:26:38] one of the challenges we have around product is actually thinking about how would our products be used by different aspects of business. One of the things where I have a big thesis around is that we need to understand a business' operations in order to best embed our product so it gets best used in order to get best customer experience from our products. Following that, operations becomes very important. That said, it then also goes down to, are you speaking to an operationally heavy business, that say someone like Far Fetched who's very operationally heavy because they're effectively trying to provide the slickest, most operational way of getting products from boutique vendors to their customers, versus someone let's say who is selling luxury holidays where actually the process and operations are far less important, but instead the aspect of luxury is what the entire brand is about. You can't be selling luxury holidays unless you're going to be putting that in the front.

I wonder if there's actually another one here, actually something like business model, or what is the most important attribute of the business which defines the order? I don't know if that blows up this model a bit exponentially. There could be some sort of catalyzation around industry here. You take commodities for example, again going with the one I mentioned selling petrol, a [inaudible 00:28:21] station. There's not going to be a culture there of ... Okay, actually that's interesting. In the UK where it's very self service, there's no culture of customer experience. You go and drive up your car and you go and put your petrol in your car and you know what you're doing. In the US, I think, I hope so anyway, you drive up and then someone comes out and fills the car up for you.

Gareth: Or you go and pay and you get it yourself depending on [crosstalk 00:28:48]

Lucas: There's different aspects. Perhaps different [inaudible 00:28:51] have different levels of what you ought to expect.

Gareth: In that situation customer experience could still be self service, but if you walked up and the pump was broken and the [inaudible 00:29:02] was dirty and it was more expensive than normal and it pumped out only 1 second in every 5, there still has to be a working system for you to walk away from that [inaudible 00:29:12] happy.

Lucas: In that case [crosstalk 00:29:17]

Gareth: You don't choose [crosstalk 00:29:17]

Lucas: The customer journey map, as a business we decide to be only self serve. We want to have a self service model. That is almost like ... Which one's first? If I'm saying that I want to have a [inaudible 00:29:31] which is self service, then that defines what kind of culture I'm then going to be putting in place in order to drive customer experience. If I'm defining that actually I want my [inaudible 00:29:43] to be the best customer experience, the user never has to leave the car. That then effectively drives the culture which is then used around customer experience after that.

Gareth: Interesting. I think this is worth exploring and definitely for the recommendations for my model. Actually is there something that drive what type of customer experience? What culture do you need for the customer experience that ultimately the customer wants from your type of industry? Or something like that.

Lucas: Is it commodities play, is it highly competitive?

Gareth: Luxury, is it price sensitive?

Lucas: Something like Google for example which have such a strong area of the market share, everyone uses Google because they get a good customer experience from that. That's also in respect to the fact that they're also now defining what the expectation is.

Gareth: Which is think is what Peter [inaudible 00:30:39] talked about in Zero to One where he's like, "You have to have a monopoly and then you get the pleasure of doing that." Okay, is there anything you would change in there other than what we were talking about? We have to potentially look at this coming before culture?

Lucas: [inaudible 00:31:00] before culture in terms of changing this stuff. I think in many places they might understand the customer journey, and then only later would they have a defined customer experience strategy.

Gareth: Yeah, I do wonder whether question 4 in this is actually too high, because it seems like understanding the customer experience journey is actually a fairly basic tenant of delivering ... If that's meant to be a level 2 question actually, if you can't understand the customer experience journey, how do you manage customer satisfaction? Maybe they even go together and the define the customer service experience strategies is a level 2 question. Okay, interesting.

Product and service. This is like effort. How easy is it to do business with you? How easy is your product to use? Remove the feature, easing of language, meeting expectations, not just the whole idea of bad profits, but of good profits. Yeah, people have to use your product so that's bad profits. Whereas they want to, which is good. Here you're looking at ... We have a complex product/service offering. We understand the expectations of our customers. We're able to serve the customer in the way they want. We deliver services our customers expect. We're easy to do business with. We understand the values of our customers.

Lucas: [inaudible 00:32:32] I think is actually quite driven by the rest of the industry. While your operations find what kind of experience with the product that someone would want to have, there's also this external influence which comes in here. There's also, we understand the expectations of customers means you have an understanding of what environment you're dealing with. Complex product/service offering. What do you mean by [crosstalk 00:33:04]

Gareth: Yeah, I'm not sure. This was a bit of an odd question, because what I was trying to get across was that actually a complex product isn't as easy, it actually gets in the way of [inaudible 00:33:14] customer experience, but I don't think that's true because a lot of software offerings are quite complex, but you can set up a good customer experience from using them. I actually think this question is slightly misplaced, because on this one you almost want to be answering low on it with what I was trying to get across. I think it doesn't quite fit properly.

Lucas: There's also the word complex can be taken in ways ... I think back to Apple when Steve Jobs came back in and he completely re-factored their entire product line to simplify it. They were still complex products, but they were simplified from the perspective of the end user so that it was easy to understand what it was they were buying. Was it consumer, was it professional, was it a laptop, was it a desktop? [inaudible 00:34:02] complex products, it was made simple. There's definitely a perception angle into this.

Able to understand the customer in the way that they want?

Gareth: Actually there is do we simplify our product offering for our end customers, something like that.

Lucas: We're easy to do business with. Again, this actually gets a little bit caught up into the definition of customer. Customer typically in my mind is somebody who's now a user of the product. In order to become a customer you would have to have been easy to do business with. That would be lower level protocol in any case. It comes on that customer journey map.

Gareth: More like a level 1 type question than a level 3. If level 1 is the base level for just getting going, and then 3 is good, this ought to be a base level question.

Lucas: Yeah, because I can imagine if you weren't easy to do business with, then many people wouldn't be using your products because you weren't easy to do business with. It's a fundamental thing in order to get to the next step. Maybe on that customer journey map there's almost some sort of waterfall process where if you don't get above a certain score on the previous, on acquisition for example, you don't become a customer. That can actually help you identify [inaudible 00:35:39] in your business where customer experience is failing, which means that the next tier ...

For example, you won't be looking at your metrics thinking, "I've got a low retention score," but then you look up very abruptly and it's because people are dissatisfied with the product, and that's because this expectation was set earlier on when they actually found doing business with you in the first place was very difficult. That all waterfalls down. A domino effect there.

Gareth: That makes sense. Moving it further up. It seems like we're getting to this idea that the questions need a little bit more thought around what comes first, as opposed to being level 1, 2, and 3, it's like actually you can't have this without this, and therefore there needs to be more of a chain effect? Actually, I guess that is level 1, 2, 3. It's just that the questions here are potentially the wrong way around.

Lucas: Yeah.

Gareth: In which case, let's have a look at the technology piece. This is again measurement. This was one of the key things that came out. Channel switching, touch points, MPS. Here we're looking at we can track [inaudible 00:36:57] channels, we can analyze customer data from the touch points, we can collect qualitative data, we can deliver a consistent experience with multiple channels. Customers can move seamlessly between those channels, and we can offer [inaudible 00:37:08] a personal customer experience.

Lucas: The <technology vendor>s example, how would product and technology differ? Would it be the same thing, or would it be more service than technology?

Gareth: I think it would probably be more service than technology. I think the last one around the ... This disappeared. This one is operations. Yeah, so I think this one is more, this would be talking about <technology vendor>s example, this would be talking about the <technology vendor> product. The technology in this case is not ... Because our offering is the technology. The technology here questions are more like, "What are you using internally to be able to measure customer experience?"

Lucas: Okay. Then if this is an internal aspect, then this is quite tightly covered almost a feedback loop back into the operational layer and how much is listened to is then considered by the culture of the business. You have to have good culture in place to say, "Okay, I'm going to listen to customer experience." This is where [inaudible 00:38:47] actually culture drives operations comes in. At this level, if the culture isn't driving that customer experience is listened to in operations is not going to happen. Playing thoughts out there.

If I am let's say I'm Nike and I'm trying to figure out what the customer experience is when I'm trying to sell a pair of shoes, you want to understand ... What this first couple of questions really ask is do I have an understanding of what my potential audience could be by tracking that. Does that influence customer experience, or does it just set a foundation for what total market is? I would potentially say those 2 are the 2 separate things. When you get into the qualitative data and providing a consistent experience, that is much more into customer experience. I'd probably say questions 1 and 2 is much more about audience reach. I'm not sure how audience reach and customer experience necessarily directly correlate.

Gareth: Would you potentially putting something there are instead of we can analyze this data, etc. it would be more like we understand the segments of our audience and then we can provide different experiences to different segments or something along those lines, like ...

Lucas: We understand [crosstalk 00:40:28]

Gareth: There is not a unified customer.

Lucas: It could be a case of we understand how our different audience base is broken up in order to define a strategy for [inaudible 00:40:46] the strategy part of it is obviously ideally the way you'd like the business to be. Potentially at level 3 we cover a unified strategy which is able to create a customer experience seamlessly across all those different audience segments. Question 1 and 2 is probably do we understand what our customer segments are. Understand what our customer segments are. Level 2 is we understand what those customers, each of those segments expects from us and we have a way of deploying communications in order to satisfy their needs. Then 3rd level is we have a holistic unified way of delivering that and we are doing it on a modus operandi basis.

Gareth: Brilliant. Thank you. Then finally the customer. This is around customer perceptions, customer management. For these ones, I think it's important to have the customer in there because quite often they seem to be left out of customer experience talks. Actually understanding their perceptions and what they need. To take your example of the different industries, something like a British gas. I don't want you to necessarily wow me. I just want you to let me pay my bill and let me get out of the way. If you don't understand me as a customer, if you're focused on customer experience and not actually what I need, I think quite often you fall down and focus in the wrong areas.

This would be I understand ... Our customers understand our values, we understand what our customers intend to do. We measure referrals, we manage the expectations. Customers enjoy using our service, and we measure the emotional engagement we have with our customers.

Lucas: The measure of referrals is like word of mouth, like, "This company is doing a great job"?

Gareth: Yeah, can we measure that ... I guess actually measure referrals would be, probably MPS is a better way of measuring, because you don't necessarily thoroughly measure every referral, but you can measure the likelihood of somebody to give a referral.

Lucas: Yep. My brother's job, he just got himself a new job. He's just starting work this month at DWP, department of working pensions, with the idea of putting in place digital transformation for people who are collecting pensions or collecting benefits to understand what it is. I'm trying to think about how that fits into, again this is a completely different framework in how it works.

If you were engaged with DWP on their website for example, you understand what it is that they do there, the service that they're offering. Probably that's even a foundation of 1 as well, understand what the business is.

Gareth: Does your customer understand what the business that you do is?

Lucas: Yeah.

Gareth: Then actually work through the layers potentially like, "But do you understand the why of why they're using that service?"

Lucas: Yeah. Once you've got that base understanding in place, then you have values, and then [inaudible 00:44:17] customers intend to do, that's the reciprocal. That all makes sense. The 2nd layer, manage expectations, that's an interesting angle actually. It's almost like for each of these layers there's a 2 directional question. One is what the brand expects of the customer, and the opposite way is what the customer [inaudible 00:44:43] almost like this reciprocal thing that can be woven into this.

Gareth: That's really interesting.

Lucas: Question 5 and 6, enjoyment of the services, yeah. Measurement of emotional engagement. I'm not sure about measuring emotional engagement. I think that's basically an impossible thing to do. I think what touches on this might be ... You optimize ultimately from an engineering point of view, you optimize what you measure.

There's an example of this book that I'm reading at the moment where a CEO chose not to measure the length of time that their customer support team spent on the phone with the customers on the basis that if they did measure it, they'd soon end up optimizing those [inaudible 00:45:37] phone calls, and on shorter and shorter phone calls. By choosing not to measure it, it meant that they never had to worry about optimizing for the wrong thing.

Gareth: That's interesting. That's almost taking you can't measure what you can't manage, and saying ... I'm sorry, you can't manage what you don't measure and saying, "You're absolutely right, so we're not going to measure it."

Lucas: Exactly. It's not quite related to measuring emotional engagement. I don't think you can measure emotional engagement but it's around making sure you're continuing to optimize for the customer's experience.

Gareth: Then finally, it would all feed into this score, as I said. That way then you'd be able to say, "Right, you score high in technology, you don't score that high in culture. Therefore you should go and speak to, or you should focus your efforts on getting this right at each level before you can just focus on 1 specific area." Or it might say, "Actually we think we're really good at technology, but your culture is not right at the moment." That's the overall framework. What are your any closing comments or thoughts?

Lucas: The only other things I'd probably say around this is raising this at the broader level is definitely a good thing to do and having a customer experience as 1 additional metric has been useful. If for example profits decreased quarter on quarter [inaudible 00:47:05] business, but at the same time customer experience metric had increased significantly, that's a very powerful thing for a CEO to go and tell their customers. You can have some assumption or try and base some kind of model of this, say, "By investing in the customer experience, actually that means we're going to have a higher lifetime value in the business, and therefore the business value in the long term for shareholders shouldn't be impacted negatively."

Customer experience is one side of things. I would probably also argue that actually there's value in not just being a financial ... A typical metric [inaudible 00:47:43] is the financial one. This is more of a customer satisfaction angle. You've probably also got employee satisfaction, as I said at the beginning as a 3rd one, because that could potentially be a leading indicator for how satisfied your customers are going to be. If for example revenues stay flat, customer satisfaction stays flat, but your employee satisfaction fell, that could become a, because the employee part is so immediately wrapped up in the culture of the business, if your employee satisfaction falls off, you could potentially end up in a situation where your customer satisfaction fell in the subsequent quarter. You can end up with almost quite a predictive [inaudible 00:48:24]

Gareth: Fantastic. Thank you very much. Awesome.

Interview 5 - Edward

Interviewee: Edward
Interviewer: Gareth
Date and Time: 20th/May/2016
Location: London
Customer Experience Group: Vendor
Gareth: What's your name?
Edward: My name is **Edward**

MEASURING CUSTOMER CENTRICITY FOR COMPETITIVE ADVANTAGE

Gareth: What company do you work for?

Edward: <technology vendor>.

Gareth: What's your job post?

Edward: VP of product marketing

Gareth: What are you responsible for?

Edward: The messaging, positioning of the <technology vendor> product globally.

Gareth: What does customer experience mean to you?

Edward: Customer experience, I think to me means that you're building a lasting relationship with your customers rather than treating them like numbers. If done right, I think it's more personalized experience. It is in some ways going back to the future, in a way. You have to go back to the fundamentals of human interaction and the need to build a trust between two individuals or two entities to create a better experience.

Gareth: Have you seen an increase in customer experience being discussed both internally at <technology vendor> but also in the greater market and with customers?

Edward: Absolutely, it's a huge topic of conversation, I think everywhere including this is really what drives our product development and our company.

Gareth: What do you consider to be the key element of delivering customer experience?

Edward: I think you have to be able to have a good knowledge of customer insight, I think is important. With that you can layer then empathy on top of that insight. If you know more about your customers and what they're trying to achieve and their typical day-to-day frustrations and things that will become friction for them, then you have a better shot at being empathetic to that and then doing something about it.

Gareth: Can we use some examples of companies and they don't have to be <technology vendor> clients, but could be personal or through experience, but those that you think are delivering good customer experience?

Edward: It's a spotty sort of things because there's so many examples of bad customer experience that I've most recently been subjected to. The good customer experience is almost overshadowed by the times when they get it wrong. There's also the thing about, so some experiences seem to work pretty well. Ocado I think is a great example of the customer experience that I have through Ocado is generally very strong. They have the products I want. They make it easy to reorder things that I, groceries that I'm commonly using. They know what my favorites are from past experiences. They kind of understand me or at least give the appearance of understanding through retention of past behavior and products. To me, that's a pretty good experience. Ordering the weekly groceries is just almost a delight.

Gareth: You mentioned that you see, you've had some pretty bad ones that tend to stand out as well. What were some companies that you see or even sort of where do you see companies most often failing when it comes to customer experience?

Edward: Most often when they treat customer experience as a necessary evil, it seems to be doomed for failure. The example I'll give is just a night or two ago. I've grown accustomed to getting a lot of customer support through chat because I do it after hours as most people are working during the day, so you go and you try to sort out something, in this case it was with a bank. I've had the same experience with utilities. I've had the same experience with insurance companies where there's sort of the brick-and-mortar old school companies who have to their credit, a contact center, so they know that there's a necessary evil in the contact center, but they don't empower them enough to do anything useful.

The bank experience I had where I was trying to activate a new secure key for my bank, it quickly turned into a nightmare of the support rep not being able to do anything and basically said "Hey, you're going to just have to call." Pick up the phone like it's the 90s, right? "Actually talk to somebody, and by the way, because you're doing this at night, they're not there right now. Although I'm the guy that is providing you the prep line to support, I can't do anything for you. You're going to need to resort to the other way of doing it." That's incredibly frustrating. That's an example I think.

Gareth: A recent Dawn survey on the role of marketing and customer experience found that by 2016, 89% of companies expect to compete mostly on the basis of customer experience, but it was 36% four years ago. What are your thoughts on this?

Edward: I think that's right. I think that the emphasis on customer experience is a good one. What's happened, I think, is we've gotten so connected and yet, so with that connectedness doesn't necessarily imply interpersonal. We've become more connected yet less personal. I think what people are recognizing is that bringing the personal touch back into these experiences are a competitive advantage for them. If I take that bank example, the disruption in the banking industry is going to be the guys who have 24 by 7 highly empowered reps on their contact center and I can just go handle my banking issues any time of the day because that's what busy people do. The bank no longer sees it as a necessary evil but a competitive advantage to do that. Those are going to be the winners in the future, I think.

Gareth: According to that same research, fewer than half of companies see their customer experience capabilities as superior to their peers, but two-thirds expect these capabilities to be industry leading, or more successful than their peers in five years. How do you feel about that?

Edward: They're saying, I guess, that they don't feel like they're differentiated right now on this basis, but they feel like they can be differentiated it seems like. That's a good sign. I think that is optimistic. There is a question of when everybody has top notch customer experience, then what happens? It would imply that it's no longer a differentiator at some point and the raising of the bar is the end game here. There's going to be a lot of room I think from now until that bar level reaches a critical mass of good enough. The question is what is good enough? There's a lot of room I think there for them. It's good to see that they're optimistic about that.

Gareth: There's an interesting question here, and this is actually outside of my questions, but by what metric, because there isn't a unified customer experience metric. There is a basket of metrics that we use to measure business, but how do you ... Is it by a top-down, our customer's voted us the best customer experience? Is it a bottom-up, we think [inaudible 00:09:23] thing? That's the interesting question for me. Is there a unified CX metric?

MEASURING CUSTOMER CENTRICITY FOR COMPETITIVE ADVANTAGE

Edward: There isn't a unified CX metric. Quite often the customers voting sort of thing turns into a popularity contest. What I worry about under that sort of scenario is the most popular brands become the ones that are seen as given the best customer service when it can really mask the reality of that. For instance, I find Apple to be a fantastic brand, a fantastic product, a fantastic product company, and yet I dislike their customer service immensely. I hate the genius bar. I hate the way that they try to push everything towards their knowledge base online and not really give you any personalized support for their products. Yet, I would guess that most people in the world if you asked them, "Is Apple providing good customer service or a good experience?" They'd say yes.

Gareth: That's pretty much how the gold standard is, right?

Edward: Exactly right. I think separating those two things is really important. Going back to the metric for that, I think the metric has to take out the notion of popularity of brand in order to get to the real of question of are they giving it a superlative customer experience and a customer service. I don't know what that metric is.

Gareth: It's been an interesting part of my research is actually the interweaving, everybody from the interview seems to be coming to this same ... Without what it is, but there must be something there. We use the current rational metrics around business, they sort of miss out the idea of experience and they miss out the idea of the customer.

Edward: There's some cases like MPS where if I'd been shown an MPS score the other night when I wast trying to do my banking stuff. In fact, at the end of the chat session, it said "How satisfied were you?" And I gave it like the lowest marks. It wasn't an MPS but there was several formed questions that I just wrote them a scathing review on. Their response of collection of insight into whether or not it's a good experience or bad experience, a lot of surveying going on in that process, but what that doesn't touch on is the more casual kind of experience that you have with the brand.

These customer service engagements are only one type of engagement, from my perspective, that lead up to a good customer experience. I think on other accounts, Apple does a pretty good job. Software usually works, it's usually easy to use, the hardware is elegant, there are things that Apple does right on a customer experience level that aren't simply customer support experiences. Those are a lot harder to measure by definition. You don't stop people on the street and go, "Hey, I want to do a quick survey. Do you like the new release of Keynote that Apple just put on there," you know, whatever it was. That's tough. How do you gauge and how do you then blend and what's the waiting for things like good customer support versus good product delivery.

Gareth: Back onto the presentation. I'm going to talk through the framework. How useful, what would you change, what would you move around, all the questions, do you think they're in the right order? Feel free to tear it to pieces.

Edward: I always have an opinion.

Gareth: Research findings and the experience. Recurrency model, we've been through this together before, but just for the record, I've gone through a study of customer experience, reading all the literature around it, identified key themes, key topics, classification to competencies and created a series of questions that are 1-10 scale rated that run through a model to then create a score in different areas of the business. Hence the framework with which you can then create a guide to where you should be allocating your resources for improving your overall customer experience delivery. I've built it around a level 1 2 3 option where 1 being the base level you have to get going, 3 being you should be delivering good customer experience. This is different to your typical pyramid model, but I think the pyramid model, people forget the bottom and tend to focus straight up to the top, and it becomes this idea of wowing customers. Wowing customers is not a sustainable business practice at its logical conclusion to stop a 2.99 newspaper subscription in turn you give them a Porsche.

Edward: Yeah exactly.

Gareth: Because I wowed the customer I kept them but within what framework?

Edward: Yeah, it's an extreme emotion. It's sort of like you shouldn't strive to be happy all the time because happiness is an extreme emotion. You should strive for contentment, right?

Gareth: Contentment, exactly.

Edward: It's the same sort of thing.

Gareth: I think too many companies try to do that sort of wow factor and forget that actually, I don't need you to wow. If I'm paying my bill, I don't need you to wow me. I want to get on my phone and I want to pay my bill and I want to leave.

Edward: Yeah exactly. One thing about the maturity thing. To me, sometimes that throws off the conversation because it's almost sometimes I think not a maturity thing rather than a capabilities kind of question. Maturity is often closely associated with time on the problem or there's a time element often associated with maturity that doesn't necessarily play in what we're trying to achieve here. Some of these things are easy to accomplish, you can do it in a matter of days. That's not a maturity thing, that is a did I build up that capability thing. That's just a comment on that.

Gareth: Yeah and actually as we've gone through this, we've gone through my research it's becoming more apparent that actually this is almost a capability map instead of a maturity model.

Edward: Right.

Gareth: What are we doing, how can we score internally, and where should we be focused. I think there probably does need to be some changes in the naming of it. The key themes that came out I've built around the onion type model, starting with culture and then that feeds. You get the culture right it feeds into the operations that feeds into the product and service that feeds into the technology that then lets you deliver that to the customer experience to the customer. If we were going to talk about people, process, and technology, but I think we, and I mean that as an industry and not specifically <technology vendor>, forget the cultural part that is the heart of the business and the customer at the end of the customer experience and we focus too much on the other pieces. We forget that you have this emotional heart dealing with an emotional endpoint and we focus too much on the KPIs we've been discussing, all these rationale business things around optimization.

Edward: I absolutely agree with that and I couldn't agree more. I think the interesting questions are the core questions like, how do you get people to emotionally connect culturally to a better experience that have a long standing necessary evil kind of point of view, so how do you get it back, a culture who says I need a contact center because I have to provide some support for my clients. They keep that emotion at arms length because it's not to them about, you know, they pay lip service to the, I'm really trying to delight my customers, to the, I've an operational kind of need to have customer service. To me, that seems like a very interesting and challenging mindset change. It's a psychological thing that is at the core, absolutely, but also perhaps the most difficult of all of these layers to actually solve, right?

Gareth: Yeah, I agree. What we're going to look through next is the questions that go into determining your capabilities within these different layers. Around culture, some of the key topics in here were things like voice of employee, empowering employees, your hiring around a customer quotient, almost the ability for people to deliver customer experience. Some people aren't capable of delivering it and hiring around that and having some board level responsibilities for the CX.

Edward: This is really good, but what I'd like to see is sort of the next, because this is sort of an operational question of do you have things in place operationally that will help you build a better culture, but it doesn't address the psychological problem of how do you get people psychologically invested in the idea that they should provide a better culture because all of these things, you can put them on a project plan, but if the people involved don't really feel it emotionally, it will fail. Or it will be less effective, right? This is what I worry about with this sort of thing is it can kind of become a checklist, and it shouldn't be a checklist.

Gareth: Yeah, I think it's actually back to what we're talking about, do you even want to turn CX into a unified metric because it makes it another standard thing, and I don't think any kind of experience should be that. It shouldn't be a necessary measurable thing, it ought to be a thing that you enjoy and experience.

Edward: There's two sides to that. There is the, admitting you have a problem is the first step in recovery, right? What we're trying to do I think is a very noble goal, is getting them to admit they have a problem, but then the recovery process has to be more than, in my mind, more than a checklist of things of process flow or processes that they should put in place. There should be something more visceral about it that makes it a real, human motivator to make it happen. I don't know what that is, but my sense is that there's something, maybe it's a peer pressure thing or some sort of political gain or something that they can really identify with.

Gareth: The questions that are on here are customer experience as a company value, a senior person's responsible for customer experience, this is the base level, level 1. Level 2 we have a central customer experience team and we empower decisions to be made in the best interest of the customer, and then training and recruiting a human resources development that are guided by the CX strategy, customer experience is linked to company's incentives. What do you think of the questions, the ordering, the layers?

Edward: These are good. I guess question three, it's related to two. If you have a senior person responsible, do they have a team? If they have a team, is it a team? I guess the relationship between two and three is interesting to me. It's almost like you could reverse those and still have a similar kind of impact because a lot of times there are customer experience teams, but they're not led by senior people. The question is are they showing a minimal effort by having the team or are they showing minimal effort by having a senior, responsible person. I'm not sure.

Gareth: Maybe you could even get rid of the piece around the team and just say, "Is there somebody responsible for it?" Because that then feeds out across the organization. If somebody's responsible for it, there must be not necessarily a team but it must be happening.

Edward: My gut is it feels like you want to ask a more precise question on question three, something about the size or scope or something of the team like, how pervasive is that team or how influential is that team in the business. Something that says "okay we're not just doing it lip service." Question two is we can still do lip service. Question three is we've actually made an investment. It needs to be more about the investment to understand whether it's lip service or not.

Gareth: The restructuring the questions would be at level 1 are you just paying lip service or are you getting on the right track. Level 2 is actually we've made an investment. Level 3 where really everything is tied to it.

Edward: To me that would be a good outcome if you could understand how much investment is being made and if you could benchmark that investment to other things, so how much of it as a percentage, it's like defense spending or something like that. Part of your GDP is spent on this, but it tells you how important it is to the company. If we can somehow get to the question of how strategic really is this. That would be useful.

Gareth: Interesting, yeah, at what percentage is your customer experience and maybe you're above it. .1%, well then you're probably going to have put a little bit more behind it. Operationally then, so this is more, I guess content, so strategy, measurement, segmentation, channel switching, all of these sorts of bits and pieces. This is then through, you know we have a defined customer experience strategy, we measure customer satisfaction, we listen to the customer, we understand the customer experience journey, we measure customer experience, and we continue to optimize that customer experience.

Edward: Yeah this is good. I think that question two, that's where it gets tricky because we're talking about how do you measure customer satisfaction in non customer service kind of scenarios and for it not to just become a popularity question. Question two, I think there's a lot laced into question two where it has to be done very carefully.

Gareth: Yeah I guess the challenge is, as we've said, at what point are you measuring customer satisfaction. To be honest, before I even buy something, I'm already thinking about the product, I'm already experiencing the brand and what do I feel there. Well probably some sort of excitement and I'm very satisfied and then when I'm picking the product up and then delivery. There's a whole cycle.

Edward: That's right. We measure customer satisfaction but do you measure the whole cycle of customer satisfaction, are they categorized and what weight should you place on these things. Should those interactive customer support, customer service kind of interactions weigh heavier than brand affinity or the excitement you get from deciding that that's what you've chosen as the product, that sort of thing.

Gareth: Like I've never bought one, but I'd probably feel pretty satisfied with Tesla at the moment.

Edward: Yeah I feel the same exact way. I'm sure that until buyer's remorse kicked in, I'd be a very satisfied customer until I realized how much I just had to spend.

Gareth: Do you feel like these are layered in the right way? Do you think that somebody that is really apt, I guess customer experience heaven or nirvana, whatever it may be, is continuing optimizing or do you think that's more of actually of a base level piece than something beyond that?

Edward: I do think there may be something beyond on this which is continuously optimizing the customer experience. It's broad enough that it might cover a lot of the things that you want to do, but it sort of understates all of the ways in which you want to do that. I think there's a lot of areas of customer, I think you have to define customer experience very broadly in order to get question six right because brand affinity and all that sort of stuff, people wouldn't think of as customer experience but it is. If you're continuously optimizing that, you're continuously trying to make Teslas more sexy and that's a valid part of this but isn't necessarily intuitive in that flow.

Gareth: I think what I'm taking from your points around this is that there isn't enough nuance in these questions. I don't know if I'm nuance or being specified enough.

Edward: Yeah, I know it's improbable or something. Well, I guess I geek out on nuance in general, so I may be an outlier in that way. To me, the nuance or the specificity of this is the actionable part. I look at it with an eye towards, how would I do anything about it, so if I had the question six and I said, "yeah, we continuously optimize for customer experience," then the answer because it's a slightly ambiguous question, the answer is likely to be ambiguous. Therefore, the derivative action is likely to be less effective. When I look at this, I think the more specific the questions, perhaps the more specific the responses and therefore action would be.

Gareth: Thank you. Then the product and service, so this is here I've got a lot of interest in the idea of customer effort, so MPS is brilliant for how happy you are with the brand. But customer effort is equally as important. How easy do you make it for me to buy your product? If I'm buying a service, I go through all of the sales process with a software company, and then I have this horrible billing method at the end. Actually I was really pumped to buy the product at this point, and my experience to that point was really good. That's kind of where we're going with the product question is actually can you make it simpler.

Edward: I like that. Part of what's baked in here is that when you add all of these things up, then you get the overall impression of experience. It is true that any given point in all the interactions with the brand can be a bad experience within the larger good experience, so how do you deal with that.

Gareth: This is we understand the expectations of our customers. Question two is we have a complex product service offer. That's actually written slightly wrong, it should be we have complex product service offer, but it's simple to use.

Edward: We've simplified.

Gareth: We've simplified a complex product. We're able to serve the customer in the way they want. We deliver our services as our customers expect. We're easy to do business with and we understand the values of our customers.

Edward: Some of things sort of remind me of Nike. If you got in particular the serving the customers in the way they want, this whole idea that you can just build your own Nike is a delightful kind of experience with your own, just build your own. Same thing with like car configurators and all of those online gimmicks for making you feel more in control. That's what it comes down to, it's the appearance of control provides you a more emotional investment in the relationship with the product, and therefore, the thing is it may not be a faster or more streamlined process, it may just be that you're more emotionally invested in it. Like the Nike solution, you can say, "I went to the Nike site and I could do a one click purchase of some Air Jordan something or another and that was a fast, efficient process." But if I'm customizing it and putting my own initials on it and choosing the colors and all that sort of stuff, I'm much happier at the end of that process and it took maybe ten seconds longer than the other process. What's the right experience in that case?

Gareth: I wonder actually if that relates to smartphones and dumb phones, there is obviously the functionality bit, but my iPhone is my iPhone. It has my apps, it does what I want it to do. I'm so invested in it that I would rather lose my wallet than my phone because it's built around my life whereas the phone previously was just a thing, like they were my phone, right?

Edward: Yeah I think that's right. I think these are good questions. Again, it's the nuance thing so you can think of counter examples to lots of these things. Like the simplicity thing, you can actually miss out on that emotional connection with simplicity so it has to be smart simplicity when it matters for simplicity and yet immersive when necessary.

Gareth: Again, I guess that would then depend on your industry. I work from a continued product, I potentially want to be able to personalize it and for my gas bill, probably not, but I want that to be a simplified process because I just want to get in and out.

Edward: Yeah that's right.

Gareth: From a technology point of view, these things like measurement and voice of the customer and segmentation. We can track our customers across multiple channels, we can collect and analyze customer data from touch points, we can collect quality feedback from our customers, we can deliver a consistent experience with multiple channels, customers can receive this between channels and we can offer a personalized customer experience. Again, do you think these are the right layers, do you think actually maybe personalized should be number one?

Edward: The problem with level 1 doesn't imply that you're actually doing anything for your customers because you can take all of this analysis and you could just sit it on a shelf somewhere. You try to contract your customers, you can collect, analyze customer data but it doesn't mean that you're doing anything about it. I think it's an inherent part of doing something about it, but I would want the action to be at level 1. The requirement of that action is these things, but these things aren't actually affecting experience at all in and of themselves. They're a means to an end. My preference would be that you get to the means to the end. There are lots of levels of better delivery that happen along the way and many of which listed here so that would be my only criticism of that.

Gareth: Finally, the piece I think we tend to miss out on the most when we talk about customer experience is the customer at the end of it. This is looking around their perceptions, do we actually understand what the customer wants when coming to our site. Do they even know? It goes back to that wow thing I mentioned. Maybe they don't necessarily want to be wowed, maybe they're just ... Most people don't care to about the brand because they just want to achieve that they want to achieve and do you understand what is is that they are trying to achieve when they interact with you? Sometimes I think the best customer experience is when they don't actually notice anything.

Edward: I think that's absolutely right. It does really, and yet I think because we're kind of neurotic about this, every brand is neurotic, we all think we're the center of everybody's universe. Every brand, it's almost like they're the center of the universe. It's natural when you're passionate about your brand and building a company and all that. It's a natural byproduct of that passion to feel like you should be the center of the universe. It is, I think a very healthy thing to step out of that and say, "what is my real place in the overall scheme of the customer interaction? Am I the gas bill or am I Nike? Do I just want to get in and out, or do I actually kind of geek out on different shoes that I want to buy?" What is the difference between those two. Sort of the hard truths and all that is baked into that.

Gareth: Our customer point of view then. Our customers understand our values, we understand what our customers intend to do, we measure referrals and existing customers, we manage the expectations of our customers, customers enjoy using our service, and we measure the emotional engagement of our customers.

Edward: I think again, baked into this is emotional enjoyment. For the gas bill, it's much different than if you're trying to delight somebody. I think the first level sort of have to be that what's the correct or the best expectation or the most reasonable expectation. You should start with what's the most reasonable expectation, and it has to be a pretty cold assessment of your place in the world. Then layered on top of that these questions can be honed correctly. Just like we've been saying, I think these questions are much different for the gas company than they are for Nike.

Gareth: Yeah. I wonder whether the unified model sort of falls apart because different industry have that different expectation or there is that, if there is a way that you can structure it with because we understand the intent of our customers in our respective industry, we can therefore be delivering good customer experience despite the fact that we are in different places because we understand that intention in the first place.

Edward: Or you take some things out of here like enjoyment. Enjoyment is akin to happiness or wow, right?

Gareth: Yeah.

Edward: They may not need to enjoy using your service. If you say that in a different way, you know the gas bill, did it live up an expectation of ease or something like that. I don't know what the right word is. Trying to get to the initial expectation and not necessarily and enjoyment because you may be building things for the purpose of enjoyment. If I'm a video game manufacturer, it's all about do they enjoy my game? That's much different.

Gareth: Distance is a horrible way of phrasing but something like we meet the expectations of our customers and understand what those expectations are or something like that because meet our expectations is a horrible phrase because it has this feeling of almost being average, we meet their expectations, but actually that's kind of key in this model.

Edward: Yeah and exceeding the expectations are key. I think the early questions are we understand our customers' expectations, and then maybe question two is something like, we understand our place in our customers' life or workflow or ...

Gareth: World.

Edward: World, yeah. World is fine. We understand our place in our customers' world. We understand our customers' expectations. Those are good sort of first level because then you go, "Okay now I know what to do. I know where to aim."

Gareth: Wonderful. Then that also fits out of your CXMA score, which will then lead to it. That's the end of it. Is there any final thoughts?

Edward: I think it's great stuff. I really do. It's wonderful work.

Gareth: Thank you very much.

Interview 6 - Paul

Interviewee: Paul
Interviewer: Gareth
Date and Time: 20th/May/2016
Location: London
Customer Experience Group: Vendor

Gareth: What's your name?
Paul: Paul
Gareth: What company do you work for?
Paul: <technology vendor>.
Gareth: What's your job title?
Paul: VP of People Operations.
Gareth: What are you responsible for?
Paul: Everything to do with people, given the title, so pretty much any touch-point that a person has with the company. The way I look at it is anything from office, to hardware, to IT, to meeting rooms, to getting them in through the door and out of the door, and everything in between: food, benefits, pretty much everything.
Gareth: All right. Excellent. What does customer experience mean to you?
Paul: To me, as I said to you before, there are two ways I look at customer experience: the way in which we as a business deliver to our customers, but also say I look at customer experience as my how I can deliver happiness to our employees, because I say I sort of tend to call our employees customers or clients. Customer experience in both instances, to me, if I had to sum it up, would be delivering happiness. That's the way I'd look at it.
Gareth: Given your role, would you see there being a link between the happiness of employees internally, your customers, and the capability of delivering excellent customer experience?
Paul: Yeah, exactly. If you've got people working for you who are happy, driven, and excited about what they're doing, then they're going to be obviously, when they're doing their job, which, depending on obviously their job role, whether it's building the product, or actually then servicing the product and making sure clients get the most out of it, if they're that way in terms of happy, driven, then they're going to be doing their best job and delivering excellence and happiness to our customers and giving our customers the experience that they're expecting.
Gareth: You've been with <technology vendor> for five, six years?
Paul: Six years.
Gareth: Six years, so almost since the founding. Have you seen an increase in customer experience being discussed internally and externally with clients, given your role previously in Client Services as well?
Paul: Yeah, definitely a lot more so. Just I think that's naturally because of the fact that previously, going back in the first probably three years at <technology vendor>, we were heavily reliant on external, third-party products. We didn't have pretty much anything in house apart from Opentag, which was built two-and-a-half years down the line. Back then, I think customer experience

was all about, as I say, making sure that we delivered on the promise that we would give them, and we were, as I say, using third-party products.

Now we're building our own in-house ones. It's more about making sure that, A, they're getting the most out of ours. We feel a lot more passionate because the products and service that we're delivering is something that we feel ourselves. In the early days, when I was on the client team, it was more sort of mixing together stuff in Google Analytics, Clicktale, wherever it may else be, sometimes occasionally using the reliance on the fact that those technologies weren't working to possibly say, "Look what we can do, X, Y, Z."

Now I think, because we've got our own products, people feel a lot more prouder to be delivering on those, so customer experience is a lot more important. Then obviously, given our shift and change with obviously the way in which <the CEO> delivered the experience economy speech at the conference, is definitely now much more ... everything is experiential.

Gareth: What do you consider to be the key elements of delivering good customer experience?

Paul: Understanding from the start what the customer wants, I'd have to say is probably the best way to define that. Not every customer is going to be the same. I think there's not going to be one template that fits all, so from the beginning, in order to deliver, the way I would say it, good customer experience is understanding what that customer is actually expecting. What do they want from our product? What do they define as success? If you can achieve those, then they're going to have a good experience with <technology vendor>.

Gareth: Which I guess actually quite nicely maps onto your treating internal people as customers as well, because you say, "What are your expectations from your career? What are your ... ?"

Paul: Yeah, so whether it's expectations ... "What are your expectations from your career? Where do you want to go? How can we help you to get there in order to keep you happy?" ... whether it's using Office 5 to understand why people are unhappy with the particular benefits or part of the <technology vendor> environment, and how we can then change that and make sure we then obviously don't replicate that. Then obviously they get a good experience internally of <technology vendor>.

Gareth: Have you got any good examples of companies that you think are delivering good customer experience? They don't have to be <technology vendor> clients, but you personally, is there anyone that you think, yeah, they're delivering what I would consider to be a good customer experience?

Paul: Without sounding cliché, and it's always the one that people go to, but I'd say Amazon is for me pretty good. I've not had a bad experience with them yet. That's probably pretty high up there with me: just the convenience, the quick easiness, the way in which things just work and happen right. I haven't had a bad experience yet, so until that day, they're up there. Also, probably a company like AO.com as well. I don't make electrical appliance purchases that often, but when I have done, I've gone to them and had a very good online experience.

Gareth: Where do you see companies usually falling down?

Paul: When they personally are trying to do something outside of probably their capabilities because they're trying to play catch-up with other competitors in the market. Consequently, not delivering on their promise, so poor service, whether it be customer service or the delivery. I think a lot of companies get it right up to the ... personally, a lot of companies, not all of them ... get it right up to the buy position, but I've always experienced problems with the actual execution and delivery of the end product.

Obviously I think for that, companies like us exist to help, but the actual end delivery I've had problems with, and then consequently getting fed information around, "Oh, it's not our fault. It's the delivery company that we use. They screwed up." Then it's a sort of finger-pointing exercise, which I'm going through right now with B&Q. They only delivered three of the four packs of decking I wanted, and they're like, "Oh, that's the delivery company," and the delivery company saying, "No, it's B&Q." I'm just ... I don't care. I just want it. I put the order in well in advance so I could do the decking this weekend, and right now it's looking like they're not going to be able to do it. It's quite frustrating.

Gareth: Do you think that because our expectations of the customer experience have changed, that maybe if that happened 10 years ago, you'd have gone, "Oh, do you know what? This always happens," whereas now you're like, "This is absolutely unacceptable because I can go to an Amazon and I know that I'm going to get [crosstalk 00:08:07]."

Paul: Yeah, exactly, that the expectation economy, knowing that someone else could have done that, and not screwed up, and it be seamless, because other companies get it right. I've never purchased from B&Q online before and would never do it again because of that, so there you go.

Gareth: There you go.

Paul: There's other companies that have set the bar high and delivered on it, and you then use them as a benchmark. If something's not up to that level, then your experience is bad and that will remain with you.

Gareth: Now a recent Gartner survey on the role of marketing in customer experience found that by 2016, 89% of companies expect to compete mostly on the basis of customer experience, versus 36% four years ago. What are your thoughts on this?

Paul: I'd probably tend to agree with that, with the ways things are going. Up until we had the conference, I hadn't really thought too much about it, but <the CEO>'s keynote in that definitely got me thinking a lot more on how that, as the economy sort of evolved over the last, what, I think it was sort of a couple of hundred years that we went back, it makes sense to me now. If I hadn't probably had that speech and listened to that, I probably wouldn't be as in ... not in agreement, but I'd be indifferent about that comment that you just said then. I'd be like, "Yeah, I guess so," but now I'm like, "Yeah, 100%. I do believe it."

That's not just because of that, because it got me thinking, and then I was thinking, yes, everything here is now the competition, the stage, is on experience. It's not about product ... price is still there, but price is now pretty much leveling out. You can get the same product in most places around price, but the price competition is maybe ... Two years ago, everything was price, maybe three years ago or whatever, online, but now that's leveling out. Now the arena is on the experience side.

Gareth: Fantastic. Thank you. Again, I'm going to take you through a presentation of this experience framework that I've created. As I said, I would love you to tell me how useful it is: the questions, if you think they are at the right level, if they ring true, if there's any feedback, thoughts, recommendations, basically a [inaudible 00:10:45] thesis as you see fit. We're going to look at my research very briefly, some of my findings, and then the customer experience maturity index model.

What I've done is I've gone away and done a lot of literary research around customer experience, trying to understand what it is, some of the key themes, the key topics, how do those topics link to those themes, and then I've created a survey that an organization can take where you'll answer from 1 to 10 around these questions, and then we can then run that through the model to produce a report on your customer experience score and in each of the different areas. The way that I've done that is through a Level 1, 2 and 3, where Level 1 being you're just about kind of capable, 2 being you're delivering good experience, and 3 being that you're really nailing it.

The traditional model, and this is a Forrester model, tends to look more like a pyramid, where you have this, sort of Level 3 is this peak piece, but my issue with this is that a lot of organizations take that piece, the peak, as being the most important piece. We wow our customers quite often here, but if you take that to its logical extreme, it means that to stop somebody churning on a 299 subscription, you could give them a Porsche, because I wowed the customer, but actually you've given away all your margin.

I'm trying to get away from this idea that there's a peak point and that you don't need to consistently exceed expectations because it's not sustainable, but rather you should aim to have everything working at Level 3. Now you will naturally peak at times, and that's the way the story's come from, but that's not or shouldn't be your goal.

The model that I've built is a five-stage kind of onion model whereby you need to get your culture initially focused around delivering customer experience. That then feeds your operations, which then feeds your products and your services, and feeds the technology that delivers customer experience and extra service, in which case ... or again, actually technology can be quite important, but that then feeds out to the customer.

Now we talk about people, process and technology, as most companies do, as being the most important, but I've added culture and the customer because actually you have an emotional heart to a business that's dealing with an emotional being at the end of it. If you're too rationally focused, actually you lose sight of what you're doing, and so that's why I think you need to measure five stages instead of just the three in the traditional sort of customer experience model. Any thoughts?

Paul: No, not really. It makes sense. Now I think I would always see the heart of a business the culture and the people, so yeah, it makes logical sense to me. I guess measuring that emotional would be quite interesting to see how you're going to suggest that.

Gareth: How do you see in your role the customer feeding back into our internal culture? In fact, is there even a feedback loop there?

Paul: There isn't really, I don't think. It's a good question. I think the only time ... whether this is related or not, I'm just trying to think ... the only times where there's a crossover between the customer and feeding back into our culture and seeing our culture is otherwise when they're physically on site. They get to see the office and comment on it, and 10 out of 10 times, it's usually positive. A lot of, "We wish we had this. This looks fantastic. What a great office."

MEASURING CUSTOMER CENTRICITY FOR COMPETITIVE ADVANTAGE

I think as well, I'd like to think the way in which our ... Again, I'm talking about the client team here because obviously they're ultimately the ones who usually are with the customer and building those relationships. Them as a person, we've hired them for a particular reason, and how they act and behave and deliver, to say my definition of customer experience is delivering happiness to the end user.

Hopefully that end user, that customer, can see that as reflective of your organization as a whole, so the reason why they're getting that value is not just because of the person, because they're incredibly intelligent and they've been educated well, or whatever, but it's also the fact that they work at <technology vendor> and there's certain aspects of the culture that have I guess not been adopted but ...

Gareth: Have been internalized.

Paul: Yeah, internalized.

Gareth: I wonder whether NPS would be a good feedback mechanism to put into that, into this framework, because NPS is a pretty good indicator of customer happiness.

Paul: Yeah. We ... Don't we do that?

Gareth: I think we essentially did. I don't know if we still do. I'm not in the client team, but ...

Paul: On an annual basis, we used to send out a customer survey to our customers on pretty much a really sort of straightforward, "Would you recommend us?" That was the other ... I think there was five questions: What are we doing well? What can we do better? Would you recommend us? Then obviously that was a good gauge to understand how well we're doing, but whether that was going to the right people always, whether it was going to, shall we say, an end user who's probably going to have a completely different view on whether they'd recommend us to someone who's higher up the ladder.

Yeah, I'd say that would probably be quite a good start on an indicator on a culture, but I tend to feel that sometimes that something like that might be quite skewed by their last interaction and whether it's been product-related. "No, I wouldn't recommend you. I've had a bad experience because of the product. It's not you. It's the product." That's how that NPS score, that Net Promoter Score, I think could be skewed to, it's because of the product and technology, and not because of the culture and the people delivering on that.

Whether that would affect culture and put it in a bad light, you'd need to have a specific, "Were you happy with your client team? Were you happy with the people that you worked with?" "Yes." "Were you happy with the product?" That's where you probably need to have a bit more of a ...

Gareth: A separate, almost like two NPS scores, almost.

Paul: Yeah. [inaudible 00:17:58]

Gareth: Now for the culture, within culture and customer experience in the literary research, it's really about employee engagement, empowering your employees, having management control and a board-level approval of customer experience. The questions that come out of the back of that are, a Level 1 type question would be, customer experience is a company value. A senior person is responsible for customer experience. We have the same for customer experience team with how to make decisions in the best interests of the customer. Training, recruitment, and human resources development is guided by the CX strategy, and customer experience is linked to company incentives.

Would those questions make sense? Do you think they're in the right order? Do you think maybe some are ... Are they at the right level? I'm interested to see your thoughts.

Paul: I'll just have a quick read. Just off the bat, and maybe this is just because it's ... I'm just thinking customer experience is a company value. Yeah, I guess that underpins everything, but then I can't help thinking ... I'm just thinking for that Level 1, when the customer experience is a company value, whether even that Level 1 would be in there or not. Some Level 1's might not have that. They might have a senior person responsible for customer experience. When you say customer experience is linked to company incentives, does that just mean it's linked to their remuneration?

Gareth: Yeah, potentially, like there is a KPI around it, and you remunerate on your KPI. Potentially, "Customer experience is a company value" actually might be slightly more advanced than a lot of companies, saying you don't necessarily need it as a company value, but you need to have somebody in there that's at least thinking about it, whatever one ...

Paul: Yeah, quite possibly. I can't really think of swapping any of the others around. That's just the only one that people at Level 1 might not have it as a company value. I don't think a lot of companies have got their company values right, but as a bare minimum, perhaps it should be in there. Whether they do that or not, I wouldn't say a lot of them do.

Gareth: Do you think if you answered these fairly strongly, that you would be in a good position? Do you think these are a good indicator of your customer experience capabilities?

Paul: Yeah, I think so. I definitely think the Level 3 training, recruitment, and human resource department are guided by the CX strategy. That CX strategy, though, it seems to be sort of missing from Levels 1 and 2.

Gareth: Interesting. So even "We have the CX strategy" might even be the Level 1, and then it's the company value, Level 2, and then actually we train and [crosstalk 00:21:59].

Paul: Yeah, quite possibly. I think at a bare minimum, a Level 1, you need to, "Do you have a customer experience strategy?" as a bare minimum. Then that obviously then defines how it's led by a senior person, and then there's an experience team. I think empowering to make decisions in the best interests of the customer, that could be probably a Level 3. If you're doing that, then you're empowering ... Well, I'm reading into this, but we empower to make decisions, so is that anyone can make those decisions, or ... ?

Gareth: Yeah. The idea there was, in terms of customer satisfaction, customer experience, it's like we let the front-line team, whoever is dealing with the customer, make decisions on the fly. We trust them to be able to make those decisions, as opposed to having to go up three ranks and trying to get sign-off for things.

Paul: Yeah. I can't help thinking that's probably in Level 3, because that's quite something ...

Gareth: It's quite bold.

Paul: That's quite a bold change to say I'm going to let someone make that decision on the fly, which could ultimately, if they've been trained and empowered ... no, if they've been trained and onboarded, well, then they know what they're supposed to be doing, then 99% of the time they're going to make the right decision and it's going to have a good impact. If they're going to say, "Let me get back to you on that" or delay something, that then could have quite a knock-on effect. So I would possibly put Question 4 up to Level 3. Do you have to have two in each section?

Gareth: No, and also, there might be an argument to make more than three levels.

Paul: Yeah.

Gareth: If it's more nuanced than the three, which is what I think you're getting at with the questions, actually maybe we'd expand that to a different number. Then maybe there are six levels, and have a question for each.

Paul: I think empowering to make [inaudible 00:24:12], I reckon, achieve it, personally that's one of the biggest things that we struggle to do. If that was a Level 2, then we're definitely not near Level 3.

Gareth: That's really interesting.

Paul: Because we say we do, but ultimately people feel scared to. It's one of the things that came up in the leadership training.

Gareth: Wow. That's so interesting, because I think that must vary between individuals and departments, because I [inaudible 00:24:45]. It's one of the things I love most about <technology vendor>, is I do feel empowered, completely. I can go out and make decisions I need to make, and so therefore I assume that's the same across the organization, but actually, potentially not.

Paul: No, I wouldn't say. It's one of the biggest things that came up in the ... people not feeling ... They get all this autonomy, all this autonomy, all this autonomy, and then you ... Can I make that decision? Should I make it or not? No. I need to go and ask Person X, and then ...

Gareth: Interesting. I wonder if that comes from ... This is off-topic. I wonder if that comes from the general maturity, though, because we skew fairly young. I guess if you're not used to making decisions and needs checking, like, okay, I'm confident about this being the right decision, but I better go and make sure that it is ...

Paul: Yeah, that slows down everything.

Gareth: It slows down everything.

Paul: That can slow down the customer's experience. That's the difference between getting the job done, or getting the job done quickly. In this expectation economy where things need to be done quick, the client wants something pushed live or changed, it's like, "Yeah, sure. We can do that," whereas somebody might be like, "Let me get back to you on that." It's those two different conversations which ultimately will affect ... I don't think you've reached Level 3 until everyone feels empowered to make decisions in the best interests of the customer.

Now, actually coming around, I would probably say, if I changed any of them, would be, Level 1, you have to have a customer experience strategy in place, and then ... so I'd probably move not the whole of Question 5, but "Do you have a customer experience strategy?" Then I probably would move Question 4 up to Level 3.

Gareth: I guess then linking company incentive to customer experience is fairly ... that's quite a strong indicator?

Paul: Yeah.

Gareth: Do you think that's something that we do?

Paul: We've started to.

Gareth: What's the metric that you use for customer experience? This is another, a whole different question, but is there a ... ? There doesn't seem to be, from my research, a unified customer experience metric. It seems to be a basket of metrics.

Paul: I'm out of touch with the current customer experience or customer success team, should we say. I think going back to what you said about an NPS score, that definitely would be a metric, and in all honesty, a sort of Office 5 sort of star score would be great. If you had an Office 5 star thing going out to all your clients once a week or once a month, then you could keep tabs on how they're feeling.

Then I think that would be a good metric, because all too often, from my previous role here and even now, you hear things and it's usually there's kind of a fire drill. Everything's fine. Everything's fine. Then all of a sudden something's going wrong, and it's like everything sort of boiled up and we didn't realize they were pissed about this, or this, or this, and then all of a sudden it just happens.

So there. I guess that's the way end users would feel about anything. They probably have a certain threshold of things perhaps not being to the standard they want or what was expected, and then all of a sudden, all sh*t hits the fan. If you could make and understand before that happens, I'd probably say an NPS-style score.

Gareth: Yeah, or even ... Yeah, not an external Office 5 sounds really interesting. Moving on to the operations, this is a lot more quantitative. This is like strategy measurement, customer journey mapping, different sort of values, incentives, so this would be ... I may have to look. We have a defined customer experience strategy. We measure customer satisfaction. We listen to the customer. We understand the customer experience journey. We measure customer experience, and we continue to optimize the customer experience.

Paul: That's where that would define customer experience strategies in Level 1.

Gareth: Yeah. Interesting. I almost feel like that wants to be a Level 1 question in a lot of these. Could we just go back to the keywords quickly on that?

Paul: Yeah. Sorry, could you just describe sort of what the operations are again, for you?

Gareth: Culture is the people that are doing things. Operations is the processes. A good example would be, if you are a customer-centric organization, is it quick for you to get an invoice in and get an invoice out? That's an operational process. Is that being developed? Are internal processes being developed with the customer in mind, or are they being developed with the business in mind?

Paul: Right. [inaudible 00:30:24]. Just a quick one on that, you got "We measure customer satisfaction," and then "We [inaudible 00:30:53] measure customer experience." How are you defining those two measures, just out of curiosity?

Gareth: That's one of the questions that's come up, actually. It goes back to that metric question. Actually what do you use, the defining metric? You're absolutely right. What is the difference between those two things, and can

it be defined in different ways, or actually are they one and the same? is something
that's come out of my interviews for this research model.

Paul: For me they seem one and the same. Yeah, sorry, just my ...
Just looking at this, my ... Between "We measure customer experience," "We listen
to the customer," "We measure customer satisfaction," for me they're probably all
of the same. You're listening to the customer when you're measuring their
satisfaction.

Gareth: Okay, so you're almost repeating yourself, then.

Paul: Yeah. That's personally how I see it. When we measure
customer satisfaction, there you're measuring it in a way in which you're having a
two-way conversation, so you're listening to them and asking them, "What can we
do? What would you rate your satisfaction? What can we do to improve?" That
kind of falls into the same area for me, so I would probably say Questions 2, 3 and
5 probably all merge into one and probably would sit within the second band
there. But as a bare minimum, we have a defined customer experience strategy,
and probably we understand the customer experience journey, so Question 4 into
Level 1.

Gareth: Yeah, I guess if you don't understand the experience journey,
how are you meant to do anything else?

Paul: Yeah.

Gareth: What if we map the customer experience journey actually a
bit internally?

Paul: Not ... I don't know.

Gareth: Not that you [crosstalk 00:33:36]?

Paul: I've been out of the game for a while.

Gareth: It's not something I'm aware of. Interesting.

Paul: I'd like to think that when [inaudible 00:33:42] was here, she
would have probably worked on something like that, how that whole journey
looks and works, from initial engagement, sales, through the hand-over process, to
like you said, the operational process around the sort of contracts, the invoicing,
the regular meetings and things like that. I'd probably say that there's repetition, as
I said, between Questions 2, 3 and 5, and also, "We understand the customer
experience journey" should probably be on Level 1, for me.

Gareth: Great. Thank you. Then the product. This is really ... I find
this one really interesting. We talk about NPS quite a lot in terms of understanding
whether people would recommend you, but I think there's another piece to
experience, which is, how easy are you to do business with? If I'm really ...

British Gas is a great example. They're really hard to do business with.
All I want to do is go on, pay my bill, and get off, but I have to call different
people. I have to speak to different people. I don't know if they're the right
people. The effort involved is a lot of effort, and I would rather go somewhere
that was easy. This whole product business is kind of around that. It's around how
easy you are to do business with.

Also, meeting expectations with the product as well: If I have a single
use for a product, I want to have that single use met. If I have many different
things, I want to be able to use all of them [inaudible 00:35:17] buy a suite:
Photoshop, for example. This would be like, we understand the expectations of
our customers. We have a complex product service offering. That question's
actually worded wrong. It should be, "We have a complex product service

191

offering, but can be simply used" is the one there. We're able to serve the customers in the way they want. We deliver our customer service in the way customers expect, and we're easy to do business with, and we understand the values of our customers.

Paul: I don't think there's a huge amount I'd change there. Just thinking. For me, that makes-

Gareth: Makes sense?

Paul: Yeah.

Gareth: Great. Then technology is a lot of what we talk about at <technology vendor>, so voice of the customer, easy to do business with, multiple channel, being able to switch between channels, different touch-points for the customer. We can track our customers across multiple channels. We can collect and analyze customer data from all touch-points as Level 1. Then moving up to Level 2, we collect qualitative feedback from our customers. We deliver a consistent experience across channels. Level 3 being, people can move seamlessly between those channels, and then we can personalize the customer experience.

Paul: Yeah, that all seems to ... Just on Question 2, "We can collect and analyze customer data from all touch-points," what ... ?

Gareth: I'm thinking if somebody's using their mobile, or if they're using a tablet, if they're viewing ... and it depends on what business you're in, but set-top boxes, potentially, if you're a broadcaster. Wherever your customer touch-points are, you're able to collect data from that touch-point, which all leads back to the thing you said at the beginning, which is that customer experience is about understanding your customer, so if you can't collect data about everybody, you're going to have blind spots.

Paul: Yeah, that makes sense to me. That lot is okay.

Gareth: Finally, the one that we seem to forget the most when we're talking about customer experience is actually the customer, and so this is about understanding what their emotional engagement, their loyalty, their perception, their expectations. What are they trying to get out of using you? Do they want a wow? Do they want a great experience, or do they just want to turn up, do what they got to do, and leave? B&Q, you aren't looking for a wow. You're just looking for your decking.

Our customers understand our values. We understand what the customer intends to do. We measure referrals. We manage the expectations of our customers. Customers enjoy using our service, and then we measure emotional engagement with our customers.

Paul: I don't think there's anything I would change about this [inaudible 00:39:44], actually.

Gareth: Nothing stands out, then?

Paul: No. I think it's hard to get customers to understand our values. If that's a prerequisite to moving on to Levels 2 and 3, then I think a lot of companies will fall straight to Level 1. They might be doing the stuff on the levels 2 and 3 there, but I wouldn't say a lot of companies do that well. They think they might do it well, but ...

Gareth: Actually, it's an interesting point. Do you actually understand Amazon's values? I'm not entirely sure that I know what Amazon's values are. I just know that I get a great customer experience. It's a really interesting point.

Does it matter? I think I understand Apple's values: "Think different." But they're Apple. They're in a position where they can do that.

Paul: Yeah, that's a pretty ... Just that's the only thing that jumps out at me. As a number one question, I think a lot of companies would be like, "Do our customers understand our values?"

Gareth: Do we understand our values? [crosstalk 00:40:59] I just mentioned earlier-

Paul: The customer, let alone the people who actually work for the company, yeah.

Gareth: "Do our employees understand our company?" might be an interesting first step.

That then all spits out into your experience score, so you get an overall score which you can index against other people in your industry, like the expectation economy, where are you actually scoring within your industry and outside your industry, and then it breaks down into the different component parts that we've seen in that model. Are there any final thoughts on it?

Paul: No, not at the moment. It makes sense to think in terms of, it would be interesting to understand what you've got as the end goal for this, as you see it as something that's being widely used, or is it just something for your ... is it a thesis, would you call that?

Gareth: A thesis, yeah.

Paul: Then it sort of sits in there and dies, or are you actively trying to actually get this out and to be widely adopted or used?

Gareth: Yeah. The basis of this model has already gone through McCaig and Lorne, and it's gone off to a research agency to be turned into reality, to be turned into something that we can actually use as a <technology vendor> product, so the <technology vendor> Customer Experience Maturity Index will be the goal. [inaudible 00:42:20] diversified [inaudible 00:42:22] from that slightly because that's already gone off, but the goal is for this to become a standard of measurement so that you can use it as a sales tool: Is <technology vendor> the right answer, or are you brilliant in technology, but actually your culture's knackered? You think that you're customer-centric, but you can't get your value proposition. That sort of thing is the idea behind it.

Paul: So it's to be used by businesses that we might or might not work with, to actually tell them where.

Gareth: Yeah, exactly, to elevate the conversation beyond the CMO into the CEO's [crosstalk 00:42:52] snapshot of your business: Is it ready for delivering customer experience? If not, where should you be allocating your resources and focusing?

Paul: Not playing devil's advocate here, but do you think sometimes that might result in quite awkward conversations, trying to tell a business where they're ... "You're not ready for customer experience because you're not being able to actually do this particularly well," and then they'd be like, "Who are you to tell us what we're doing wrong?"

Gareth: Yeah, absolutely, but I think that's the role of any consultant, is to make things awkward, because if you just went in there and acted as a yes-man, they'd never fix the business. You talk about being customer-centric, but your accounts department can't invoice. Your marketing messaging is around features instead of the why. Your sales team are focused on cost reduction. That might be what's relevant for your customer. Are you true to your word about being a customer-centric, customer-experience-led organization, or actually does this make you realize that you fall flat in some areas? If it does, okay, well now you have a guide to where you should be putting your effort.

Gareth: Thanks very much.
Paul: All right.

Interview 7 - Patrick

Interviewee: Patrick
Interviewer: Gareth
Date and Time: 20th/May/2016
Location: London
Customer Experience Group: Consultant

Patrick: My name, **Patrick**.
Gareth: Wonderful, what company do you work for?
Patrick: <consulting> company?
Gareth: What are you responsible for?
Patrick: I co-lead, with two other gentlemen, our customer experience practice globally, for <consulting company> . All of the geography and all of the sectors.
Gareth: What is customer experience mean to you? It's a term that's used with increasing frequency, but what does it mean for you?
Patrick: It's a perception of your customers, of a companies customers, about how satisfied they are with a company they're meeting with, or in this case your companies you are supplying. For me, it's a very- even though it's a perception, which makes it a little bit difficult to grasp. For traditional companies, it's a very powerful tool to understand how health your company is and how well your performing with your different customers.

To be even more explicit, this perception is guided by a very simple equation of: The observed performance that the customer has with the company, minus the expectations. Basically, he had this certain number of expectations, that you may have put in his head directly or indirectly; Either through a person that said something, or marketing message that made them expect a certain quality of service, or a certain speed of service, or a certain performance. Then they compare it to the real performance that they got. The negative version of this equation is negative performance, negative satisfaction. You put it against the one where you exceed the expectation, it's basically a positive satisfaction.
Gareth: Wonderful, that's actually one of the key things that I took away from your podcast; The observed performance that the customer has with it's supply, minus expectation. I think it really nicely sums up why- and we'll come into this a little later, but why if you're looking at something, like a utilities company, expectation is fairly low; You don't have to do a huge amount in order to get a positive customer experience. Potentially, you don't necessarily need to focus on wowing the customer, but rather just exceeding their expectations, which can actually be quite low depending on the industry.

MEASURING CUSTOMER CENTRICITY FOR COMPETITIVE
ADVANTAGE

Patrick: Yeah, although I would argue with that, that your obviously right. Expectations are different at those industries. The main point is that across the board they're increasing; Expectations are rising, why? Essentially, because you are having new players in the industry that are now raising the bar. All these new, let's call them [inaudible 00:08:12] to make it simple, but not only Google, Amazon, Facebook, and Apple, many others. [inaudible 00:08:19] just reinvented, completely, the number of sectors. Now you expect the type of quality you get from Uber or Airbnb, Across your experiences. You expect it from your bank, you expect it from your tel-co, you expect it from your energy utility, you expect it from your fuel retailer, or from your grocery retailer. You expect it everywhere.

Even in B2B, you expect it from your professional relationships, in the B2B relation. That's quite interesting, because then, if expectations are rising, it becomes a bit more difficult to deliver on expectations.

Gareth: Well, it's commonly referred to as the expectation economy at the moment.

Patrick: Yeah, interestingly yeah.

Gareth: Have you seen an increase in customer experience being discussed with customers over the last one to two years? Have you, also, seen a rise in customer experience being discussed internally as well?

Patrick: What do you mean internally-?

Gareth: What I mean is, has there been a rise in customer experience inquiries and people talking about the need for customer experience with customers of McKinsey? Them coming to you and saying "We need to address this?" Also, internally in McKinsey are you talking more about how do we deliver a good customer experience for McKinsey, given the importance of it?

Patrick: Certainly, it's been a topic on the rise for years now. It's continuing, so we are. The simple fact that we are a practice on customer experiences are already quite a good revelation, right? Signs of this including very prominent companies coming to us and try to move the needle on this. Now interestingly, multiple competitors have been pushed to position themselves on the dimension, some of them for quite a few years. Including the typical measurement system. I have to say that a lot of customers have followed that path.

A lot of our clients have followed that path, and have been having a measurement system for ten years now, for some of them. The needle simply didn't move. The fact of having a measurement system, or measure for some of them, doesn't help in itself. "Okay, at least you know the temperature, okay very good." Most people thought having the temperature would help move the needle. It's far complex than this, because they use it as a lightning indicator, wondering what they could've done differently, and get a little bit lost in thought, why it moves, why up, why down, and so on. What you see is it's more and more requests from clients, saying "Can you help us move the needle on this?"

Gareth: What do you consider to be the key elements to delivering good customer experience?

Patrick: One key element there is, obviously, the journey thinking. At least, that's what Mckinsey has been pushing with quite a lot of success. We continue pushing it, because it works. Customers think in journey, they don't think in touch points. Most companies are organized in touch points, recitals even. They

195

optimize for the recitals. Usually, even the worst case, you optimize for recital touch points and focus.

You end up with a call center, with average handling time, where the essential job of the level one is to catch the client and dispatch. Basically, they don't do anything; They just send you to the next guy, wherever that next guy is, and so on and so on. Manages the average handling time to the second, without thinking at all that this client is likely to come back, because you didn't manage to solve the issue for them. You're just pushing the send button.

Thinking Journey is completely different. You think end to end, exactly like you said you mean to. You take a different perspective about how you deliver on this customer journey, and what are the different services that the client will need? What are the different steps through which this journey will go? What are the different channels he will go through, because they want sometimes, on certain journeys, to extend different channels. There, I just want to say, I am definitely not a big fan of Omni-channel, which means nothing. It just means- omni means any, any directional, all directions. I don't think customers behave in all directions. They have clear paths, clear ways of going through the channels to achieve something.

That's what you need to recognize, optimize, sometimes transform, or innovate. You may want to find your weekend, probably digitize, some of these interactions; Instead of having everyone calling in for a password change. You can optimize this directly, but for some interactions they will require a multi-channel interaction and a [inaudible 00:15:01] interaction. Like ordering a new car; the clear path now today is going on the web, configuring your car, playing with the options, the colors, and everything else, at least for some segments of customers. Then going into the dealership, and shipping your car. Then that's a very satisfying way of ordering a new car.

Gareth: Okay, so needing a move from- I actually cover that. I mean if you look at a lot of vendor advertising and look in the Maltec space, everybody is talking about Touch-point management, and Omni-channel management. Actually, I think, what you're saying makes a lot of sense. We really should be considering what's the journey, what's the goal of the person. What are the wanting to achieve, and how do you then take them through that. Rather than actually, what are they going to use on the way through that journey.

Patrick: Exactly, if you're just confused, because of our conversation on the example of ordering the new car. Most of this come- I mean most of the auto manufactures have today, considerate of. It's extremely stupid, if you look at it, because it just stops there. There's absolutely very little link established with you at that point. When you, basically, go in the dealership, you start from new, again. There is little way for them to find what you are- Or if they do it, they're doing a very non-customer centric way. You have to register fully as the customer, again. [inaudible 00:16:41] , and actually, the guy in the dealership doesn't hardly recognize it.

There could be, today, an absolutely amazing way of doing this, recognizing customers: ID, an apps on your smart phone, maybe recognizing the customer with a beacon in the dealership. Almost loading your configuration on the sales guys Ipad. Even if you were new into the dealership. All of this is absolutely possible; Nobody is thinking about it really end to end.

Gareth: I would absolutely love to continue these discussions. I agree with you on so many points, but I need to get into the framework piece. I appreciate I only have about 15 minutes of your time. If we can go into this. Maybe what I'll do, if it's okay, is send over some of my other questions to you, and you can just, maybe, give me your thoughts; A brief email or something on the last bits, that would be great.

Patrick: Okay, I read through the document, by the way, in the background.

Gareth: Okay, I'll just very quickly go through and talk you through my thinking. I've been away doing all of my literature research on customer experience, identifying key things, key topics. Then working through and trying to pull apart what are the key areas that customer experience touches. What that's done has then lead me to this framework. Within there, there is a piece about the customer experience pyramid.

Talk about this pyramid, very much like a Maslow's Hierarchy. The issue that I have with it is, that I think too many companies, when they look at a pyramid like this, instantly jump to the top bit. Around the wowing the customer, and then customer experience becomes this idea of exceeding expectations all the time. If you take that to a logical degree, then if I have to do anything to wow the customer, I could give away a Porsche to save a subscription on a magazine. I wowed the customer. I've kept them as a customer, they've had a great experience, but it's not sustainable as a business practice.

What I'm trying to do with my model is get away from this idea of a pyramid, and move into a level 1, level 2, level 3, potentially more levels. To say, "Actually, there is a base level that you should have in delivering customer experience, and then you can move up and deliver more." It isn't something that pivots around this idea of a Wow. It should be moving up the whole organization level by level.

Patrick: I would agree with that. Yes, be specific with your levels, because it's probably right. For me it's more than level 1, or 2, or 3; It's either your expectations, or your not. It's more black and white kind of. A little bit like NTS is doing it, which is forcing it to be structurally by even the calculation method to be positive or negative. [inaudible 00:20:27] the black and white story. I think there's something true about this. Either your delivering, or not.

Gareth: I wonder, if in that case, and this is exactly why I'm looking for the feedback so that I can make recommendations against my model to improve it. I wonder whether there is an initial stage, which is binary, that says "Are you even doing this or not?" If the answer is then yes, or binary, it then says "But to what extent are you doing it?"

Patrick: Yeah it could be, but it's a bit complex. What's the use of what your doing? Where do you want to bring it, apart from getting graduated?

Gareth: What I want to do, actually that leads me onto the next bit. I'll explain them in tandem. The onion diagram that's in the next piece is- I'm trying to get away from this idea of just people processing technology, and saying that, actually, key in components of delivering customer experience are your internal culture, your employees and your business culture. Then also the customer, at the end of that do you understand their expectations, for example. You have a very emotional core to a business dealing with an emotional endpoint, which is people. You need to make sure that's translated through the different layers. It goes back to what you were saying around the call center; If you have a rational thing at the heart, if your metrics are all around just getting people off the phone as quickly as possible, you're in a bad place for delivering customer experience through to the end point, the customer.

What I'm trying to do is say, "On each of these rings of the onion," and again this might not be the best model for explaining it, which is what I'm trying to get at within the research; To then say, "Level 1, 2, and 3 are you very, very good at the technology piece of customer experience, level 3; Actually, your operational piece is very weak, and that's why your overall customer experience is lacking."

The goal of this being, is that I can take this to a business, and say "take my survey, get your scores, index against the rest of the market, and how they are." Also, take it as a roadmap to say " What you should be doing is investing in technology," or " You should be, actually, doing a cultural change piece," potentially speaking to someone like in McKinsey, and say " Or your operations piece," and saying "We've got a long way to go internally around organizing around the customer before we even think about doing the next bit." It's always the score card, a dashboard against these different areas, that's working out where you should be investing for improving customer centricity.

Patrick: Yeah, why not, I think it's interesting. We have something quite equivalent on the- If you read our articles, all the articles published, because we actually didn't do only the podcast. We also did publish multiple articles. Actually, a complete companion on the topic. You will find the hallmark of what the great customer experience companies are doing. Then in front of each hallmark you could do an assessment; Like how good is the company against each of the hallmarks? [inaudible 00:24:02]

Gareth: Okay, I can find it, is it just called The Customer Experience Companion?

Patrick: I don't think the Companion itself is online, no. We are publishing one-article-by-one, so you will find the article on our McKinsey.com website. As well as inside, you need to go to Lorneeting,Sales, and then within Lorneeting,Sales you look at customer experience. You will find, probably, most of the articles.

Gareth: Okay, I will check those out.

Patrick: They've been all published in the last three months. We publish one per month, and we have twelve articles. It's going to be going on for a year, probably.

Gareth: Okay, I will definitely check those out. I guess, for some feedback on the model, you are in general agreement with it? Are there anythings that you would change, or is it just that binary-

Patrick: I'm fine with it. I think the difficulty is more in the- But from your position, it's fine. You are in the assessment and diagnostics world, right? You probably should be. The student or the university person. The difficulty of business is not really the diagnostics; It's much more in the doing, which you might find strange for such a difficult subject to study. It's the truth. The difficulty is aligning the organization around the End-to-End idea. You should think, obviously, end-to-end is the difficult way of implementing this. The way it's going to implement this is quite difficult to go against the organization recitals.

The whole public of customers think organization, is the table that I would add if I were you. The way the organization is structured, and the way the [inaudible 00:26:44] can be pushed, or even governed within an organization is quite tough. It's quite the new thing. You definitely need a structure, a structure is very vague, right? You could put it on the wall everywhere, nobody would care. The wall is fine, there's a poster there; The customer would think "Okay, big deal."

How are you going to make decisions? How are you going to delay the launch of a product, if the product is not customer ready? Your competitor has it in the market; He's scoring big sales through it, so your marketing guy wants it in the market immediately. Your sales guy wants it in the market immediately; The CEO wants it in the market immediately, and the product is a piece of sh*t, right? It's a piece of product that would generate a lot of calls in the call center, because it's bat sh*t, It's not very- You get me, right?

Gareth: Yep.

Patrick: How do you make the decision not to launch this product, which is precisely what Apple did when they decided not to wait, whatever three or four years, to launch an Iphone. It's a bit of an extreme example, but you get the story.

Gareth: Yeah, they must have missed that for the Iwatch, but that's a different discussion.

Patrick: Oh the Iwatch, but no, it's the same. It didn't, you know- The product breakthrough was not the same, but the experience was good. I mean, it worked. There was no major issue. Now, the design, you know- You cannot put everything learnt from experience. This experience was good, including the buying experience.

Anyway-

Gareth: Listen, I-

Patrick: This organizational element, because this is one of the key [inaudible 00:28:54]. The way you measure, as well, the link between measurement and the structure. Measuring just for the top management doesn't mean anything, right, it doesn't help. You cannot change the culture with just, again, with a poster on the wall. You need some real thought groups. This is the main element behind measurement. Measurement is telling you what to do, so what to change. Measurement, if you pitch, is easier to achieve by piece. Bring back to the single person, or the last customer that interacted with the client, and ask him to act on it. Then he will repeat differently, because he knows that- think about Uber, right? Every guys has direct- You need to give feedback on every Uber, I don't know do you use Uber?

Gareth: Yeah, absolutely.

Patrick: You see what I mean, right? Call every guy, as soon as the guy is not behaving properly, they call you back.

Gareth: Interesting, so I think there needs to be a feedback loop within the model to say, "The customer is feeding back into this-"

Patrick: Exactly.

Gareth: Plus you can take their metric score, you'll also then need to feedback the responses, in order to increase the score within each area.

Patrick: Exactly, Look, I am needing to-

Gareth: Need to end there?

Patrick: I am coming to my next meeting. I think this is very interesting. I think you are on the right topics. I think that there are a few links between your levels that either reinforce themselves if they're all there, or kind of hinder the impact if they are not. You should think about this. Apart from this, that's very interesting and I'm glad. I will send you the Companion, so that you can a read.

Gareth: Wonderful, thank you. I will be sure to send you a copy of the Thesis when it's finished, as well.

Patrick: Thank you very much.

Gareth: Wonderful, thank you very much. I really appreciate your time today, thank you.

Patrick: Your welcome, bye-bye.

Gareth: Thanks, bye.

Interview 8 - Alex

Interviewee: Alex
Interviewer: Gareth
Date and Time: 29th/June/2016
Location: London
Customer Experience Group: Vendor

Alex: Alex

Gareth: What company do you work for?

Alex: I work for <vendor>,

Gareth: What are you responsible for?

Alex: I am responsible for the effective operations of business, the value that drives our customers, and the innovation in the product that we deliver.

Gareth: What does customer experience mean to you?

Alex: Customer experience is a broad topic, but what I see it as is businesses that ... Consumer business that put their customers first. They think about how their customers are going to interact with the brand, with the product, and with the general operations of that business.

Gareth: Have you seen an increase in customer experience being discussed with customers?

Alex: Yeah, I think we live in an age now, we call this the expectation economy, where the customer has got a very low opportunity cost to move on to another solution, brand or product. What that's created is sort of a very impatient customer, as a result of that. If you look at 100 years ago in retailing, your opportunity costs of going to a different retailer was very high, because you'd have to physically, without even having a car, get somewhere quite far away than your local High Street or department store.

Today, you're only a click away on your phone. It's very easy to switch, as a result of that switching cost being so low. Customers are extremely demanding, and a bad experience will lead to that customer detracting and never coming back to you again.

MEASURING CUSTOMER CENTRICITY FOR COMPETITIVE ADVANTAGE

Gareth: What do you consider to be the key elements of delivering customer experience?

Alex: There are many formulas for this, but the key elements from my perspective is that you need to understand who the customer is. If you're a business, you're dealing with multi-generations of customers. A customer from one generation wants to interact with you on the phone, and the customer from another generation … And wouldn't know how to interact with you on chat, and another customer only wants to interact with you through chat, and wouldn't even want to touch the phone. You need to know who that customer is. You need to cater for those absolute opposing interaction points for the customer. The heart of customer experience is about, who is the customer?

Gareth: Can you give some examples of companies that you think are delivering good customer experience? They don't have to be <vendor> clients, but for you, where you go, "Wow."

Alex: Yeah, it depends on what type of customer experience you're going to measure them on. General customer … I think the way we measure most businesses is that you have a bad experience, you have a bad interaction; how do they make up for that? How do they solve that problem? I fly a lot, and Virgin Atlantic knows how to rectify a problem pretty effectively. If something isn't working, I don't have the right seat, they will fix that. They care. Their culture cares about solving the problem, while you might fly another U.K.-based airline and they are less likely to fix the problem. They're just kind of like, "This is the way it is."

Culturally, businesses, or the people in the business, have to care about the customer experience. I think that's when it comes to dealing with a problem. From a digital perspective, I think obviously a business like Amazon has a good customer experience because the customer experience is about speed and price, so they're very good at that. If the customer experience sucks, or discovery, like I don't want to go to Amazon and have a look around. It's really uninspiring.

I think it's very hard for a business to be good at customer experience on every single level. The ones that can get that right can build everything, their culture, their product, their brand, their delivery mechanism all around that, are going to be the ones that crush it, and beat the businesses even like Amazon.

Gareth: Do you think that's why Tesla are killing it? I know your experiences with Tesla have been pretty phenomenal. Have they nailed each section of that journey?

Alex: Yeah, that's actually an interesting question. I think Tesla is very good. The buying experience, the production and the creation of the car, all of that is very good. Actually, the car has got a lot of bugs in it. I call up, and I try and get the car fixed, the problems fixed, they don't call me back. It drives me crazy. I'm still a promoter of the car, I think it's great. The experience of the car is generally very good, but there are a lot of problems with it.

That's actually quite interesting. It makes me furious when there's a problem with the car, and I call up the support, and the support doesn't help me, but I'm still an overall promoter of their brand and their business and what they're doing, and so are most of the customers.

Gareth: That's interesting. The next question was to be, why do you see companies most often failing when delivering customer experience? Actually, from what we're talking about, you kind of can fail in certain areas, but still have an overall high view, I guess, a good experience.

Alex: Yeah, because it's what … I think what's so important in the customer experience, this age, is what does that brand stand for? Tesla stands for a revolution. It's a new way of driving. It's good for the environment. It's actually an incredibly amazing, fun car to drive. What they stand for is very unique, and it's something that you have a lot of patience for.

When there are problems, there's problems with the car, the software in the car, which is annoying, and then there's problems with the service, which should be more fixed, an easier fix than the problems with the car, you have a lot more patience for that. Now, if you're a business that is a traditional retailer, all you are about is low prices and range. You don't stand much of a chance in this customer experience age, because you don't stand for much. Unless every part of the customer experience is perfect, is great, your customers will move on. You have a lot less wiggle room when it comes to your business. That's why I think brands and what you stand for and identity is such an important part of customer experience. That, I think, is overlooked.

Gareth: Yeah, I agree. For me, this whole idea within customer experience around sort of meeting the expectations of your customer, and if you don't understand what those expectations are, it's very hard to deliver. If you're a retailer … Actually, my expectations for retail aren't that high. If you just go slightly above my expectations and do what I expect you to do, you're probably going to have a very good experience.

As you said, with Tesla, it's like you're revolutionary, so you've got a bit of wiggle room in there. My expectations are pushing the boundaries of what I'd usually do.

Alex: Normally, Tesla, broadly speaking, normally exceeds expectations. Many parts of it are like, "Wow, I didn't know a car could do this." I think what you're coming from is exactly what you say with a retailer. Generally speaking, a car, your experiences are pretty low, because cars are generally not that exciting, haven't really done much of a great job for a long time, so you've got low expectations that are often hugely exceeded.

Tesla, I know they've changed their customer services system recently, because now when you call up, they know who you are. I used to have to identify myself. Something's changing there, and I think that I wouldn't put up with this for much longer, and they see … It looks like they're reacting to it, and that's an important thing. They should have the ability, and I think this is where we're going to get to, where everything is connected together. They should be able to tell me that they're changing something, because I've gone in and I've said on numerous phone calls that I'm really disappointed with their services, their never calling me back. I've said it four or five times on the phone.

They should be logging that, and it should somehow tell me that there's a problem, that there's an update to the way they're treating their customers, and servicing their customers. That would make me happy.

Gareth: You would hope if you'd messaged like five times, "Please call me back," that would go in a five-time call bucket somewhere as well.

Alex: Yeah.

Gareth: He's called in this many times, it's a priority person.

Alex: Yeah, exactly.

MEASURING CUSTOMER CENTRICITY FOR COMPETITIVE ADVANTAGE

Gareth: The recent Gartner survey, which is one that we talk quite a lot about around the world of marketing and customer experience, found that by 2016, 89 percent of customers, sorry companies, expect to compete mostly on the basis of customer experience, versus 36 percent four years ago. What are your thoughts on that?

Alex: Give me an idea.

Gareth: Say, the Gartner survey on the role of marketing in customer experience found that by 2016, 89 percent of companies expect to compete mostly on the basis of customer experience. What are your thoughts on this?

Alex: It goes back to the expectation economy. I think that it's not like they're choosing to compete on customer experience. I think they're forced to compete on customer experience, and so you have to measure how much the customer expectation is, and how far off they are on that, to figure out how effectively they are going to be able to compete.

I think that the biggest risk for most businesses today is that the delivery, digital revolution, is changing the delivery mechanism to the customer. I think that what seemed like your obvious competitor set is now not obvious anymore. There are digital-first businesses that will compete with very traditional industries, and it will come out of nowhere. That's very disruptive.

Gareth: It's interesting, this is a side note, but we look at these amazing advanced digital leaders when we're trying to go in and sell customer experience. For me, based on my research and this whole idea of the expectation, actually things like utilities companies ought to be the easiest to fix, because the audience has the lowest expectations.

Alex: Yes.

Gareth: All you have to do is make it easy for me to pay my bill, and that's it. You don't have to wow. It's interesting that those businesses, the laggards should in theory be the easiest to fix, but actually they're the ones that seem so mired in what they're doing. They're thinking, "We need to wow." It's like, you don't.

Alex: A lot of commodity companies sort of five, ten years ago, were selling themselves on their services as a … For instance, I look at Rackspace. Rackspace; completely a commodity company in terms of selling servers, and hosted serving. They came out as the … They even changed their slogan to being all about customer service. I think that enabled them to continue, because they changed their mindset around that.

I think utility … I think there are some utility companies trying to do this, but they're not … I don't know why they're not doing it. I find, I've switched to Ecotricity, which is a completely renewable electricity firm. Again, my expectation with that is that I've got a lot of … They've got a lot of wiggle room with me, because I'm buying green energy, and I care about that. I care about buying green energy, and they're investing in wind turbines and solar. That's what I really care about. I care about the fact that I'm not damaging the environment.

Gareth: That's really interesting. There's actually some values piece built into the framework. You understand their values, and they understand your expectations. By doing those, by understanding those [crosstalk 00:12:07]-

Alex: They're actually very good, though. They don't send me a paper bill, which is great. I don't want a paper bill. They send me an e-mail with a bill, and they also, I input my meter and electricity readings in an app. They send me an e-mail saying, "Can you please put this in the app?" It takes me two seconds. I just go look at it, put it in the app, and send it to them. They are amazing at customer experience, actually.

Gareth: That's very interesting. I might have to go and have a look at them, because my-

Alex: They cost less than the other providers.

Gareth: My [DF 00:12:35] experience is terrible. According to that same Gartner research, fewer than half of companies see their customer experience capabilities as superior to their peers, but two-thirds expect these capabilities to be industry-leading or more successful than their peers in five years. How do you feel about that?

Alex: It sounds like a lot of hope there. It's not just going to happen. It's going to require transformation. I think if businesses want to become customer experience first, they need to change their culture. They need to change their organizational structure around the customer. That's the only way they can succeed. It's not going to be something you can just buy in. It's going to be something that you have to actually build from the core.

Gareth: Wonderful, which actually segues quite nicely into the framework. Now, I'm going to show you a presentation of the framework that I've developed, and the survey that goes with that, and measures that. That's HDMI.

Alex: Oh yeah, you have no options.

Gareth: No, I'll just take you through all that, in that case. We're going to have just a very quick look at the research, what my findings were, what the model looks like, and then what the survey would be. What we'll do is, we'll go through each section. If you can just give me your thoughts on the framework, on the questions; do you think they're in the right order? Have I missed the point? Are there things you'd add in there? I can take the recommendations at the end.

What I've done, I've been out studying customer experience, identifying key themes, key topics, and then classifying those, looking for key words, key things that can be measured. There's a customer experience permit for us to do, which you may have seen before. My problem with this permit is that I think if you showed this to a lot of people, they would jump straight to the top of this as being the most important. This is the easy one to do, right?

Alex: Yeah.

Gareth: Wowing customers is easy, and to take this whole idea of wowing customers to its logical extreme, you must keep the customer happy. As a timed subscriber, if I'm going to quit, you could give me a Porsche. That would keep me very happy, it would wow me, but that's not a sustainable business practice. This idea of pushing things to the top, I'm not overly keen on collecting people trying to skip the bottom piece of the pyramid.

What I've developed is just almost a proficiency levelling system, so level one, level two, level three. You go through those as you go up. The survey that I've done is based around, if you answer the questions and you're very strong at level one, they will be weighted in a certain way, level two in another. What it should do at the end is spit out effectively a snapshot of your organization, from a customer experience point of view, and say "You're very strong in this area, but you're not very strong in this area."

MEASURING CUSTOMER CENTRICITY FOR COMPETITIVE
ADVANTAGE

To your culture point it would be, "You're very strong in technology, but actually, and you've bought all the things you need to deliver customer experience, but your culture is broken. You need to invest and focus on that, before you invest in everything else." It almost gives you a road map of customer experience.

Alex: Exactly.

Gareth: What I've done, we often talk about the people, process, technology, which I think is Schneier's framework, and I've expanded that out, because I think it needs a little bit more nuance when you're looking at customer experience. I've got, I put culture, you have to have a customer experience culture, to lead to having customer experience-centric operations, which then will feed out to your product and service, which is delivered through the technology, to the endpoint of the customer.

Alex: Exactly.

Gareth: I think too often in customer experience, we forget the customer when we're talking about them. The reason that they're different colored is this idea that you need to have an emotional core to the business, then there's rational pieces obviously in your operations and your products, because you are dealing with an emotional being at the outside.

I think if you have a purely rational culture, you can't be customer-centric. If it's entirely operational efficiencies, you're not … To take call center as an example, you're going to be looking at how you can get me off the phone the quickest, because that's very efficient for you as a business. That's terrible for me, from a customer experience.

Alex: Exactly, and then it actually … The thing is, it's a false metric, because you're actually just going to hurt your business. If you are ineffective on the phone, effective in terms of time and cost savings on your customer services on the phone, but you'll pay for it. You'll pay for it down the line, in future revenue. I agree completely, culture is at the core. I think I said that earlier, it's absolutely necessary to have that culture at the core. That's like the Virgin experience. The culture is at the core, that their job is to serve the customer.

That empowers everybody within the team to make sure they're delivering on that. You can't … The question is, could you create a rational strategy within your company about serving the customer? I think that's more like British Airways, a bit more like that. British Airways is a bit more rational about serving the customer, rather than emotional. It leads to more friction.

Gareth: Yeah, I definitely don't get that. Visceral is the wrong word, I guess emotional is the right word, attachment to British Airways. I like using, their app works fine, I have a good experience, but I don't think, "Wow, you really care." Whereas Virgin, you do get on board and you're like, "Yeah, absolutely."

Thoughts in general, other than the culture piece? Does that make sense?

Alex: Yeah, I feel like where the products and the service fits, is something that's going to be changing over time. I think businesses will become more core around their products or service, and the operations will follow off that. You're seeing a lot more companies emerge that are literally, the product is a brand, the brand is the product, it's all blurring.

You take like GoPro, for instance; GoPro is the product and the brand at the same time, and they kind of have a couple different products now. I think that it's almost like that forms everything else. It's kind of like culture, product, operations, technology, customer.

Gareth: Yeah, I have some of the thoughts around this is actually, it might be too formulaic to say this, or it pulses out from the inside, because actually not every company delivers their product or service through a technology, either. A management consultant is a person, it's a personal transaction.

Alex: There would be some sort of technology though, involved. There would be some sort of, even a management consultancy is going to have some sort of customer delivery through some form of technology.

Gareth: You think tech is always, more often than not, the interaction point with the customer?

Alex: Yeah, you're still … I'm sure most of the output is delivered through an e-mail, sent by e-mail-

Gareth: PowerPoint.

Alex: … Or PowerPoint, like it is involved.

Gareth: Looking at the different sections, so culture; some of the key words when looking at customer experience and culture are things like actually you need to have empowered employees. You need to have trust. You need to have management-level oversight of customer experience, and ignore the quotes.

The questions that came out of this, on a scale of one to ten, how would you rate questions one, two, three and four, these being the levels that we talked about? Customer experience and company value, senior persons responsible for CX, and you can read the rest.

Alex: Just rate these?

Gareth: Yeah, so you would take this. You would rate where your company is on this. That would go through the model and spit you out effectively a culture score, it might be two out of ten, four out of ten. The idea is that then you can then benchmark that in the expectation economy against your peers, against the market, against the standard.

Alex: How important I'd say these are in general?

Gareth: Yeah, so what I'm looking for is, do you think these make sense in terms of travelling upwards? Would this be a base level piece? Would this be a high-level, a company where customer experience is linked to [crosstalk 00:20:50]?

Alex: I would say a customer is the company value. Our customers are our value, rather than customer experience, I'd say that.

Gareth: More like, customer-centricity is the value rather than the experience.

Alex: Yeah.

Gareth: My thinking is that if a company is really doing five and six, everything is linked to company incentives is a CX, everything you're doing is guided by the CX strategy, that's fairly advanced. I don't know what your thoughts are on … Actually, that might be a base level.

Alex: Yeah, I think so. I agree with these, but I think customer experience is like the company incentives. We're seeing that more. That's where you're measuring interactions with the business, and you're rewarding people based on their interactions. That does … it is the behavior mechanisms that drive change. It is sort of, that's the way to make sure it is actually … I think the way …

I think sort of like recruitment, I would put recruitment of people who are customer-focused way earlier in the importance.

Being able to … I'd switch like four and five over. I think "We empower people to make decisions in the best interest of the customer" is actually a pretty complex thing to do, to actually empower people to like, "Now, what should I give this customer?" is very hard. I think recruitment, finding people who are guided by customer experience, is a more fundamental thing.

Gareth: One of the things that's come out quite a lot in my discussion with different people-

Alex: I think people have central … Sorry, people have central customer experience teams, that's dangerous.

Gareth: That was about to be my point. This is a question that I've been discussing with so many researchers, where two and three have created quite a lot of question around actually, do you want a central team, or maybe do you want a team of teams, almost like you want a CX person in each team?

Alex: Yeah, if you have a central CX team, then you're not taking CX seriously.

Gareth: Okay, cool, that's really interesting.

Alex: That's my view on it. You're just paying lip service to it. It's like a board just saying, "We better do more about our customers. Let's hire a team." I don't think … You need to have it built in to all parts of your organization. A senior person responsible for customer experience could be the catalyst starting it, so I think that …

Gareth: Yeah, this was like, for the culture point was if you looked at someone that didn't have a particular customer-centric culture, and then people said, "We're going to become culture-centric," and you didn't put somebody with some sort of power in charge of that.

Alex: Yeah, you need to bring that in. I think that's fundamental, yeah.

Gareth: On operations, so this is a lot more on the strategy, the measurement and voice of the customer, and this is then … We actually have a defined customer experience strategy. We measure customer satisfaction. We listen to the customers. We understand the journey. We measure it, and then we continually optimize.

Alex: Yeah, I would put, up at the top, I would have some more like … I think the ultimate is you're reporting on your customer experience. If you're a public company, you're actually reporting on customer experience, as a public company metric. That's really supposed to get it.

Gareth: What would be, I had this discussion with [Janet 00:24:16], what would be the CX metric? It's always a basket of metrics at the moment, there's NPS, customer metric score, customer service, feedback.

Alex: Yeah, like what's the EBITDA of customer experience? It's tough, I don't know. That's one that's still being defined.

Gareth: It's actually in the "future research needed" section of my thesis. That's one of the questions, is that has to be developed. You can tie CX to performance, but actually until you can create some sort of actual measure, there is-

Alex: … There's something that's … You have people that are interested in … I was talking about this the other day in New York, in a meeting.

You have people that want to spend time on your property, in your environment, in engaging entertainment and content. Then, you have people that want to go through and buy and shop as quickly as possible. How do you cater for these different experiences? How do you measure the fact that someone is actually enjoying their shopping experience, and maybe they're not even transacting, but there's value in that? It's tough.

Gareth:		There is, and this is what I think is one of the problems with NPS as well, when do you take that CX measurement? Is it post-purchase? Is it when you're first exposed to the brand? Is it … To go back to Tesla, I had a pretty good customer experience at Tesla. I've never even bought their car, I'm just reading about them, knowing about their brand. I'm kind of an advocate. How would you measure my CX experience of them? It's usually done post-transaction.

Alex:		Yeah, that would be social media monitoring and PR and things like that. A lot of people have tried to figure that out, and didn't really succeed. It's a tough thing to do. I'd say your questions one and two, I would be more like we have to find more of how to … We have to find how each part of this business is interacting with the customer experience. It's like defining departmental responsibilities for customer experience. I think that's really fundamental.

Gareth:		That's actually a key part of, the Forrester, Bodine and Manning I think wrote this, which is you need a customer journey, but then you need to actually go below the line and say, "Who's actually responsible for delivering against that?"

Alex:		That's the biggest fundamental thing that needs to be solved.

Gareth:		Product and service; this is, I really like, NPS is awesome, but customer ethics score for me is really powerful. How easy are you to do business with? You have a great experience with the sales team, but then it's really hard to get any employees out. At that point, the CX is great. In that point, the CX was terrible. It's actually all the way along, you need to make it easy to buy from.

This goes back to the expectations piece. If you understand the expectations of the customer, we have a complex … This is actually slightly misleading. It should have a complex product service offering, but it's easy to understand, or it's simple to understand, along those lines.

Alex:		Yeah, when you break the problem down, you help guide people through the purchase process of your solution. Buying a car is like that. It's a complex thing to buy a car. It's expensive. It's got lots of features, so you need the problem broken down for you.

Gareth:		That's exactly what the guy from [McKenzie 00:27:42] was talking about. Instead of thinking about touchpoints, always think around journey.

Alex:		Exactly.

Gareth:		At each stage of that journey, what is it you want to do? What are you trying to complete?

Alex:		Yeah, that's a good point.

Gareth:		He said … I can give you the transcript, actually. It's very interesting. He was saying "touchpoint" is just the wrong language, because it just gets you … It locks you into this idea of a device. Actually, it should be like, "What am I trying to do?" Once it's all written up, I'll share all the transcripts and everything.

Alex:		Yeah, that would be interesting.

MEASURING CUSTOMER CENTRICITY FOR COMPETITIVE ADVANTAGE

Gareth: This is the way we understand expectations of our customer. We're able to serve the customer in the way they want. We deliver our services our customers expect. We're easy to do business with, and we understand the values of our customers.

Alex: Yeah, so this is related to the product.

Gareth: Yeah, this is product [inaudible 00:28:33].

Alex: My question here would be, as a product business, how do you use your customers' needs to influence what you build? That's a really important phase here. I would want to know, I think the businesses of the future are going to be very customized. Your customers are actually telling you exactly what they want from you. You are a producer of something, and your customers are able to gain scale, or unit economics that are affordable, because they can say what they want from you.

This is communication; communication with the customer and the product designers and the developers, that exists. It's not necessarily about building exactly what your customer asks for, but it's about interpreting their needs and then solving a problem for them. I think that's like a connected customer and product innovation that's really important.

Gareth: Actually, I think one of the things that's missing from that framework is the idea of a feedback mechanism across any of the [crosstalk 00:29:45].

Alex: I think it's incredibly, it's absolutely critical.

Gareth: In here, it would be something like, we have a feedback mechanism, or we have a feedback loop with our customers for developing the product, something like that.

Alex: Yeah, exactly, that would be sophisticated.

Gareth: That would be up towards the top end?

Alex: Yeah, definitely.

Gareth: Technology; this is a lot of the stuff that <vendor> [inaudible 00:30:12], of course it's new around here, so voice of the customer, listening segmentations, channel switching, et cetera. We can track our customers across multiple channels. We can place and analyze customer data from the touchpoints. We can collect quality feedback. We deliver a consistent experience across channels. Customers can move seamlessly between channels, and we offer a personalized customer experience.

Alex: Yeah, I think that these are … Yeah, because I think the fundamentals are just going to join things together, be able to create … That's really hard to do. I'd say qualitative feedback is more fundamental.

Gareth: Is more like a level one, actually, and that tracking customers is actually fairly complex?

Alex: I'd say yeah, we can collect and analyze data from all touchpoints. I'd switch two and three around. I'd say question six is all about, we can offer a personalized customer experience into every touchpoint.

Gareth: I wonder if we could squish those together, actually? It's like, we offer a personalized customer experience across channels, would almost … Question five would then be part of question six, and we could expand some.

Alex: I would, because I think here you want to say it's all about continuity. It's all about wherever the customers, whatever touchpoint the customer is interacting with, what's the continuity from the last place they were at? That's the holy grail, advance off of that.

Gareth: Is that like ... That's when I'm on my phone, the Netflixing, I'm watching a halfway through TV show actually, and then I pick up my tablet and I put it down and I'm looking like-

Alex: Exactly.

Gareth: ... But for every-

Alex: Everything.

Gareth: Everything.

Alex: Yeah, so it's like, where do you leave off, being able to do that? That, where did you leave off concept?

Gareth: Is that incredibly complex, if you're talking about retail journey?

Alex: No, it's not. If you have ... As long as you have a user joined between the touchpoints, it's very easy.

Gareth: That's what we thought.

Alex: If we know that the user is that user on a phone, that user on a ... Our platform is in real time, wherever you left off can be made immediately available on another device.

Gareth: Anything else on the technology bit that you would add in as either being fundamental, or the sort of Nirvana levels?

Alex: Yeah, I think it's just like on the technology side of things, you've got to have a profile schema. You've got to have a way of defining the profile of the customer across all these different touchpoints. I feel like that's something that lives at the heart of this. It's obviously the way we think at <vendor>, but also you can track, but the tracking can be pretty lightweight and not very useful. You have to think about, what do I need to know about my customer, at any touchpoint? I think that's a really fundamental thing.

Gareth: Interesting, and this is not in here, but I wonder how you would, from a technology point of view, measure people's expectations? That's something ... My expectation is, they vary depending on the day and depending on what kind of mood I'm in. It's that, what am I expecting from the brand, and how do you know what my expectations are so you can meet me in that way?

Alex: Yeah, I think that's what net promoter score attempts to do. What you can do is, a person can go through what is considered an experience, a journey, and then you can ask them, "Did this meet your expectations?" and you can refer off that.

Gareth: The NPS is more like, "Isn't this more, would you recommend?"

Alex: Yeah, so it's sort of like, maybe that's as simple as what you do is you say, once you see a person who has gone through a journey of some sort you say, "Did this meet your expectations, yes or no?"

Gareth: The free text box would be, "What were your expectations?" You could almost collate that as group expectation data.

Alex: Yeah, that's interesting. You can start to say, certain customers, clearly this did not meet their expectations, or it did, what was the commonality between the groups that did understand it?

MEASURING CUSTOMER CENTRICITY FOR COMPETITIVE ADVANTAGE

Gareth: Yeah, and that's very different from a customer complaint like, "I'm unhappy with this." It's like, "Actually, I'm not unhappy, but I wasn't expecting this and you did this." That's pretty cool.

Finally, the final piece is the customer, so this is persuasions and values. This is, our customers understand our values, which goes back to the Tesla conversation. You understand what Tesla do. We understand what the customers intend to do. We measure referrals from existing customers. We manage the expectations of our customers. Customers enjoy using our survey, and we measure emotional engagement with our customers.

Alex: I think there are other, more fundamental metrics around just like, our customers buy from us again. It's like repeat purchase and things like that.

Gareth: We measure loyalty, we have loyalty, we-

Alex: Yeah, we measure loyalty, I think that's a really fundamental thing. You want to make sure that your customers keep buying. Nobody really … No businesses really like single purchase only.

Gareth: How does loyalty work in a subscription, not a publishing subscription, but something like I bought my bike insurance, and I am a repeat customer. I pay them every month, but I don't choose to. I have to. Am I loyal to them?

Alex: You're loyal, yeah. You're loyal in the renewal period. You could go find other bike insurance, so you're loyal to them. Maybe you're loyal to them because you don't think there's anything better.

Gareth: I just don't care, I think.

Alex: Yeah, that's the thing, then that's important. You have a … In that scenario, if you're loyal because you don't care, and you don't really feel like looking, you don't think it's that expensive, then you're pretty … That business is doing its job. They run the risk of being disrupted by getting complacent. If they don't think they have to provide a good experience, they could get very complacent.

Gareth: That's a good point. They've done a good job of just getting out of my way. I don't think about them, ever, and so I don't … The disruption isn't-

Alex: You haven't had to make a claim?

Gareth: No.

Alex: I guess that's where I'm … That's a critical point for those businesses, is when you have to make a claim. That's when their customer experience is critical. If you have a bad experience, you'll make a claim and then quit, if they treat you badly. Then, they've lost a lot of money.

Gareth: Is that when most people leave insurance companies, is after a bad claims handling?

Alex: Probably.

Gareth: Yeah, that would be a pretty good hypothesis.

Alex: Yeah, I'd say.

Gareth: Anything else in the customers?

Alex: No, I'd just say measuring repeat purchase and loyalty.

Gareth: Wonderful. That would spit out at the end, you would end up with your overall customer experience. This used to be maturity, it's now not, it's competency. This would say like 6 ½ out of ten, and then you could break it down and say, against the market, against your industry, against people, companies of your size.

You would then get a piece that would say, "You scored … You only scored six out of ten in culture, but you scored one out of ten in technology." Then you could say, "Actually, in that case, we should probably go and speak to someone like <vendor>," or whatever.

Alex: Yeah, that's great, very cool.

Gareth: Overall thoughts, any feedback, any-?

Alex: I feel like the questions are very high-level. I feel like, will you get enough sort of variance in the model from the questions that are pretty high level?

Gareth: I wonder whether the answer to that would be to expand beyond three levels, and potentially go to five or ten?

Alex: Potentially.

Gareth: If somebody really cares about the CX, they're probably going to be happy to wade through a number of questions.

Alex: Yeah, I think you will need more.

Gareth: That's really good, that will go into the recommendations. Actually, the gentleman from Accenture said the same thing. "This is great, but you need to go further."

Alex: Yeah, I don't think it's deep enough yet.

Gareth: Cool, great, wonderful. Thank you very much.

Alex: Yeah, really cool; I can't wait to see it.

Interview 9 - John

Interviewee: John
Interviewer: Gareth
Date and Time: 23rd/June/2016
Location: London
Customer Experience Group: Consultant

Gareth: What's your name please?

John: John.

Gareth: What company do you work for?

John: <consultancy>

Gareth: Right and what's your job title?

John: I am MD here.

Gareth: What does customer experience mean to you?

John: It is about providing a … it's about the outcome for me, the outcome is creating content and committed customers which ultimately generate a sustainable profit for the business. In order to do that what customers are engaging with an organization for in the first place needs to fulfilled in a way that meets their expectations, that's what customer experience is to me.

Gareth: Have you seen an increase in customer experience being discussed as a topic? Are you finding more and more people coming to you as a customer experience consultancy? Are you finding it's generally becoming a wider discussion?

John: It is, I think the most interesting thing is that where it's coming from has changed. Originally, we've been doing customer experience for some time, we

212

probably did as part of ... we used to do a lot of customer value proposition work and it was part of that solution. It would normally be either just digital guide or customer service and over time it's broadened out.

With Leen and Kaizen we found operational people were getting involved in customer experience and because the easiest thing to show improvement on is communications, marketing got involved as well.

More recently, reassuringly product are there and brand are there so it has evolved to become a wider piece, there still is that lack of understanding. If you go into a business and say "Who looks after the customer?" they go "We all do" and then you say "Well who looks after sales?" One hand will go up and you'll say "Well how does that work then?"

There's still a lack of understanding of ownership within an organization of the customer, some obviously have their Chief Customer officer. There's also many who are at the point where it's about fixing the broken stuff and it's quite difficult to get the conversation with people at that point to say "Look, I know thinking about what this is going to look like in the future is very hard for you at the minute because you've got a great big long list of stuff to fix but can we give you some indication on how you should fix it because otherwise in the future you'll be marginalizing the potential of your CX now".

There's a lot of people who are in CX who haven't completed CX programs, they haven't come out the other side so they don't know that they're about to step into another bear trap, they don't know they could have made their life easier if only they'd have spent a bit more time on the wiring at the start.

So in short, yes much broader, the quality of the conversation probably hasn't moved on that much though.

Gareth: What about the quantity of the conversations? Are you seeing more customers approaching you because it's become such a hot topic?

John: Yes absolutely, as I say it's one of those things, it's a bit like the new CRM, it's a but like the new sponsorship, it's a bit like the new quality management. You have parts of the business who latch onto it for the wrong reasons and, we'll do a little bit of customer experience on the back of this as opposed to very few who do see it as a business model.

We just had a Croatian Telco company come over and took the guy, shocking the CEO around some really poor customer experiences before he went "This is not a KPI on a dashboard, this is about how we do business". Too few are at that level, the quantity of conversation is "I should be talking about customer experience shouldn't I".

We've worked in organization with people like Visa, when it then blurs into a digital world all of a sudden they get confused between UX and UI and CX, they're not quite sure of what it is they should be delivering against. They think if things are well navigated they're probably delivering a good customer experience and they get these terminologies confused.

We once had, going back about 3 years but one of the largest management consultancies in the world were working for the utility company and they turned up and said "We've brought our guy over who's a specialist in this area", here is ... I can't remember his name now but he's head of CSR, we said "What?", "Corporate social responsibility, that's what we're doing here isn't it?", "No customer experience", "Well it's the same thing isn't it?". They had to very embarrassingly back track, when I say that what it's really about it was embarrassing and I'd flown him halfway round the world but that still does happen unfortunately.

Gareth: What do you consider to be the key elements of delivering good customer experience?

John: For me measuring the right thing is absolutely fundamental, everyone is chasing the wrong target at the moment, or a lot of people are chasing the wrong target and I've seen CEO's lose their job because of it. It's understanding what is it you experience? What should it achieve? It should achieve a behavioral change that's more favorable to you and to the customer. That favorable change must be recorded in terms of this is commitment and profitability, if it's anything else then it's a falsehood.

Trying to understand how something will increase my chances of verbalizing it to other people how good you are is not a measure of profitability and yet most organizations will build their programs around net promoter score. If you're going to build it around net promoter score the second component is absolutely fundamental and that is to make sure that from the very core customer experience as a discipline is built in.

We've just completed a project with one of the UK banks where their brand positioning was just too flaky and people were making their own interpretations of how it should be delivered. Those customer experiences that were being delivered, some of them were just so impossible to sustain that it was creating frustration for customers because on day one they get a marvelous delivery, on day two they get a very poor delivery.

Going right back, I go back as far as I can, I go back and I find people like expenses clerks and data processors and company solicitors and say to them "How are you deliver the customer experience?". Having a set of standards which are the things that customers are looking to achieve and to obtain as a consequence of this interaction is a great starting point. That for me is a really key area, to make sure that internally, not the front office staff but the back office staff get that they actually make a contribution.

It's just what what you were saying really, I've got a really good example there was a guy talking to me the other day, he was sitting down and saying to the ops director that actually 14 days for the customer to get a response on this particular issue just wasn't good enough and she was saying "Well fourteen days, I'm sure customers don't mind that, I'm sure it's fine", anyway she get a phone call and she said "What do you mean my dry cleaning's not going to be ready until tomorrow? I brought it in this morning you said it would be here today, a whole day to do it, that's outrageous, I'm disgusted". She out the phone down and he went "Do I need to carry on this conversation?" There's that real lack of understanding that actually you have a massive impact.

The cultural piece is really, really important and the other element that we find is really essential and this is probably ... those two I don't think anyone would argue but the third is probably a question mark. That is branded customer experience, there's a lot of investment goes into making things work and making things work better but brand really struggles to find its way to the table when it comes to we're migrating from the website onto an app or we've found that the payment processing in the background was actually taking three days longer than it needed to so we've made it one which is good because we can have more money in our account.

Whatever those things are brand really struggles to say "So how can we deliver that in a way which really epitomizes what we stand for so that when customers think I have a choice they think well that's the one I want go for?" When they're very customer facing executions it's a bit easier but many organizations are very poor at building brand into their externalized customer experience. On the internal stuff, it's just not there but that ability to be able to think how can we do it in a way that really reinforces why we are different and why that's of value to the customer at the same time as how do we improve this for the customer? Professor Klaus talks about vanguards, that's what the vanguards are doing things in a very specialist way.

They're the three areas I would say, there's a whole list of other stuff that I think is just housekeeping underneath that in terms of the way you set up continuous improvement systems. We spend a lot of time helping clients understand the value and how to structure VOC programs, the component parts, you get those three things right or get those three things as a priority and lot of other things will take care of themselves.

Gareth: Speaking of the vanguard, can you give some examples of companies, they don't have to be clients but just companies in general that you think are delivering good customer experience.

John: Yes so one organization I'm particularly a fan of is the BECU, Boeing Employee Credit Union, I don't know if you know those guys?

Gareth: I don't no, wow, I was expecting the usual body of South West Airlines, Apple, you know the usual ones, I was not expecting Boeing.

John: I'll come back to that because Apple do this and I think it's fabulous but not probably, it may not have come up before, so BECU it's Boeing Employee Credit Union, it's not just a standard credit union but obviously a credit union very much set up as an organization that's helping the local community.

Gareth: Yes.

John: They took a step back and they said what is it that we can do that is a contribution to the local community that others can't do? They decided financial literacy, that's what they actually can do better than anyone else so that becomes the thing that they will build in to all of their customer experience executions or the way in which they'll bring it to life as a customer experience. The premise is basically that if you have an interaction with the organization you will be more financially literate as a consequenece of it, that may be "I didn't understand how that works" or "Thank you for telling me it's going to be here on Tuesday", or "That reaffirms what I thought it said", or "This has created an issue for me which I now need to resolve" but it makes sure that you actually move forward in that relationship.

They way they bring that to life in a really ... there's quite a bit on YouTube you can go and have a look, it's a campaign they have called Closed for Good where they close the bank for half a day a year, you can't go there, you can go online but you can't get help, it's closed. Every one of the employees from top down to the bottom goes into local school and runs financial literacy programs. Basically all the students in the school are given a persona reflective of their banks customers, so it's all very tied in with what they do and they're given challenges such as, you're going to university and you've only got an evening job how are you going to raise the funds? How are you going to manage your finances? Or you're a mother with three kids and your husbands left you how are you going to manage the healthcare?

They're given these real life scenarios and asked to work their way through and what sort of tool? It's a fabulous demonstration of the importance of financial literacy, great opportunity for the bank to see actually how the next generation will be thinking about it and applying some of their own solutions and also a real brilliant opportunity for employees who sit in the back office to see the impact they have with the decisions that they're making, so they are a favorite of mine BECU.

Whilst you mentioned Apple I'm a big fan of the Apple geniuses. No other organization operates like that, if you go to a utility company or a telecom company, somewhere, probably up in Peterlee or Sunderland they will stick their complaints department in a call centre and it will have FTR first time resolution targets and it will have a budget in terms of compensation and it mustn't go above. What do Apple do? They stick them in the store and they make them geniuses, they put the complaints department in the store and they say if you've got a problem go and see these guys at the back.

We also, like the utilities will have a call handling system which will take you maybe an hour to get through, it's no different to the Apple geniuses, you've got to book it, you can't just walk up and explain to them but you're basically taking your product up and saying "This doesn't work, fix it please" but of course you're not complaining because these are geniuses with the lovely white environment around them, at the back of the store, kept away from everyone else because it's a privilege to go and see them. Under that environment and atmosphere the ability to resolve your issue there's an expectation they're going to resolve rather than this is going to be a problem.

They turn what everyone else does as a very much invariably will create an negative net promoter score into a real valuable service. To be honest they probably sat round and went "Well how on Earth can we run a call centre where everyone sends there stuff in, this is probably the only way we do it". I know their stores are not measured on sales performance either, so they've got these [inaudible 00:18:15] service centres. I think that's a great demonstration of how you can take something that's very routine and operational and put your brand experience through it, I'm a big fan of those guys.

Direct Line I'm a big fan of, Direct Line kind of identified that the customers that really valued what they did were those claimed, which is not unsurprising. What they decided to do was to try and replicate that experience before you have a claim, the whole fix it campaign with Winston Wolf. They created a lot in their program to remind you of how important it is to have things fixed correctly so that those 8% who are very strong advocates of the brand become a much broader audience because there's now a wave of people who whilst they haven't made a claim have got much closer to understanding the value of a claim.

What it has meant, I think Gus Parks is the name of the commercial director down there, there's a proportion of their book of renewals that isn't rated on price it's rated on customers value of experience. They can actually put a higher price on because customers say "You know what it's not worth trading. I think the fact that things will be fixed properly is really important to me".

MEASURING CUSTOMER CENTRICITY FOR COMPETITIVE ADVANTAGE

An organization who can take an industry standard of pricing for renewals and say we're actually going to base it on customers perception of the value of our experience, it's probably not your John Lewis or your Amazon but it's smart, that vanguards me.

Gareth: Where do you see companies failing most often in delivering customer experience?

John: I think it's not seeing it as a model and seeing at a phase they're going through, that's the biggest area. You have a great big long list and the worst thing is you go into an organization and they say this list is reducing, you kind of go, every time something falls off something else should come on there, you shouldn't just get to a point where you go "that's brilliant we're done now", I think that's a real failure.

The biggest one for me is measuring that promoter score, we've been called out to two banks now, one the CEO called us in directly and said "I have a problem, my problem is we're number one for customer satisfaction and that causes me a problem because I know that there are certain things that we do that make our customers more satisfied and have no correlation with their loyalty to our business". They were saying "I couldn't be more satisfied, I'm still going somewhere else". She said "There's a point where I've got to where I know every further pound I spend on improving the customer satisfaction is actually reducing my profitability, so that's bad, worse is I don't know what those things are". You can kind of go "If you'd have started by looking at finding a measure that tracked profitability then obviously you'd know what you focus on is driving profitability and what you're deciding to neglect hopefully has no impact on profitability.

We've and another organization, exactly the same scenario for net promoter score, they've gone so public with their promoter score they can't come back for it but we've been asked to go in and look underneath to find out what are the things that really drive net promoter score, that they can continue with and what are the things that have no bearing on it that they're currently focusing on so they can drop them. There's something quite uncomfortable about that because you would think they should just be brave enough to say "We go it wrong, wrong measure". Not saying that net promoter score isn't a force for good because when it's in an organization it gets everyone thinking about the customer and it tends to be all the other stuff that happens around.

It's not the improvements specifically against the net promoter score but it's the culture, it's the focus, it's the airtime, it's the COB and all that, all the things then mean the customer becomes part of the agenda but actually focuses purely on these are the things that our customers are saying are detracting and these are the things that are promoting. Lets spend more time on the promoting stuff and lets fix the detracting stuff, it's not a recipe for success as logical as that may seem.

I think that is a key area, also that first point I remember a chap who came to work us for a consultancy pool for a little while after he left Virgin Media. I said "what happened?" And he said "We just got to the end of a period and they went well we're probably done here and they just stopped and moved on". I said "What about all those touch points that need to be managed" and he said "Well there's no one accountable for them now", so anyone could come in not realizing how pulling this particular straw from KerPlunk would mean all the marbles would fall through, he said "Yes, there's no one managing them they just thought we've done it now lets move on to the next thing". Seeing it as a project rather than a philosophy I think is a big issue, capability of people as well inside an organization. There's a growing sense of "We should be able to do this ourselves" and I don't think I've had a project I've worked on where the client hasn't agreed that an outside-in perspective has been invaluable, either our perspective or bringing them examples of.

We;'re just working with a major betting organization and they came to us and said "We've got an ambition of being number one" and as a definition against that, "Can you help us understand what that looks like?" We helped them by showing them examples of how other organizations who are number one are delivering a better experience. That's very different to other organizations, with the healthcare company who said "We know what good likes like what we're looking for is someone just to help us with the functional journey mapping", we said "Okay so what does good look like?" And they showed us some very uncomfortable luxury brands and we said "I can't see why you've got there and those luxury brands do not deliver a great experience, what they deliver is a very exclusive experience and you're talking about becoming the most accessible brand on the high street for healthcare so why have you picked those?", "Because we're expensive". There's a real mismatch in understanding how to apply customer experience with practitioners internally as well.

Gareth: Like the idea of the NHS trying to be Burberry.

John: Yes but also people on our side of the fence don't help. I run a pitch for Playstation globally to bring in a new voice for the customer, vendor. The reason Playstation approached us is because they said "We're very conscious that depending on who we talk to will dictate to us the way things should be" and I was flabbergasted so we invited 30 of the worlds leading vendors in voice of the customer, customer feedback. The amount of organizations who have a view which is very much based on the kit that they're selling as opposed to what's right for the customer was uncomfortable, it really was uncomfortable. That doesn't help at all when you have vendors in a sector who have a very single minded vested interest.

We asked some questions like should we do analysis and then translate or translation and then analysis? It's a massive point, when we're doing text analytics how do you deal with sarcasm? These sorts of fundamental things when you're helping to shape output that then would define investment choices the flippancy or actual lack of investment that they've made in those particular areas was shocking versus the and the good news is that when you work with us we'll do a half day every quarter which is a bit of a workshop, you'll get to know us and we'll get to know you. It was just like, some of those fundamentals you've missed off there, or performance metrics what should we measure? "Well you tell us", "What do you mean you tell us? Give us an indication as to where you think the best profitability lies for us determined on what we measure". They didn't have a view that was beyond the kit that they were providing, not all of them some were very good.

A couple of them dropped out of the process because they "Our kit isn't designed for you it's designed for other purposes" but some were just interested in signing a deal. I've just come away from an organization who are at Christmas going to get a new vendor in and they are absolutely livid with this vendor because it's completely not the kit that they needed but the vendor assured them that with new upgrades coming it was going to be what they needed and those upgrades haven't come, that's another global company, a hotel chain.

You find organizations are therefore slightly skeptical when you have practitioners who are trying to support them, I think that doesn't help. If I'm working with a client how can I judge what you're saying versus someone else saying is right or wrong? There is the Customer Experience Practitioners Association which isn't that challenging to get into, I don't know if you've tried it?

Gareth: I haven't, I'm not even aware of them.

John: Right so the CXPA, you just write and say fill out their form and then you can put CXPA on your prolifery.

Gareth: Oh right.

John: The qualification you can get in it isn't going to do the best for clients so there's no standard. That is a slight issue for us in our sector, there is no standard.

Gareth: I will check that out off the back of this research. I think there's also a challenge at the moment around that vendor I was talking to someone about this the other day, all of the vendors are converging on customer experience in so many different directions that who do you listen to? We're the single truth, this is where you should put this, this is what you should do. "hold on if you're all converging on a singularity of CX which one of you should I be listening to and why can't you agree what the right approach is?"

John: A lot of that is to do with the client themselves. If you're a small team you probably do want a team who's more research based than tech based, if you're a large team you probably want a more tech based operation because you can take more of the heavy lifting over yourself.

The way a vendor is structured, whether they have their process in here, in Germany or Luxembourg or Salt Lake City it very much depends on your setup and structure if you are going to be providing dashboard intelligence, if you're an organization with a retail network versus an inline presence, all of those are variables that will impact which vendor is right. Most of the vendors will say "We're right for you" anyway irrespective of those choices.

These are big bits of kit, to plug in a force of the customer programming is quarter of a million pound a year for a decent sized one, you can get them much cheaper of course. When you look through the criteria that the client's going through in terms of the selection it falls short massively of the criteria they need to be considering and really stress testing their vendors against. It's almost like going for a current account and saying "what's the rewards program like?" They say "Well it's quite good" and you say "Well I'll take it" without inquiring what the charges were if I go overdrawn.

Gareth: Yes.

John: Some of the platforms the way they work, because they're not actually owned by the vendor they are taking components from other people they're dependent on those other vendors making upgrades before they can make upgrades to their system. They just don't get into thinking like that, a lot of the clients we've found and therefore they end up buying a piece of kit that doesn't quite work. That's really hard then because your CEO is going to turn around and say "I can't keep investing in this".

The last company I saw hideously, in order to keep a program going the client had sent up their trust pilot so that if as a customer you gave a negative response you didn't get a trust pilot questionnaire but if you gave a positive you did. It goes against what trust pilots are set up to do it just reports everything but this client was very conscious of the fact that they may not get budgets for next year because it was costing too much and they weren't able to make changes. You end up with that sort of poor practice just to keep the program going which probably wasn't their fault it was because they appointed the wrong vendor and that may not have been their fault the vendor just said "Yes I can do that" and there was no delivery.

Gareth: Just a couple more questions and then we'll go through the framework. A recent Gartner survey on the role of marketing and customer experience said that by 2016, so this year 89% of companies expect to compete mostly on the basis of customer experience versus 36% four years ago, what are your thoughts on that?

John: I think the statement of expect to compete on customer experience versus will compete on customer experience is probably a casam, that's where the gap lies because organizations will believe they're delivering a customer experience, of course any interaction is going to be a customer experience.

I think in some sectors we have seen a definite shift, in the hotel sector, price and location were forever and day the only two things that mattered and the experience now means that I will sacrifice the location I'm going to and I will may less or more if the experience is better. In some sectors I absolutely agree that has become the competitive battlefield, in others I think they do struggle with it. The more utilitarian the more commoditized a service is those industries do struggle to compete on customer experience but I agree with the sentiment that organizations believe they will compete on customer experience even if they don't actually know what that is.

Gareth: According to that same research fewer than half of companies see their customer experience capabilities as superior to their peers but two thirds of those expect those capabilities to be industry leading or more successful than their peers within five years, how do you feel about that?

John: It's quite interesting we did a piece with William Hill quite a few years ago where they kind of got all rah, rah around where they wanted to be with their customer experience and we showed them the cost of being market leading and the risk of it not coming off which meant bonuses were at stake and it meant investment choices would be pulled from areas that they were currently funding. Unsurprisingly everyone in the organization said maybe we don't need them, maybe we shouldn't be market leading.

Actually in that sector there's such a lack of decent customer experience that we ended up with a positioning which is one step ahead, that's all they need to be, to keep one step ahead of the competition, that doesn't need to be an incredible experience. I think they're claims without conscience because as an organization you don't necessarily need to be at that particular point and being there and sustaining it is very, very difficult.

If this is the competitive battlefield for the future then I have to be the most fiercest, capable warrior in that battlefield, of course you must have the best kit and everything that supports it. When you sit down and work out the cost of doing that, I've just sat down with an organization, looked at their VOC evolution from now over the next two and a half years and to get to where they wanted to get to required employing a continuous improvement team, it required lassoing all of the feedback that's happening globally and centralizing it so we had a standardization and can certify its MRS certified. All of sudden you go well "that's more difficult, I'm not sure that we've got the head count to do that" and you start to see that what's required ti fulfill that claim is probably beyond what the client anticipated would be involved in it.

I think they just think with that it's going to be about providing a better outcome but you look at the Institute of Customer Service Satisfaction and the expectations of customers are increasing all the time so what was before an extraordinary experience is now considered to be an okay experience. You've only got to look at home deliveries where now you can get a home delivery within a two hour window, whereas historically it's been a real pain in that space trying to know when things are going to be delivered. The benchmark is moving up and up and up and I'm not sure those organizations who are making that claim are thinking about what the benchmark will look like in three or four years time, they're probably thinking what the benchmark is now.

Gareth: I actually just got my groceries delivered by Amazon for the first time last Sunday and they've got it down to an hour.

John: Brilliant.

Gareth: They started doing trials in East London and it was the best online ... I love Amazon anyway and just being able to use mu Amazon account. They had amazing produce, amazing selection and I got to chose within an hour and if you order before 1 o'clock you can chose an hour slot after 5pm on the same day for free which is amazing.

John: Yes it's very good, I don't know who's making money there but it's great. I guess it's such an organization they can subsidize those sorts of things but again an hour slot, that's great. We had an Ikea delivery and this is where I guess organizations like Ikea get it just right, a week beforehand they tell you it's going to be there between 7 and 11.30, three days beforehand they say we've checked the amount of stuff coming to your area we'll be going to you between 7.30 and 9.30, the day before likely to be leaving the depot at 7.30, anticipate being with you for 8.30, on the day we're 20 minutes away, we're here.

Managing that whole journey is just fabulous and all you've done is just manage my expectations, just moved it along a little bit recognizing that actually they didn't need to do anything apart from turn up and say here's the stuff but they just reduced anxiety for me through that. I hope they've looked to see that that means that I'm more likely to purchase again from them because obviously if I said "Well it didn't matter whether you caught me or not I was going to buy from you again" then you could argue that's wasted investment because the customer experience could have been reduced and the customers commitment and contentment would have been equaled.

Gareth: That's a really interesting point and it's also interesting that this seems to be such a key part of my research findings has been around this idea of expectation management as being the core tenant of customer experience. If you are a utilities company you don't need to to wow the customer what you need to do is manage their expectations, meet their expectations which actually could be fairly low for something like British Gas.

John: It could, I noticed one of the books you've got there is Klaus's book on ...

Gareth: Measuring customer experience.

John: Measuring customer experience, so one of the things in there you've got that list of attributes that determine share of category. In that list of attributes, I think it's 26 or 27 and they account for 88% of the share of category decision making so obviously 12% just kind of whatever makes up chose that we're never going to be able to find out but this 88% can be defined by these 27 attributes.

I've seen it, I've worked with Doctor Professor Klaus on the output and I've seen it in practice, in there you do have two or three things around expectation management. Sometimes they have no bearing on the customer behavior so they are where appropriate things like keep me informed, keep me up to date which is slightly different, manage me well through the process, have coherent procedures, those sorts of things do bubble to the surface. Other times they're not there at all, they're just not important to customers either because it's something that I am very familiar with and therefore I know how this thing works or other factors are far more influencing and I'll tolerate a little bit of uncertainty because the other things are far more important.

Product quality for instance, I think it's one of those areas that the coffee shops and the payments company should have probably sat down first of all and worked out because I can go into Costa now and pay for my coffee, beep and there you go it's done instantly, isn't that brilliant? Actually the way Nero's model works is you get allocated a barista per customer so that Barista will do everything for you, it's not the same with Cost and Starbucks but in Nero's it is. They will take your order, they will pay for your order and they will make you a coffee, if they're getting the coffee as quickly as they're getting my payment made I don't want to drink that coffee because I don't think it's very good quality.

I'm expecting this to take a bit longer, I want it to take a bit longer, it shouldn't be that quick and I think that's where it isn't always essential to have that speed go through but also separately those expectations managed so strongly. The EXQ studies really good because it bubbles to the surface where it's important.

I remember Travis Perkins is a good case study where Travis Perkins said if you order it it'll be with you tomorrow, and bust a gut to get them to the client the next day. What they found out was about a third of their projects are just people like me doing DIY, I haven't got a project plan, I'll order it thinking I might need this next week and it turns up the next day, I don't want it here, I've got it on my drive now for a whole week.

They did some research and said to the customers "What would be right?" And for that segment they went "If you can get it through within a week then you're not going to make me fall behind with my project schedule". They were able then to contact their suppliers and say "Rather than bring the stuff to us and then drop it with us at our depots and we drop it to the customers, would you mind taking it straight to them?" They went "Okay" and also "Do it within seven days" and they were like "This is brilliant, I haven't got to pay so much for getting overtime and stuff for my staff, that's absolutely fine I can do that", Travis Perkins went "We save an absolute fortune on haulage can we give you some rappers just to put on the vans when they turn up just so they look like Travis Perkins?", "Yes no problem at all". Actually the customer was happier with a 7 day delivery than they were a one day delivery.

Gareth: Really interesting insight.

John: I think efficiency areas, efficiency measures, manage expectations, get it faster, get it sharper, sometimes are red herrings.

MEASURING CUSTOMER CENTRICITY FOR COMPETITIVE ADVANTAGE

Gareth: Wonder, thank you very much.

What I'd like to do now is go through the deck with you and talk through and get your thoughts and feedback on this. Just to talk you through my process then, the research has been literature research, so I've been studying customer experience with various articles, periods, podcasts, books etc and I've really pulled out key themes or what I think are key themes and key topics around those. I've created a series of questions around those topics to be able to measure each of them and I'll show you how that works as we go through. The goal, as I said at the beginning of creating a roadmap for actually we need to invest in our culture before we go investing in our technology stack for example.

John: Yes.

Gareth: Funny you mentioned outside-in, the customer experience pyramid piece from Forrester with the meets, needs, easy, enjoyable is good but for me I struggle with the idea of a pyramid because too often I think business leaders will jump to the top of that pyramid because it's the fun bit to do, it's the easy bit to do. It's why a lot of people say "We wow out customers", well actually wow is not a sustainable business practice, taken to its logical extreme, as a newspaper subscriber worth £3.00 to me I could give you a Porsche, that wows you but it doesn't make any business sense.

John: Yes.

Gareth: What I have suggested is that we get away from having this pyramid model into a level based, one, two, three whereby it's like a proficiency measure. One is you are delivering it and it's okay, at least you're on the right path, two being it's good and three being, as I've had it described in the past nirvana, you're really on fire with it and you have that proficiency level and capability to deliver it.

The questions that I've developed will then go into a model that will say you answered X number of level one questions and these are weighted in this way for this topic and then that would be used to spit out a score that you can indexed with at then end. The idea being you'll be able to index yourself against your industry and against the market in general.

Any thoughts so far?

John: That makes perfect sense, I'm in agreement with you on the Forrester model. Paul Massara who was the CEO of NPower went out with a bunch of flowers to see an old lady to say "Sorry that we didn't get your bill right" and she said to him very quickly "Why are you not fixing it for all of us? Why are you out here with a bunch of flowers that probably cost a fortune". There is that kind of this model, you're right, people do dive to the top and it's the quickest way to go out of business without a doubt, I'd agree with you on that.

I see the competency levels as being an appropriate way of thinking of things. We have four stages of maturity which I haven't used for a while but it was newbies and then you get to the numeric and then it becomes natural state, the layers you go through because people tend to do the numbers first of all. The newbies are the wow lest give flowers out, you always need to have that little bit of this is great customer experience, then you do the numbers and then it becomes more disciplined in terms of how you do it.

I find most clients do go through that process, there's a real sort of expectation that when you get a customer experience team in that's it but I think the customer experience team that starts the journey is not the one that finishes it.

Those who are really good at delivering operational excellence do not have creative flair so they're not the same people, don't expect them to be able to go all the way through to the end of the journey, they won't be able to make it.

Gareth: Okay, wonderful.

Then what I've done from there, and again this is based out of the key themes that came out of the research is that we have a tendency to use the model around people, process and technology but actually I think there are important parts beyond those when it comes to customer experience which is your culture, the heart of the business and the customer which we seem to sometimes forget when we're talking about customer experience, how important they are and then expectation peaks as you were discussing.

I've built this sort of onion model to explain that culture, customer experience comes ... you have a customer experience focused culture that then feeds into operations and feeds into product and service, then you deliver it through technology out towards the customer. The colors in this model are because I think too often we forget about this sort of emotional and rational idea and the people, the employees in an organization are emotional beings and the customers we're dealing with are emotional beings. Actually if we build the business around rational business processes we can be successful as a business but we miss the point when it comes to customer experience.

You mentioned first time call resolution, that makes absolute sense from a business efficiency point of view but absolutely no sense when it comes to dealing with human beings so I've tried to build that idea into this model as well.

John: I like this Gareth, I'm just looking and thinking I can put Michael O'Leary from Ryanair in the middle there. They have a very strange but they have a very structured and clear customer strategy which is we have terms and conditions, you stay within them, happy days, you stray outside of them, you're going to get punished. The way he set his stall out at the start means that all the products and the operations and the technology is structured to do that and culturally all of the staff personify that. They're changing obviously or trying to change but they wouldn't even look you in the eye, if a member of staff had an issue with a customer, Michel O'Leary's view was that the staff member is always right, what's the customer problem? Irrespective of what they actually had to say.

I think that does sum it up quite nicely.

Gareth: I wonder if they've done ... with Ryanair I usually consider that I've had a pretty good customer experience with Ryanair because I don't have any expectations of a good customer experience.

John: Exactly, yes. Make it very clear at the start what you're going to trade.

Gareth: Yes.

John: If you're not prepared to trade those things, if you get on board and go "Oh my God, the food's awful" and "The space isn't very good" or "you were very abrupt in the way you dealt with me", they say "Well it said that at the door, we couldn't have made it clearer when you came in, that's how it's going to be. You get in here and now you complain, it's not on". If you've taken an Emirates flight, you get to the other end and go "It's really expensive isn't it" it's like "did we tell it was going to be any other way?"

Gareth: Awesome.

John: I have huge respect for the way they operate, it's not something I'd ever want to get close to but I do recognize they way they operate is a customer strategy, it's just they view customers in a very different way to the way most organizations do.

Gareth: One thing that I think is missing from my model is a concept which actually Forrester being the outside-in approach, I think there isn't a demonstrated feedback loop in this model. I think that emotional layer around the outside of the customer needs to feed the inside culture and the other bits otherwise, the voice of the customer piece that you've been talking about I think is that feedback loop.

John: So you're worried at the moment it looks like you're kind of radiating from the center, out.

Gareth: Exactly.

John: Yes but I just would perhaps put a note to say this works both ways, it can push from the outside in or it can be pushed from the inside out, it's kind of pulsing both ways as opposed to the customer will have an impact on ... I guess I can see actually the way it's laid down there, the technology's intentionally the last layer before the customer?

Gareth: It is intentionally because I was thinking about it that that's usually the interaction point that most people have is with their technology but actually that's only really true if you're dealing within a digital channel, quite often the last part touch point. If you're dealing with a management consultancy it would be a person.

John: I might be tempted to simplify it and take this is I say, you don't have to adopt it. I might out technology, products and services in the same ring made then a third each just because if I am buying a product through a distributor then there is no service, I buy the product and now I'm going to experience it.

Lets say I've just bought some DVD players for the car, so actually I bought that through Argos, the first experience I'm going to have is in actually unpacking them and going though the instructions and setting them up, it's not the technology, it's not also service. Obviously if I am dealing with First Direct then it's going to be probably more the technology end of service. When I was in Argos it was actually a combination of the technology and the service because obviously it's someone else's product.

I might be tempted to say operations and then the next layer is technology, product and service in the same ring and that's what the customer then experiences.

Gareth: Interesting, I like that a lot, thank you. Actually the final part of the MBA is the recommendations based on all of this and all of the thoughts of the experts I was speaking to about how I would recreate that model so I will definitely use that.

In the culture piece the key words within culture were around expectation setting, voice of the customer, empowered employees, ignore the quote, we don't have to go through that. What that then led to if we go down to the culture questions, sorry it's a PDF, it's not that easy to flick through. On the culture questions a level one, on a scale of one to ten, a level one set of questions would be customer experience as a company value, a senior person is responsible for customer experience. Then it goes up through questions three and four and five and six, as question six customer experience is linked to the company incentives and training, recruitment and human resources development and guided by CX. To me that seems like quite advances roadmap pieces but it would be really interesting to get your thoughts on do you think these questions are in the right order? Should they be compressed? Are they relevant?

John: Yes, obviously the brown ones are the bottom of the entry level aren't they?

Gareth: Yes.

John: A senior person responsible for customer experience. So are you assuming that permission to trade here is that you understand customers and the value of customers and therefore customer experiences fits in the business alongside other areas, it might be have an invested interest in customer such as customer PRM or customer service. So those things are in place and now we're saying, we know customer experience is important to us and therefore there are two things that we've done to demonstrate it's important to us. We have a small team who are dedicated to customer experience and also if you look at who we are as an organization, they way we present ourselves, we say we believe the experiences our customers have with our business is of value to them and to us, that's your entry level. So it's kind of like a recognition and supported with head count or some investment to support it.

Whether those things are actually making a meaningful contribution doesn't really matter it's the fact that as an organization you've recognized them and you've out them in place, that would be the level one, yes?

Gareth: That would be the level one but I do wonder whether actually if you based it on your experience an interesting question, actually customer experience is a company value, company values are pretty enshrined a lot of the time. That actually may be a much more advanced question and almost ...

John: I think it is, we've just done a big piece with the Co-op bank and the values have kind of been adjusted as a bit of resolve as we've gone through because the starting point doesn't really have customer recognized in there in the way you would customer experience. Doing the right thing for the customer is not a customer value it's a suicide most probably. I guess what I'd be worried about is that we have a proficient understanding of customer experience as a company value versus, we've put it in there, we want to be customer first thinking, you'll get all this kind of stuff put in without the organization really thinking through what it means.

I fit's a considered and structured view versus a superficial "We'd better say this because I'm being told we'd better say this" I think there's a gap between those two.

Gareth: Yes but I'm pretty sure Enron had customer based service or customer value as one of their values and that didn't really work out so well. I wonder whether it needs some reordering.

John: Isn't it just more kind of it's a priority agenda point or it's common partner in the business, that's at that level you want it. So if I come in and say customer experience you say "We do that, that's us I think somewhere, we've got a guy who looks after it and it's important" there's that advantage that we do it rather than it being enshrined, mandated as our raison d'etre, just what this perhaps is conveying at the entry point.

Gareth: Okay, interesting, see I think maybe moving some of these around would make sense, I think potentially the sentiment is right but maybe they're in the wrong order and these are maybe a little bit too nuanced when you're trying to create a score against them.

John: Yes, that level one you typically will find, you can say to any company do you measure customer experience and they say "Yes we do that we record calls and we score on the back of customer service" or "We have a study that goes out once a year". You will find that we measure customer experience in some shape or form or we measure the performance of customer experience, that I think you will probably find is a fairly straight entry question. It all depends on the size of the organization obviously because if it's a big, big provider quite often they really struggle in that space, the measurement just because of the volume of contacts.

Gareth: Okay.

Moving on to operations, so here is a lot more round measurement, actually having a strategy, journey mapping, a lot more of the operations of the business around the customer. The questions here if we skip down would be around, we actually have a defined customer experience strategy, we measure customer satisfaction, we listen to the customer etc.

John: Yes.

Gareth: What I was thinking about here is the nirvana point, was the continuous optimization because that's quite a large step for a lot of companies and if you are continually optimizing around the customer experience, that's fairly advanced.

John: Yes, it might be a wording thing here but obviously in insurance they probably measure customer effort rather than satisfaction. The bank we're working with they measure and are promoted a lot on their rather than customer satisfaction.

Gareth: Okay.

John: I think maybe measure customer performance of something, make it more generic.

Gareth: Or we have a customer related measurement.

John: Yes, perfect.

Gareth: Okay and actually I wonder whether questions three and questions two here are actually the same thing. We listen to the customer and we have a customer measurement, is that not listening to the customer, maybe?

Maybe not, there's a voice of the customer ...

John: When first working with Hill, we went in there and they said "We can't cope with the [inaudible 01:01:50] if customers come to us and say that they're unhappy can we fix it we can't deal with it", so they just switched off.

I don't think organizations do naturally listen to customers ans also there's a sense of listening versus ... one of the organizations we're working with at the minute is like ringing the bell, bring out your dead. When they have these meetings to talk about the customer feedback it's just a fight between "Well the customer might have said that but that's not right" because this has happened, so they don't actually listen to the customer, they get feedback from the customer, they don't listen. I think it's worthy of being in there.

We understand the customer experience journey, yes.

Gareth: I actually wonder whether customer experience journey is actually a basic entry point though rather than a question four, if you don't understand the journey how do you even get started?

John: Yes, I know, I've always assumed that the best starting point, if you want to get a room of people who don't understand what's going on the same page you map it and they can then start to see where there's gaps in knowledge etc. You find other organizations who say there are so many journey maps that we could do it just would be endless here, they actually elect to not do the journey mapping because they know where they should be focusing their attention.

Ii wonder if it's one of those things that it's not necessarily a given that all organizations would do it, putting in a scaling an organization may be more advanced and say we've found journey mapping to not be that useful for us.

Gareth: Okay, that's good feedback.

John: You've not said about mapping yet, you've just said that you understand, if I understand the customer experience journey I could go and see I, it doesn't mean I have to map it, I know what my three pain points are.

Gareth: Yes.

John: There are only three and that's why we don't map it. I think that's valid, mapping, we work with RWE consulting and they came in with a whole series of maps that were just process maps to show how the wiring worked at the back end, no customer at all in there but it's called customer journey maps. I think maybe that's kind of get through their, this isn't a business process or the UX, this is a customer journey.

Gareth: Okay, good and I guess that's on a scale there of one to ten as well so actually as you said it's not do we map, it's we understand and actually that is on a scale.

The product and service, the thing that I like here and I actually wasn't aware of this as a metric that the idea of a customer effort score, I hadn't heard if until I started doing my research, I knew about MPS but how easy are we to do business with? I really like and around products and services this becomes increasingly important. What features do we include? Do we remove features because actually they improve the customer experience? Which goes really to the heart of the innovators dilemma, people come along with not as many features and then dominate a market so actually can we make things simpler? Can we make things easier? Do we understand the expectations? That was we can create a simplified service for them.

John: That has to do a lot with how much impact that particular purchase has on you, if it's a low impact piece then I want the effort to be particularly low, your effort can get confused with assumptions. We made it easier for you by not sending you the terms and conditions, that's a lot of stuff for you to read isn't it?

Gareth: Yes.

John: So actually making sure that in understand fully, I think this is one of those time bombs that will go off at some point where we've made it so easy for customers that they didn't actually realize what they were signing up to and then there's lots of compensation claims to be made on the back of it.

It's making it so easy and a good example of actually how it's damaging to a brand, although they've just been sold yesterday for a fortune but Visa have made it so effortless and easy. Whenever I do research now on card payments Visa is not a consideration for customers, they do not know what Visa does behind the scenes for them through their bank because they've made it so easy and effortless you don't even see them anymore.

Gareth: Yes.

John: You can marginalize your position in the marketplace by making things so effortless and easy for customers. The customers no longer value it and then they go somewhere else because it wasn't something they realized they should have valued anymore.

I think there's a danger of saying everything should be easy and effortless. I like ... we were talking about this with Visa, so a good example is something called Stip which is when you go to the shops and you use your card if your bank has fallen over Visa will step in, take all the reliability and the risk for a period of time so that you as a customer can get your groceries from Sainsbury's.

Gareth: Wow.

John: You don't know that.

Gareth: No.

John: You don't know its happened. You could say well Visa's got a B to B relationship but actually when it then comes to choosing should I stay with Nationwide and Visa or should I jump ship and go to Santander and MasterCard? You're not aware that actually MasterCard don't offer that stuff but you've traded something that you weren't aware was important because no one made you aware of it, because they've made it so easy that you didn't notice it.

Gareth: I had no idea.

John: You end up in this position where effort and ease can go too far and it's just being conscious of that.

Gareth: Interesting.

John: If you're doing this as a questionnaire you might have a category, which category of business are you in? If you say we're in stem cell cancer research then maybe making things effortless and easy in some space will go against the grain of the complexity of the sector they work in. Of course they still want their stationery to arrive effortlessly but actually to get an organization to have a culture of being effortless and easy when what they do is very complicated and needs explanation can be detrimental I think.

Gareth: Interesting, I wonder whether what I could use that for would be elect your industry and the industry selection then has a direct affect in the waiting model that's used for the results rather than on the actual survey itself?

John: Yes, you serve the question but then just reduce the weighting in terms of importance.

Gareth: Yes, okay.

Around technology then, this again comes down to measurement, how easy it is for the customer to interactive with you? Self service, multi-channel, the mapping of touch points. Here this is around we can track out customers across multiple channels, we can collect and analyse data from all touch point, we collect qualitative feedback, we deliver consistent experience across channels, they can move between channels easily and then we can personalize the experience for them.

John: Yes, I think that question one is a high bar but I think it's the right sort of positioning. The only one I would challenge as six as being the pinnacle, again the IPS questos we've run, quite a lot of the time the thing that customers aren't looking for is personalization.

Gareth: Yes.

John: They don't want fuss and individuality. We've just done a piece on packaged accounts for a bank, the answer's in the title there, I don't want this in. We've just shown them, what they were saying is what we're going to do is pull out certain benefits to customers that are more relevant to them and not relevant to them and make them a personalized package, we said "No, it's a package, that's what I'm buying a bundle of stuff, I'm buying the bundle I'm not buying the individual elements. I do not want it personalized, I actually want it standardized".

You find in the airline sector hen you find people like Ryanair do packaging it's so much more effective than some of the airlines like KLM to go for close migrations, it's just a real struggle. It's not necessarily something for everyone personalization, anonymity and also the type of category I'm buying means that I don't want it to be personalized.

I see the value of having it in but I'm not sure that's going to be ... the pinnacle to arrive at is helpful for an organization.

Gareth: I also had this discussion the other day because a lot of the marketing that I read is customers now expect personalization and my argument is 99% of customers have no idea that you're even personalizing it in the first place.

John: How do I know what you get is different to what I get?

Gareth: Yes, exactly.

John: We're doing a piece with Loot Crate where you can order a box of stuff that comes through every month and this is in gaming, that box is personalized to me. We ordered two, me and another chap and it's different stuff in there, I had no idea there's different stuff in there, I've got no idea that that stuff is personalized to me because I'm never going to look into his box, it's only if I'm looking at his box that I know that it's personalized.

I agree with you entirely, for me it feels that it's standard. I've asked to go on holiday somewhere so therefore you've sent me details of hotels, you've sent me details of car hire companies there and to proclaim that as being personalized, what would non personalized be? Sending me details of practors from youth hostels on the other side of the world, we could have done that but we didn't we personalized it to you.

That's the thing customers don't know what this personalization is and as I say some of the times that personalization can be just a case of "Have you got the package for me?", "Yes I have" that's as personal as it needs to be. There's stuff in there that I think I'm going to need, maybe stuff I don't but actually my decision is I'll save time and effort by going for the package from the brand I trust.

Gareth: What was the name of the company you mentioned? The gaming company?

John: Loot Crate.

Gareth: Loot Crate, I'll have to check it out.

John: It's an American company, there's a UK version I can't remember the name of it but it's an American company, you get this shoe box every month of Marvel or Batman or Pac-Man or Fifa type merchandise and it's almost an extension of the gaming industry, it's a way of making it a bit more changeable.

Gareth: That's cool.

The last piece is the customer themselves, here it's around again, perceptions and expectation management and emotional connections with people. Emotions has been playing quite a large role in my research, I think Doctor Klaus actually talks about the importance of emotions.

Here is, our customers understand our values, which goes to the Ryanair thing that you were saying, like do the customers actually know who we are? Then we understand what the customer intends to do, we measure referrals, we manage the expectations of our customers and then customers enjoy our service and we measure emotional engagement with our customers.

John: Where does enjoyment come from? Why have you dropped enjoyment in there because obviously if Co-op funeral services are doing this how does that work?

Gareth: That's a really good point. I think what I've come from from enjoyment was the feeling of having my expectations met and it being an easy thing to do, is an enjoyable experience. Actually I would agree that maybe enjoyment is too much of a emotional word in here because actually maybe this contradicts my point around the wowing the customer because enjoy is ...

John: Bear with me one second, sorry my pager, let me just check what they want.

Sorry about that.

Gareth: No problem.

John: We were saying about enjoyment, so is there another way you could phrase that?

Gareth: Yes, I will have a think about that because enjoy and wow and pleasure and all those types of things have quite heavy connotations with them.

John: They do, it's not to say you can't in that space but it's not something you'd want an organization to say "Done all of that what do we do next? We've got to figure out how we can make customers enjoy the experience".

Maybe the enjoyment is the right word, it's just a sense of if I've gone through a funeral experience, given the circumstances "they were incredible, they were really good". I did actually have one I remember being in a workshop and a customer did say a funeral service in terms of an example of a good customer experience.

Gareth: Wow.

John: Someone also said the passport office so definitely organizations like that have permission to deliver fabulous experience. If you look at the Nunwood Six Pillars, the KPMG Nunwood six pillars, their model?

Gareth: The what sorry? The KPMG?

John: Nunwood six pillars do you know that model?

Gareth: I haven't I'll have to have a look.

John: Well they've got six pillars which they use, which they believe are the six pillars, a bit like Doctor Klaus's 27 attributes these six pillars will measure or provide a correlation with, I think it's customer retention, it's a bit weak. It's not, as I understand it it's not very scientifically proven or independently proven but you have these six things which are things like show me integrity, make it easy for me, personalize it to me, manage my expectations, resolve my issues. The big things you'd expect to have but enjoyment isn't in there and enjoyment isn't in there.

They run a global study and they were finding that organizations would say "We're not enjoyable", Walt Disney would definitely want enjoyment in there but it's not in there because they also have in there Scottish and Southern Energy and they have in there T-Mobile, it's not going to be enjoyable is it? If they had it in there as one of the variables then it would skew organizations that weren't able to deliver an enjoyable experience.

Gareth: That's some really, really useful feedback, thank you.

Finally then this all feeds into this idea of a customer experience maturity index score whereby you then have an overall score that you could then say right what's the industry average for the industry I'm in? What's the market average? In the expectation economy it's not just your competitors that you need to benchmark against and then you would be able to drill down and say well actually we only scored three out of ten for technology but we scored eight out of ten for culture. Maybe we need to look at an investment within technology because that's where our problem is or maybe our product scored low but elsewhere scored high so where should we be focusing in order to really get everything up to that level three proficiency and maturity.

John: Yes, one of my observations is that there's nothing in here in terms of what you've actually delivered because a lot of this is very much around structure and culture. I could do really well on a lot of this but I haven't delivered much, I haven't actually achieved much and got stuff out there.

It's one of the biggest areas of frustration I find with clients is the ability to actually launch something, to make a change, have it in place. There could be a sense of action ability of we've demonstrated the significance of our deliver, just measuring it is one thing but actually to say that we had a problem, we fixed it in a way that was best for the customer and good for the business and then we delivered it, that then moves the dial on from being strategic reviewing to actionable review. If you feel that's covered then that's fine but I'm not getting a sense of that coming through.

Gareth: No, I actually agree and I wonder whether that would slip quite nicely into potentially the operations section of this or even into the product, we actually have done this.

John: Yes, I also think you've got the starting point as we have someone in the team, the best structures I've found are where each of the different areas of the business has someone who's responsible for continuously proven from customer experience. You have your central hub and then you have your operatives out in field and I might work in operations but actually there are several operational customer experience improvements and I work in operations but I'm also aligned to the hub for the customer experience team so I can go back and make sue any changes I'm making are developed in a way which is consistent with the overall ambition of customer experience.

The first one was around a senior person responsible for customer experience, I was anticipating to see that move on from a team into it being many operatives operating across the business with the responsibility for discipline but also alignments for customer experience strategy.

Gareth: I was actually just having that discussion very recently with regards not to customer experience but to business intelligence and saying actually a centralized BI team is actually a roadblock and isn't quite what you need for BI. What you need is a BI person in every team to help every team understand data that then goes back and it's like you're a team of teams.

John: Yes.

Gareth: A very, very similar argument to the one you've just made.

John: That's just one point on their job spec but actually having that alignment to the greater strategy piece otherwise, I should have said at the start but one of the big problems is silo's. You just go "I've got it, I've got it, I know what we've got to do here, we're off, we're fixing it". Then you come back and go "what the hell is that?"

Gareth: Yes.

John: You say "We fixed it, we fixed it against our criteria", "Well yes but you've not considered everyone else's criteria" and as a consequence what you've developed is selfish, it does what you want it to but you've created problems down the line.

I think within here, I think this probably would be operations ... maybe it's the customer experience journey but we understand and accommodate the impact of change across the business as opposed to our own area.

Gareth: Okay.

John: Again that integration piece going on.

Gareth: Excellent, wonderful, I will put that in. Just as an overall observation as a tool, as a framework, what are your thoughts?

John: There's a few of these. I think it's the ICS has one, invested in cuestomer, have you seen invested in customer?

Gareth: I haven't, no.

John: Invested in customer have a cultural or a business maturity model for customer experience that they use. I've spoken to the guys who run it, it's very customer service led, they don't know what they're doing really and people are taking these things away and putting them on as creditation.

I think getting the algorithm that sits behind this is probably the most important thing. Your criteria you've got, the questions you're posing I guess have come from what you've read, talking to clients and talking to practitioners like myself and you're honing those as you go through.

Gareth: Yes.

John: Looking at how Phil Klaus did his piece, I know it took years to get those questions right and that's where they really struggled over getting those questions right and they weren't putting them on a ranking, just every one is equal.

Gareth: Yes.

John: Obviously it's slightly more complex when you're saying that actually if you tell me you do questions six and question five it's going to mean less if you're not already doing question one and question two. I think what you've got here is, we saying for each of the different areas these are the six things that you should be doing, if you're doing the top two and the bottom four then that doesn't mean you're very mature it means that you've skipped a few steps.

I think probably what's worth seeing if you can investigate is what is the implications to a business if it has skipped those bottom four? If it's gone straight to the top ... I'm just looking at the last one on the customer, so as an organization if the two things we do are we focus on are making sure our is enjoying our services and we make sure of their emotional engagement. Lets say we are Disney, that's what we do, we don't do one to four, does it matter? Could you argue, you kind of have to do one to four in order to do five and six correctly?

I'd probably just tease that out a little bit more to make sure that there isn't interdependency in these.

Gareth: Okay.

John: As opposed to them being independent variables.

Gareth: That's a really, really good piece of feedback and will definitely make it's way into the limitations part of the essay. I hadn't considered that before but I think you're right.

John: You can test them as independent question can't you and just see against the maturity of organizations. What you'd hope is that having looked at them and looking at organizations who are mature as opposed to organizations who are immature, those that are mature could tick all six, those who are immature might tick one or two but obviously if those immature come back and can tick six or five then maybe the structure needs a little bit of work.

Gareth: Okay.

John: Do you need to have it ranked? Do you need these to be three blocks of two, you're level one, level two, level three?

Gareth: No.

John: Can they just be six questions, you're view is that question one is an entry point whereas question six very few people get to, that's your view isn't it.

Gareth: That's my thought process, if you are at question six you couldn't almost get there without doing the others was my thought process and therefore you would be really one of those top companies that would be proficient and mature in delivering customer experience.

John: Yes.

         I guess by testing that you'll find that out won't you. That's the only thing Gareth I'm not entirely convinced that that ranking is right for your study.

Gareth: Okay, that's really useful and that's why I'm doing the research with people like yourself and experts is to find out actually there is nothing set in stone for it, I'm trying to get to the bottom of what is the right way of doing it.

John: Yes, okay. I can see the value of this for me as an organization as I am going through these particular lines. What does the output look like? Does it tell me where I am or does it tell me what my next moves are?

Gareth: It tells you where you are as a snapshot, the idea that would be that by telling you where you are you then know what the next steps would be. Someone like youRselves would be able to say we've done this with you, this is your CXMI score and dashboard, we therefore then suggest that we start doing X workshops or X program or we investigate this as a way to get to score higher and lets redo this again in six months or whatever it might be.

John: Yes so I guess on it it could give me a depiction of what organizations at the next level look like, then it gives me something to go towards I think. If I'm just seeing you are here, organizations at the next level are organizations like, give me some indications who they are but these are their typical practices, which I guess is just your next level of questions going in there isn't it.

Gareth: Yes.

John: Juts to give me a sense of something to go towards.

Gareth: Okay.

John: A lot of practitioners don't know what good looks like, they've got no strong definition of what a good customer experience program looks like. A lot of them are using it just to climb the ladder, having the ability to show a view of what a good program looks like, the key elements, key components, it's useful then to make sure that as an organization I can look and say "Well how far are we away from that in terms of what we would need to do to get there?"

Gareth: Okay, wonderful. John thank you very much for today, I have taken up a lot of your time so I really genuinely appreciate all the feedback.

John: Fortunately it's an interesting subject for me so that's okay.

Gareth: Wonderful and I will be sure to share the final thesis with you, how it looks.

John: All the best with it, how many other people are you speaking to?

Gareth: So there are 12 interviews and a survey with customers, the survey for customers is really finding out, some of the questions ask you around what they think a customer experience is to them but also whether actually it is important. You can talk about all this until you're blue in the face but actually if customers don't actually really care that much is it of great importance?

John: I think you're going to get a lot of absolutely it's really important because it seems dumb to say the opposite but almost it would be interesting if in 10 years time you ask that question again.

Gareth: Yes.

John: Whether people will be saying "Well?" It's one of the things it's not the thing but if people turn around and say not putting customers first is not such a smart thing, it's going against the grain isn't it.

Gareth: Yes. One response to the survey was is customer experience important to you when choosing a brand? I agree with is statement, the next one was what does customer experience mean to you and they said I don't know.

John: There you go, brilliant best of luck with it, any further questions feel free to contact me and obviously ... have you spoken to Doctor Professor Phil Klaus on it at all?

Gareth: I haven't actually, he's a big part of my research, I reference him a lot in my literary review but I've not spoken with him.

John: He's a good chap, I've worked with him a lot, I'm not promising but if there's anything in there you think what's Phil's view on this because obviously he runs PhD program on this already but I can always send it on to him.

Gareth: Actually just it would be interesting just to share my final piece with him to say there's somebody that's done an MBA piece on customer experience, I'm the only one in my cohort that's even remotely going near CX.

John: I might struggle with ... with all due respect to your people obviously he's just finished all his dissertation marking for this year on his customer experience program so if you've got perhaps a couple of slides that you wanted me to pull out and say as a highlight "What do you think of this?" I'm more than happy to do that but i'm getting to struggle to read through things which I'm paying him to read for us.

Gareth: No worries, I don't think I've got anything for him at the moment but I will definitely bear that in mind if anything comes up and as I said I'll definitely share my final piece with you.

John: All right. All the best.

Gareth: Thank you very much, take care buh bye.

Interview 10 - Michael

Interviewee: Michael
Interviewer: Gareth

Date and Time: 6th/July/2016
Location: London
Customer Experience Group: Producer

Gareth: What's your name?
Michael: My name? Michael
Gareth: What company do you work for?
Michael: I currently work for <producer> but previously worked for <producer>
Gareth: What's your job title?
Michael: Ecommerce director or previously was head of online sales, head of ecommerce for <producer>.
Gareth: Let's take your <producer> one because the next question is going to be what were you responsible for? I think it might be easier to talk about <producer> than <producer>, given that it's only been a couple of days.
Michael: Sorry, I just had some nutter trying to turn right in front of me. What was I responsible for? Responsible for global strategy on digital sales for <producer> including some key programs around data driven marketing, personalization and, to a certain extent, customer experience in the digital channel.
Gareth: What does customer experience mean to you?
Michael: Customer experience, to me, means the measure of how we, as a brand, made the customer feel during their time of interacting with us across our channels. <producer> channels typically digital, retail or call center so I would measure the interaction that a customer has with that channel within the transactions that they're doing. That's what it means within my role, really customer experience for somebody like <producer> is far bigger and broader. It's also the users that they have and the experience that they have of the service that we offer, ultimately the technology is our thing.
Gareth: Wonderful. Have you seen an increase in customer experience being discussed both internally, at <producer>, but also with customers? Do you find that customers have become more aware of customer experience?
Michael: Yeah, yeah completely. I mean it's always been a focus of <producer>, but I think it's become a major part, arguably the biggest part, of the strategy is a focus on customer experience and customer experience improvement. I do think that consumers' expectations are that any brand, certainly a major brand, certainly a big famous brand, should offer a superior customer experience than perhaps a cheaper or less established brand.
Gareth: Have you got some examples of companies that you think are delivering good customer experience?
Michael: Yeah so I think ... Clearly I'm in a digital role. I would probably point at two, yeah I'd point at two. One would be Google so I think the way that they ... If you think of the products and services that Google offer, although me as a consumer and end user, I don't actually pay to use Google per se. I think the way that Google make it so seamless to transition across devices, across browsers and various other things, I think that's incredible. The way that, to me, it's a completely seamless and frictionless experience compared to ... I know that there's a lot of technology going on behind the scenes that's making that work.

I think the other people, to me, would be Amazon in more of an ecommerce capacity. I think the customer experience that they offer is phenomenal. The range that they offer, convenience that they offer. For me, as a shopper, it's actually now more convenient to get stuff from Amazon than it is from many other retailers because I don't want the hassle and the wait time of hanging around or whatever it maybe.

Gareth: I've actually just started doing my weekly shopping through Amazon.

Michael: Yeah.

Gareth: It's absolutely fantastic.

Michael: You must live in one of the very few postal codes in London then that AmazonFresh is supporting.

Gareth: Yeah, I'm Whitechapel. It was just I got a thing, I can't even remember where I saw it, I think it might have been on my Amazon Prime, and thought do you know what? I'll have a look at it and it just ... You order before 1:00 and it arrives in a one hour block some time after 5:00 that you can pick. It's just so convenient.

Michael: Yeah, I think that's what I mean about customer experience. That's the kind of technology innovation that we, as consumers, want to have. Nobody wants to go to Tesco at least once a week, probably two, three times a week, and traipse around a shop picking products off the shelves. I think from customer experience, to me, it's a couple of things. It's, one, taking away wasted time but also, two, taking away annoyance and frustration or friction would probably be the phrase that Amazon use. It's how do you make something frictionless? It's nothing in-between from what a customer wants and from them getting what they want, if you see what I mean?

Gareth: Yeah. You've touched on some key things there, so I guess the next question was what do you consider to be the key elements of delivering customer experience? I think you've probably touched on there so frictionless buying, removing that need for me to bend my time to the business. Interlink only give me a one hour slot some time on a Wednesday, I don't want to have to take time off to meet their times. I want you to meet mine, right?

Michael: Yeah. [In general 00:10:51] I think, for me, what's a good ... I don't know maybe as a brand, if I said, "What's a really good measurement of customer experience?" It's I don't need to think twice about whether I'm doing the right thing. Am I getting value for money by doing x, y and z? With Amazon, I'm not shopping on there because I know their prices are cheaper. I know that they've grown up being competitive but they're not always cheaper. It's just so damned convenient that it's second nature to me knowing that I'm going to get something that's competitive, but maybe I am willing to pay a pound or two or ten or twenty quid more than I perhaps need to. I'm getting the service that I'm offering, and the fact that I'm not even questioning whether I'm doing the right thing in buying from Amazon probably says, to me, that they're offering really good experience.

Gareth: It's interesting. I've never once had a delivery go wrong with them and that's pretty impressive considering I've been a customer of theirs for so long.

Michael: Yeah. I mean I've probably seen the flip side of that. I have had deliveries go wrong. I've had products ordered, not show up and all that type of stuff, but the measure of the customer experience is how quickly they resolve it. They resolved it by taking the pain away from me. I'd ordered a set-top box, a Freeview recorder thing, two, three hundred quids worth and it didn't arrive. I contacted them, I rung them in this way and they didn't even question it. They just said, "Right we'll retrieve it. We'll send you a new one out today." Whereas if I think about old school mail order businesses, you would have been trying to track the delivery down, speaking to the logistics people and saying, "Where the hell's my delivery?" Blah blah blah. Almost Amazon taking that pain away, maybe even taking a hit on the product sale, turns me into a happier customer, a more loyal customer and this holy grail of promoter as a brand person.

Gareth: Where do you think that people do most often fall down in delivering your customer experience? Where are the failures?

Michael: Broken promises basically. I think if you set an expectation or you say to somebody, "I'm going to do this," and you don't deliver on that, that is just a bad customer experience. Even if it's, "I will ring you back this afternoon," if somebody doesn't ring you back, that's a bad experience. Either don't tell me you're going to ring me back but ring me back, so under promise and over deliver, or if you say you're going to ring me back, ring me back with, I don't know, whether it's resolved or an update or whatever it may be. I think it doesn't matter. What I don't want to have is, "Oh I wonder whether that thing that I queried with those people is happening?" Then you have to chase it, that's not good.

Gareth: Interesting. That's been a key theme throughout all of my research, has been this idea of expectation management and meeting in customer experience. It's like you don't have to wow me all the time, just meet my expectations then get out of my way and let me get on with my life. It's when you don't do that is when we have problems.

Michael: Or make it [good for me 00:14:00]. Somebody in our internal ... <producer> has a customer experience team, as you can imagine, and I remember one of the girls. She used a fantastic example where, and you or I, I've never used it, but Apple have this thing on their phones where, on an iPhone 6 or bigger, if you double tap the button, it shifts things down on the screen. I don't know whether you've seen that?

Gareth: Yeah, yeah [crosstalk 00:14:25].

Michael: That's a brilliant example of customer experience. It's important to this girl who, in our customer experience team, carrying shopping bags, only got one hand, can't swipe to the top of the screen. [inaudible 00:14:40] and beyond what [inaudible 00:14:49].

Gareth: Now the next question. A recent Gartner survey on the role of marketing in customer experience found that by 2016, eighty nine percent of companies expect to compete mostly on the basis of customer experience versus thirty six percent four years ago. What are your thoughts on this?

Michael: I don't know if I'm going through a dodgy signal area, but I didn't hear any of that question. [It was 00:15:23] Gartner? [inaudible 00:15:27]

Gareth: A recent Gartner survey on the role of marketing in customer experience found that by 2016, eighty nine percent of companies expect to compete mostly on the basis of customer experience. What are your thoughts on this?

Michael: Sorry mate, I'm struggling. If I lose you, do you want me to ring back?

MEASURING CUSTOMER CENTRICITY FOR COMPETITIVE ADVANTAGE

Gareth: Shall I call you back?

Michael: That Gartner question again?

Gareth: Yeah. A recent Gartner survey on the role of marketing in customer experience found that by 2016, eighty nine percent of companies expect to compete mostly on the basis of customer experience. What are your thoughts on that?

Michael: Eighty nine percent?

Gareth: Yeah, of companies expecting to compete mostly on the basis of customer experience.

Michael: I think it would depend on the industry. I think they're probably overcooking it. Eighty nine percent of what? Companies surveyed is that or ...

Gareth: It's just in the Gartner survey, yeah, just says that in their survey, yes there will be. It will be their survey, the ones that came ... Of those surveyed, eighty nine percent of them said they expect to compete mostly on the basis of customer experience.

Michael: Yeah. I mean I guess it depends on what you categorize as customer experience, doesn't it? I would probably say they've overcooked that. I think in some industries, that doesn't surprise me, it surprise me at all in telco. Where you've got heavy saturation, very little to choose from one provider to another, doesn't surprise me in the slightest that they're reckoning that's the ... That competing on customer experience in telco, sorry, and maybe to an extent, financial services. Maybe if it's a service type industry that they're surveying, then I probably could buy that.

            I wouldn't necessarily buy it in a retail type of capacity, because I think there are people that clearly market themselves based on value, price and all that type of stuff. Like Asda for example do not market themselves as you'll get a differentiated experience in our stores. They market themselves on the basis of value for money and never knowingly [inaudible 00:18:19] that's John Lewis. It's more of a value proposition that they're pushing out. I guess the short answer is, it would depend on the industry. Service industries, I buy it. To an extent, technology but not your retail, not classic grocery or retail type stuff.

Gareth: It's interesting. This isn't actually part of the questioning, but I guess if we look at it in the way that you've just been saying. Customer experience then really is a strategic choice. Are we going to compete on customer experience? In which case, let's ... We need to dial down some of the other things because things like price might go at the expense of customer experience. Or do we say, "Actually we are just going to compete on price and our customer experience may well suffer because of that." Can you compete on both?

Michael: The thing is, as you will know, they are all interlinked. You can't say, "Screw the price. We're going to offer the best experience," because the best experience will have [inaudible 00:19:16] for everyone, yeah?

Gareth: Yeah.

Michael: If Google suddenly started to charge for people using Google Maps, I'm pretty sure other map services would crop up. Even though it's a superb experience, craps all over Apple Maps and other things like that but ... So yeah. Like I said, it depends on what they frame as customer experience but yeah, I agree with you. I think probably what that Gartner study is actually probably saying is companies would rate customer experience as their top priority, as opposed to it being something that they also do above and beyond other things.

Gareth: There's a follow-up part in that as well. According to the same research, fewer than half of companies see their customer experience capabilities as superior to their peers. Two thirds expect their capabilities to be industry leading or more successful than their peers in the next five years.

Michael: Right.

Gareth: How you feel about that?

Michael: Again, that's a bit of navel Garething to an extent. I think, at the end of the day, we're all in a market ... When you talk about capability, people are people. It's how you treat them and how you develop them I suppose. [inaudible 00:20:40] your capability. Technology platforms, if you're talking about buying things in then I don't know whether one person will get better than the other. Somebody may get a head start but everyone else will soon catch up if it's genuinely become something totally different.

Gareth: It's also interesting there that ... I mean on what metric? Again part of my research, or the thing my research is leading towards and a future question that I think will be ... I'm putting in my future recommendations bit is there isn't a unified CX metric. It's like a basket of things you measure. It isn't one thing, right? You can't say, "I am a customer experience leader by five points."

Michael: I mean it kind of depends. In <producer>, the customer experience measure is NPS, [brand 00:21:34] NPS. I think you can say there, "I have got an X point lead over my competitors." You can survey your competitors just as easily as you can survey your own customers. Everyone has a connection of sorts in most of our markets. I think you can start to talk about things like that, but if you're talking ... Again it depends what you're classing as capability. I think of capability as platforms and people. I don't think that is necessarily the answer in customer experience.

It's a cultural thing in many experiences. Trying to think, First Direct do not necessarily have different technical [inaudible 00:22:16] to Barclays, but I think the perception would be that they offer better experience. Possibly because they prioritize getting you through to an advisor quickly as opposed to [through an RDR 00:22:31], routing you through to the, in theory, the individual that can help you best who may well then have to transfer you. That isn't anything to do with capability, that's a cultural thing. That's a business decision.

Gareth: It's interesting. I wonder, NPS is a fantastic metric, I wonder whether it is the ... Whether it could be the CX, the single CX metric that you use or if it would be part of it. There are limitations to it, I guess.

Michael: Absolutely. I mean there's ... Yeah, I completely agree. I think, for me, it's more important for a brand to have one metric than it is to ... If you're measuring customer experience, what I like about NPS is it is a measure of customer experience. Out and out, pound for pound, it is a measure of customer experience. You can always nitpick in the methodology and all this type of stuff, but, at the end of the day, it's a single metric. As opposed to what you'll then have, if you have multiple metrics, is you'll have well this is up but that's down or x, y, z. Like you talk about revenue, well revenue might be up but profit maybe down. You look at something like Tesco who try to focus on profit and actually end up losing ... Cutting off the top end of the funnel and the bottom end. They're trying to be more profitable, but they're losing revenue at the top end so they are losing money overall.

<End of 1st Interview session>
<Start of 2nd Interview session - 7th July 2016>

Gareth: What I wanted to do this time around is just explain my thoughts on that deck, how I got to the framework, and then to go through and ask what your thoughts were on the leveling, the framework on the questions. What we'll do is we'll go topic by topic through that framework. I'd like to get any sort of feedback you have, any thoughts on the way that it works and then we'll structure it in that way, if that's okay.

Michael: Yeah. That's fine.

Gareth: Lovely.

Michael: When you say the framework, you mean the circular, I forget what [inaudible 00:49]

Gareth: Yeah.

Michael: The customer

Gareth: Exactly, so we'll talk about the levels which was my the level one, two, three, and why I chose that as opposed to something like the pyramid that was in there. Then we'll talk about that onion diagram and then we'll talk about the different sections within that and what you thought about the questions in the survey. I appreciate you haven't got it in front of you, so it won't be specific on those questions, but just general sorts of thoughts. And then at the end, any ... What I need to do basically is I'm taking the findings from people I'm speaking to about it and using that to make recommendations for changes.

Michael: Okay.

Gareth: The way that I got to the framework was by doing the research, looking through all the books and the literature, identifying those key themes and topics and then building it up from there. The framework that was quite pop- ... Well, that came from the Forester piece which was that pyramid if you remember, the Meet, Needs, Eating, Enjoyable. For me, the pyramid approach doesn't really work, because I feel like if you gave a pyramid to a lot of people, the enjoyable bit at the top, the wow piece, "let's wow our customers", is where people jump to because it's the fun bit. It's the easy bit. But it's also not the most sustainable pieces of business. Because if you take it to its logical extreme ... If I'm given, as a customer service rep, just the direction to wow the customer then really I could give a Porsche away trying to save a five pound subscription. It isn't sustainable in that way. What I wanted to do was strip that out and, in fact, just put a leveling system in that says basic advanced and nirvana level capabilities. What are your thoughts on that?

Michael: I agree with you. I think sometimes people will shoot for the wow type of stuff and often ignore what I tend to call the operating basics. Are you trying to get into the difference between shape in a circle as a way of constructing it?

Gareth: No. Not the shaped pieces particularly relevant to this. It's just why I wanted to get away from having the pyramid approach that's used by Forester to a level-based approach for my questioning. The way that it works is you give the survey, they answer it, and then it goes through a waiting model to spit out a dashboard, if you like, that says "You scored two out of ten in culture, eight out of ten in technology, and three or four out of ten on your product" and you can compare that to the rest of the market, you can compare that to other industries. And you can look internally and say "Well we want to be customer-centric" but actually it's our culture that's broken or it's our technology that we need to look at. That's why I sort of stripped out that idea of pyramid and jumped to the top and tried to make it more linear.

Michael: Yep. I agree. I think it's a stat, kind of level-based approach. I agree with that.

Gareth: Okay. One thing I have been thinking, though, is potentially the three levels isn't enough. Maybe it's not nuanced enough to actually get deep enough into what people can ... Actually getting into the capabilities.

Michael: Yeah. For me, the thinking would be ... Whether you've got enough levels, clearly that's for you to work out. For me, it's more about is level even the right word? I may be getting a bit carried away, but a level, you can still fast-track to. And in what you're trying to get to, they are literally steps. You have to go through step one to get to step two.

Gareth: Yeah. For me it's ...

Michael: I'm not sure I'm answering your question, but a level, if you think of physical terms, you get to level four in a list. But if I'm talking about step one, step two, I know that I have to go through step one and step two to get to step five. I don't know if that's something around that type of thing.

Gareth: Yeah. That's really interesting. I hadn't actually thought about that. I was just thinking about the pyramid piece, but you're absolutely right. And it's interesting, I hadn't initially thought about it in a linear you have to go through level one to level two to level three, because I assumed from the way that the survey's put together that some people will be doing some things. Like you might have a partially level three, quite strong level two, it's not binary if you are doing level one you can't do level three, it's more a scoring mechanism. But it needs parts in investigation around the wording and the structure, I think.

Michael: What you're maybe saying is that if you are doing some stuff that's in level three but you're not doing stuff in level two, then your stuff in level three isn't as effective as it could be.

Gareth: Yeah, exactly. That's what I'm getting at. Your overall score in that area would be low because you're not doing everything.

Michael: Yeah. Okay.

Gareth: Once I've decided on the level-makings for the survey, then I would decide to look at the framework around which I was going to do. And that's that onion piece. I wanted to get away from just doing the people processing technology and make it a little bit more nuance than that. To really have the idea of a cultural piece or the heart of it feeding out through, you have to have a customary experience centric or customer-centric culture that then feeds your operations, feeds your products and services, that feeds the technology you choose to interact with the customer. And it's important to have the customer in the framework and how you're dealing with them tend to be quite often left out when we talk about customer experience.

Michael: Yep. I completely agree with the ...

Gareth: Oh. You there?

Michael: Hello? Hello, can you hear me all right?

MEASURING CUSTOMER CENTRICITY FOR COMPETITIVE ADVANTAGE

Gareth: Yeah, I can. Sorry, that was weird. Call cut out.

Michael: Yeah. I couldn't hear you. I can hear you fine right now. [inaudible 00:07:26]

Gareth: Yeah that's strange.

Michael: I'm heading into that area where I lost you yesterday as well or the day before, but let's just carry on as best we can.

Gareth: Yeah. I was just saying I got to the onion model and you're saying, "I completely agree," and then cut out.

Michael: I completely agree with culture being probably the most important part of it, to be honest. There was a part of me that had the onion [inaudible 00:07:57] is it the customer at the heart and the culture on the outside. That's pretty much where we need to start. I'm getting carried away with the visual side as opposed to what your actually trying to build.

Gareth: I think you are. I would agree and I think potentially there's a need to put into the model or to show some sort of feedback mechanism, or that it pulses always in two directions. It goes culture out to customer, but customer back to culture. I actually was trying to turn it on it's head from the customer, because as the inside out, or sorry the outside in model which is the Forester approach which is great, but again, I think you need to have that, it doesn't matter which way it goes I guess. There needs to be feedback in there, but we're trying to get to this customer centric culture being the key piece, which I think you said you agree with that.

Michael: Yeah.

Gareth: Then what I was trying to do as well is show that you need to have an emotional part to the business, because you're dealing with emotional people at the end, the customer. If you, in fact, have this rational piece all the way through if for example you're focused only on getting somebody off the phone in the quickest amount of time, because that makes sense from a business operations point of view. You're kind of missing the point of customer experience.

Michael: Yeah.

Gareth: Does that fit in line with your -

Michael: I completely agree, yep.

Gareth: Great. Then into the actual sections of it. Within culture, we're talking about meeting expectations, so expectation setting, being able to have empowered employees for example. Then the questions in there were that the levels were in a customer experience, a customer value. Then we have a central customer experience team. The top level was customer experience is linked to company incentives. I don't know how you feel about that sort of build up, how you feel about the central customer experience team that lays in there.

Michael: Hello?

Gareth: Awesome. [crosstalk 00:10:12] No problem, no problem. We got to culture and I was saying, the sort of key things in here are around empowering your employees, trusting your employees to deliver decent customer experience. Having board level oversight. The questions in there around sort of level one, two and three were customer experience, company value. There's a central customer experience team. Customer experience is linked to company incentives. What are your thoughts on culture and customer experience, the questions, the key things when you would be measuring it.

Michael: A couple of thoughts from me. One, culture, it's there for everybody. A culture is very much, it applies to everyone. If you talk about things like central customer experience team, then you kind of pull a little bit away from it. That's kind of one thought. Although, I'm not saying that you shouldn't have it. Whether you haven't got one, doesn't necessarily make you customer centric in the culture. If you see what I mean. I think what I would say is maybe part of the questioning is around things like [inaudible 00:11:30] officer, that's somebody who is directly accountable for that customer experience that's on the board. Part of their role, part of their team rating customer experience is that would be one area. Then I think culture really, I agree with how do you make it. I'm just trying to think what was on the slide. What were the other points?

Gareth: Customer experience is a company value is sort of basics. Level one. Top level isare customer experiences linked to company incentive and training recruitment and HR developments guided by CX strategy.

Michael: Yeah. I definitely would agree, but your second point is it customer experience measure actually becomes the company KPI, that determines how successful you are as a business For example in [inaudible 00:12:32] everyone's bonus is linked to customer experience measures as opposed to pure financial ones, which is what large corporates will tend to fall back on.

Gareth: Wow so everybody's tied to the MPS score.

Michael: Not everyday, but part of the bonus accelerates the [inaudible 00:12:53] has it's kind of bonus, you have a blend of company performance and customer performance to pay your bonus. Part of the company performance, one of the accelerators is customer experience improvement, which is already tied to MPS. Yes, you're bonus, or the amount that you get as a bonus, is tied to MPS.

Gareth: That's very cool.

Michael: I would say that's sort of level that in my experience that can be getting towards. Whether it's MPS their score or some other metric. It needs to be part of it.

Gareth: Would you consider a company that's doing that, someone like the <producer>, would you say that's fairly advanced in customer experience competency?

Michael: I would say for a company like <producer>, they've been around for a number of years. I would question something like Google or Amazon. I don't know whether they would be that way, inherently, because I think customer experience measures, for example, [inaudible 00:14:11] into the whole commercial model, if you see what I mean. I think that almost the mobility of the organization operation would determine are you trying to create a customer experience culture versus maintain one. Firmer than I think maintaining a customer experience culture is probably where they are. Vodaphone is very much more established than [inaudible 00:14:39].

Gareth: I guess as well it depends on, to an extent, probably the age of the business, because being a customer experience from the ground up focused businesses is a fairly new concept, I think. Isn't it. It would have to be a pure play, new organization to be really thinking about doing it from the start. A lot of it will be back filling

Michael: You certainly don't have to be purified, but the [inaudible 00:15:09] example, I'm just thinking of stuff that I've studied in the past. They have one of their commercial KPIs [inaudible 00:15:15] and expectation and you've seen it baked into their technology or that guarantee by one p.m. tomorrow for their stuff. One of their KPIs is how what percent of orders get there within that promise. That inherently is a commercial KPI that's actually very linked to what the customer experience is. That's quite different to what <producer>'s trying which is measure customer experience satisfaction you might call it.

Gareth: That's really interesting. It actually segues us nicely into the next piece which was culture then feeds out into the operation. Within operations it's like the measurement of it, the strategy behind it. Customer journey mapping, that sort of thing. Then the questions in there were a basic level would be we have a defined customer experience strategy. We measure customer satisfaction. Mid tier would be we listen to the customer, we understand the customer experience journey. Level five would be we measure customer experience and we continually optimize the customer experience. Remember these are all based around scale one to ten answers, when you answer.

Michael: Yes. I think zero is when you're nothing and then ten is probably a full 360. That's probably what I think you're getting to. You maybe I think I can allow that the scales that talking about. 360 isn't just you measure that customer interaction with you with a brand so I call the call center, then send them a text message and ask them what they thought of it. A full 360 takes every single aspect into, I'm sorry I'm just going round and round about. The full 360 takes everything into product development and suddenly MPS becomes, or whatever is set for that faction, becomes the most valuable [inaudible 00:17:22] product development.[inaudible 00:17:26] That's where it's truly embedded as opposed to 360. I get feedback on apps about it, which is how some people think about it.

Gareth: An advanced capability company would be we measure customer experience and it's baked into the development of our product. Something like that?

Michael: Yeah [inaudible 00:17:50] Absolutely. Are you talking about how to recruit people. What's the protocol or channel that you want to come in and bring it bare it to the team.

Gareth: Around product and services, what I find interesting in this is this idea of customer effort. MPS is a great measure but also customer effort. How easy are you to do business with? You can be really customer centric in your marketing but it's really hard to do my invoice with you. I'm going to have a bad experience because it's been difficult to apologies do my work with you. Here, what I was measuring was around, we understand the expectations of our customers. We have a complex product offering, but we can simplify it. It's a complex product, but it's simplified in there is a simplified offering of it. We're able to serve the customer in the way they want. We deliver a service the customers expect. We're easy to do business with and we understand the values of our customers, was the levels.

Michael: Are they linear levels though?

Gareth: Yeah, the way that I explained was that was number one two, and then level three, four and five six. The ultimate level would be we understand the values of our customers we're wanting to do business with. The basic level would be we understand our customer expectations.

Michael: Sorry about that. Ironically with we're talking about customer experience while having a sh*t network experience.

Gareth: Is it because you left motor phone, did they get angry and cut you off?

Michael: I don't know, I hope not. My reputation is not that bad.

Gareth: We were up to product and services. Saying around customer effort and the levels in this were, is around we understand the expectations of our customer, we have a complex product, but we simplified it and how you use it. We're able to serve the customer in the way they want. We're easy to do business. We understand the values of our customers. Then you asked me if it was linear and what I was saying is it's not necessarily you have to go through these to get to the top but like you said, it's about weighting. I think the base level is that we understand their expectations. A sort of nirvana level would be we actually understand the values of our customers and we're easy to do business with.

Michael: Yeah. I would agree with all of those. I think the reason I'm not feeling the linear thing is ideally I think it probably would be a gradual thing in understanding the values of that really Utopia.

Gareth: What would you think would be the measure of a company that was advanced to CX in their product and service offering?

Michael: I guess, from a company perspective it's people talking about your new as an example. I don't really know what the more quantifiable measure of that is. <producer> used to the phrase, that's not the <producer> actually, that's a government thing actually. Where they say [inaudible 00:21:36] prefer to use them. Are you aware of that one[crosstalk 00:21:43].

Gareth: I think I've heard variations on the phrase, but yeah.

Michael: I don't know. How do you measure [inaudible 00:22:00]. It's quite interesting. I would say that that is, ah sh*t. Sorry. A little town that I go through where [inaudible 00:22:13] appear to be in the wrong direction.

Gareth: Where I was going with products and services and that was that if you understand the expectations of your customer, you can build your products and service around to meet those expectations. If it just meets them or even slightly exceeds them then you're in with a good product and service. You don't need all the bells and whistles on top.

Michael: I agree with that, but I would also say some of the things that Apple come up with for example, some of these organizations I would say are customer centric. Customers or consumers don't even know that they want it. It kind of happened. If you know what I mean. I mentioned one yesterday, I think, to you, where the Apple, that you double tap the home key, it moves the screen down on the bigger devices.

Gareth: Yeah. Thank you so much for telling me that. I didn't know what you were talking about. I looked into it. It's got reach-ability and it's awesome. It's really useful.

Michael: Yeah. Exactly. You don't even know that you need it. You know what I mean? Everybody said. "Yeah I want a bigger screen." Then actually [inaudible 00:23:27] a bigger screen becomes a problem. That to me is customer centric product services. I feel like somebody who's way more intellectual than me has already told me what I want, or he told me what I need from a product or a service. That to me is true customer centricity.

Gareth: Yeah. You're exactly right because it's not superfluous functionality, right? It's not for the sake of it. It's the actually now I have it, I can't live without it.

Michael: Yeah exactly. I expect it. I expect that kind of usefullness.

Gareth: I wonder if there's something to be said in there then around all product and service like pushes the expectations of our customers. Not exceeds them, because it's not going above your set expectations. It's always expanding the expectations.

Michael: Exactly. It's probably creating new expectations.

Gareth: I like that.

Michael: That I think is true customer centricity.

Gareth: That's awesome. That's definitely going in the recommendations, because that's exactly what Uber's done. You didn't know that you need to be able to just call your car on your phone and now I wouldn't even dream of using anything else. I think we cracked it Michael. the next piece of it is the technology. Here, this is around, again, measurement segmentation, self service, channel switching. This was like we can track our customers across multiple channels. We can collect and analyze data from different touch points was number one. Then we can collect qualitative feedback. We can deliver a consistent experience. Then customers can move seamlessly between channels and we can offer a customized customer experience of being the top level.

Michael: Yeah. I guess one point of clarification would be things like devices. You said channel there. I don't know what your definition in your head of channel. I think of a channel where digital is one, retail is another. Call center is another one for <producer>. I'm not just thinking channel, I'm thinking device as well, but I'm not even thinking it. I think I said the example of Google, where if you set it on your computer on Chrome and sign into chrome on my device, when I use Google maps, my device knows what I'm looking for. It can seamlessly transfer you from desktop to mobile.

Gareth: [crosstalk 00:26:13]

Michael: That's customer centric. That's removing friction. You must have seen Google at some point, the scene where the guy's typing on a computer, [inaudible 00:26:24] then he picks up his mobile phone and he says how do I get there, and the device knows that he's talking about. Have you seen that example?

Gareth: I haven't, but I've seen numerous similar ones. I know the new release of Apple, they're latest OS is if I copy something to my clipboard on my Mac, I can paste it on my iPhone.

Michael: Yes. Exactly.

Gareth: Putting something in there about the -

Michael: It may come up as a channel, but I would almost call out the specific whether you want to say device or operating system, because as you go into this internet thing, connected world, that's more important than being able to track somebody across the channel.

Gareth: Okay. There's also something I wanted to discuss here around this, because I put the top level being the personalized customer experiences. You can deliver personalizations through technology being the top level, but I'm starting to see in discussions and through this research as well, it's that actually personalization isn't necessarily the Nirvana that we think it is. Customers don't necessarily expect it or are even aware that it's happening. They can have a great customer experience without feeling like it's being tailored to them.

Michael: Yeah. That's very interesting coming from <vendor>.

Gareth: With my MBA hat's on.

Michael: I would agree with you. It's all about relevancy. Maybe you can argue relevancy is another way of saying personalization but if it's simple and relevant, then I don't need it to be highly personalized, I can self personalize the experience, whatever that might be.

Gareth: There's also a question in there around, if I'm aware that something is being heavily personalized to me, I need to trust that I'm still getting the best deal and that you haven't given me the thing, because you know who I am, therefor you've given me something that you think I would spend, as opposed to all of the other offers out there.

Michael: Yeah. Totally agree. I think if people think that they're being mislead with personalization or what every you call it then, they will very, very quickly stop using that product or service.

Gareth: I wonder where the relevancy is a better term than personalization.

Michael: I agree.

Gareth: Because personalization does have, because it's got that personal element, is that one to one, but actually, and this is slightly [inaudible 00:29:08], a lot of personalization tests that we run on they're not as effective as larger segmentation group testing. Which would be more the relevant piece. I don't know if you found that in your own tests at <producer> as well.

Michael: Yeah. Sometimes the personalization tests wouldn't perform as well as just a good [inaudible 00:29:30] group.

Gareth: Finally, the customer, I guess the most important piece in all of this. This is around emotional engagement. Understanding expectations. It's really that there is this emotional piece and it's this understanding. They understand what they need and what they want from you and you understand what they need and want from you as the business and they match somehow. Level one was our customers understand our values. We understand what customers intend to do. We measure referrals. We manage the expectations of our customers. Customers enjoy using our service. Then we measure the emotional engagement with our customers.

Michael: Yeah. I would I agree. I think they enjoy is a good phrase, good word, good way of looking at it. I would also think about delight and stuff like that.

Gareth: I agree, although someone, one of the guys I was speaking to, a consultant, said what do you do if the company is doing this as a funeral parlor. I thought, that's an interesting news case. Do you enjoy using the service.

Michael: [inaudible 00:30:47]

Gareth: I think that's an edge case. I don't think about it too much.

Michael: I think, and again, I'm going to use another internal <producer> example. We used to talk about almost the steps to customer experience delight. Based on three key phrases that we want the customers to say. We wanted them to say, "I understand. It works." Then we want them to say, "I'm impressed." Those are a bit like you were talking about that pyramid thing. I understand that's almost irrational. It works, well that's because I'm consuming the product or service I expected to work, and then the emotional, I'm impressed.

Gareth: Okay.

Michael: Apply that to your funeral parlor and you can do that. "I understand it works. I'm impressed. I'm not delighted, because clearly it's a solemn thing, but I'm impressed with the way they handled it appropriately. Blah, blah, blah."

Gareth: I think your right in that it is whatever language you use, is that moving from that rational transactional sort of a feeling, into more of an emotional engagement and I think that's what I'm trying to get at here.

Michael: Agreed.

Gareth: Once you've taken these surveys, it feeds into your score. You'll end up with your customer experience competency score, you'll be able to drill into that to say, as I said, your strongest area but you need to focus in this area. Then that should be, "Okay, where do we need to invest? Where do we need to put the resources in order to become, hopefully to level out all of those things to become capable or competent in delivering customer experience. That's the overall piece. What's your feedback on this the framework, the piece, what you seen?

Michael: I think the framework's good. I think the transition from culture to customer is a good one. I think one of my questions observations would be operations. What does operations actually mean, because I told you that the culture, people. I know that you're trying to avoid people versus technology. That's almost like what other distinct bits, if I'm running a business, I can talk about the culture. I can talk about the technology. What exactly is operations. [inaudible 00:33:25] I think in that respect, I think the framework is quite good. I think if what you're looking for is some sort of scaled thing, it may be worth trying to, I don't know, have extreme scores I guess. What am I trying to say? I'm just trying to think of a survey where if you said zero is this and ten is that, then they're just going to give a score at some point in between. Am I making sense?

Gareth: Yeah. I think so. Are you saying that maybe the one to ten, you'll end up with a lot of people around sort of fours to sevens. Is that nuance enough to actually mean anything?

Michael: Yes.

Gareth: Okay. That's interesting.

Michael: You need to almost question test the statement. In the boundary that these are in. I guess if you're issuing a survey, the last thing you want is a vague question.

Gareth: Yeah. I wanted to say making sure the wording's more direct and the scale is potentially larger, so that you can get more variants.

Michael: Yeah, I mean, well I'm sure that there all sorts of analyses of a different sort of scale that you need. You give them a midpoint, as in if it's a one to seven scale, you can sit on the fence of it. If it's sort of even you can sit on the fence. [inaudible 00:35:17] one or another. That would also be a factor to consider. I'm not sure if I'm helping.

Gareth: No, no. It's all good. It all goes back into the findings of my research. Anything is useful. Wonderful. Well listen, thank you very much. I know it's been a few nights of trying to get this to happen, so I really, really appreciate you taking the time. I will be sure to share a couple of the final pieces with you.

Michael: That would be lovely. Thank you.

Gareth: I'll send that over. Good luck in the [inaudible 00:35:54]

Michael:				Thank you very much. If anything pops up, [inaudible 00:36:01] feel free to reach out or call [inaudible 00:36:04], you may want to clear with my ramblings.
Gareth:				All right. Wonderful. Thanks very much Michael. Thank you.
Michael:				Good luck.
Gareth:				Thank you. Bye.

Interview 11 - Claire

Interviewee: Claire
Interviewer: Gareth
Date and Time: 8th/July/2016
Location: London
Customer Experience Group: Producer

Gareth:				What's your name?
Claire:				Claire
Gareth:				What company do you work for?
Claire:		<Producer>
Gareth:				What's your job title?
Claire:		I'm Director of Customer Experience.
Gareth:				In that role, what are you responsible for?
Claire: I guess, you'd describe my job as being responsible for the end to end customer journey, so I'm responsible for making sure that the experience customers received, is consistent from application, all the way through to charge off, should that happen.
Gareth:				Okay, wonderful. What does customer experience mean to you?
Claire: To me, it's about, establishing customer's needs and then, meeting them.
Gareth:				Wonderful. Yeah, there's a lovely piece, what's coming a lot out of the research is this idea of understanding expectations and then meeting them. Not necessarily exceeding them all the time, but at least, meeting them and understanding at least, what they are.
Claire: Yeah, and I think in a financial services environment, I have this conversation with my financial services colleagues, quite a lot. Actually, customers don't get emotionally involved with credit cards and with banking, particularly, so actually, a majority of what our customers want, is for things not to go wrong. Which is not particularly, motivational, kind of, inspirational, but ultimately at the end of the day, if you're a credit card customer of ours, you want your bill to work. You want your payments to work. You want your credit card to work and there is very little that we can do to necessarily, wow you in that experience, but the most important thing is the experience is consistent and it works at all the key stages of the journey and the kind of, moments of truth.
Gareth:				Yeah, I think it's similar too, when you talk to utilities companies, it's the same.
Claire: Yeah.

MEASURING CUSTOMER CENTRICITY FOR COMPETITIVE ADVANTAGE

Gareth: You don't need to focus on wowing me, as a customer, just do what I need you to do and get out of my way.

Claire: Yeah, exactly, and probably the most difficult task that I've come across is insurance because I talk, quite a lot, the Head of Customer Experience at Aviva and he rightly, says the only time customers get in touch with them is when they've, either got to renew their insurance, which they don't want to do because they haven't used it all year and they're paying for something they feel they don't need or when, heaven forbid, they've had a break in or car accident and they need to claim. At which point, yes, they're happy they've got the insurance, but they're going through a pretty horrific experience, so actually, their interactions are completely negative, in terms of the emotion the customer is feeling at the time. That's quite difficult to manage, from an experience perspective, as opposed to, if you're in a restaurant or something like that, it's really easy to add some sort of delight into the experience for a customer. It's very difficult if you're in utility or banking, or that kind of thing. It's a constant battle.

Gareth: That's interesting. Actually, we'll look back to this when we look at my framework in a bit as well, because the way I've tried to design it is to get away from the idea of wowing being the ultimate goal. Have you seen an increase in customer experience being discussed, both internally as a priority and also, are you hearing from your customers that it's more important?

Claire: Yeah, I think, definitely internally. The definition of customer experience, I guess, is kind of shifting internally from, we used to be worried about customer satisfaction, now, we're worried about advocacy and so, we've shifted our top line metrics away from satisfaction and over to net promotion score, but definitely, internally. Customer experience is something that is discussed under the section on customer experience, not board, papers, and that kind of thing.

          Customers definitely, it's more and more, becoming the differentiating factor. Because, like I say, in an environment like ours, where fundamentally we can all buy money at the same rate, we can lend it at the same rate, there's very little to differentiate the APR across the credit card industry for a typical kind of customer. The service becomes the thing that differentiates us and we get it wrong, customers will leave.

Gareth: What do you consider to be the key elements of delivering good customer experience?

Claire: I would say there is, lack of friction, so making it easy. Meeting customers in they're, kind of, channel of choice or in the frame of reference that they're in at the time. There's a lot about how customers can contact us and deal with us. Yeah, making it easy. I've already said that. It's about the basics. It is literally about delivering, time and time again, [inaudible 00:05:07] on the basics.

Gareth: Have you got some examples of companies that you think are delivering good customer experience?

Claire: Let me think. John Lewis is always atop the tables when you start looking at customer experience. If you Google customer experience, John Lewis will always be up there. That's a difficult one for me because I'm a John Lewis customer, but the reason I shop at John Lewis is because I know the brand, so actually, I'm not sure whether their experience is actually any different to anybody else's, they just have a brand stand that carries them through. I'm not entirely sure they actually offer the high level of service that they get credited with. I think they just ride on their brand.

I guess I'd say, customers like Amazon, some of the online companies. Apple, they seem to be delivering good customer service.

Gareth: Yeah, I would agree with you as well. There's companies like, I guess, like you said, where people, they don't necessarily think of it as a customer experience and so companies like John Lewis, where there's this constant interaction. They've got that quality built into their values, people just naturally go to them. It's the same with Apple as well. Apple is always bringing their customer experience like that, actually is the genius bar. Genuinely that good a customer experience or have just, we're so used to saying that Apple is good at it, that it comes naturally.

Claire: Yeah, that's probably true. My last interaction with Apple was terrible. They're not good at it all the time, from my personal experience, but you're right. These big heavy hitting brands, once they become known for something, actually the reality doesn't almost have to stack up to the perception.

Gareth: Yes.

Claire: Whereas, I transact with Amazon all the time and my parcels turn up. They turn up really quickly. They tell me if there is a delay. They tell me things about stock. It's incredibly easy to buy through them, once I've registered me payment details. It's actually too easy to buy through them.

Yeah, this whole, I think that kind of front end of the experience is particularly where there is going to be a really heavy battleground for this sort of, payment buttons on the internet. Taking out that friction in that I don't have to have my card with me every time I transact with you. You know who I am. That you retain my details and that repeat purchases with you are easy. That's going to be the thing, more and more I think, that sticks with customers and makes them want to come back, time and time again.

If I contrast that to my experience with Tesgo, for example, who I do my online shop with every week. Every week, I have to enter my security code details from my Tesgo shop and every week I pay with the same credit card and it's Tesco's credit card. I kind of think, why do I have to do this every week? You know me. I do it the same time, every week. I have the groceries delivered at the same time every week. I think customers put up with less and less of that friction in their journey. Organizations that take that away and eliminate it for customers are going to be the ones that come out on top.

Gareth: Interesting, I just started using Amazon for my weekly shop or that reason. It's so easy and it's a lot more straight forward than a Nicardo or a Tesgo, so I've switched. Yeah, they just stared offering it in certain post codes in London and I happened to be in there. The service is fantastic.

Claire: Yeah, I bet because, I mean, their normal services is amazing. I've never yet, placed an express paid delivery with them and yet, everything turns up a day or two days later. It's brilliant.

Gareth: I agree. Where do you see companies most often failing in delivering customer experience?

Claire: Which ones, or what makes ...

Gareth: No, no. What makes them fail? What's the missing thing? So many companies say that they're customer centric, but yet, it's quite hard to think of examples of where there's good customer experience, so where do they often fail?

MEASURING CUSTOMER CENTRICITY FOR COMPETITIVE ADVANTAGE

Claire: The things that I hear, when I look at and read about this stuff. It's definitely the companies that don't get the basics right. Sky for example, are constantly getting slated for their customer experience. When you actually look at customer comments on any of the forums that customers rant about these things on, it has to be they don't answer the phone quickly enough. When they do answer the phone, they can't answer my question. They don't get my bill right. It's too expensive. They're all really, they're hygiene, then they all muzzle those high rocket needs. They're all hygiene factors. If you don't get those right, then customers will talk about it.

They're the organizations that I hear customers talk about. The lucky think for companies like Sky, is that there are some customers who unfortunately, Sky has a monopoly. They almost have no option but to stay where they are. The customers almost can't [inaudible 00:10:39]. I'm one of those. It's the only way I can get my satellite TV. I can't get cable where I live, so I have to a Sky customer and it irritates me every month of the year. It's that hygiene factor. It's that not being able to have the calls answered properly. I can't interact with you online, I have to pick up the phone and then I have to go through endless options. It's exactly the opposite of what we talked about when we talked about Amazon. It's just not easy. I feel like I have to work too hard to interact with you and quite frankly, I wouldn't bother if there is an alternative.

Gareth: Yeah. My biggest thought there is deliveries. I can only deliver between one and two or between one and four in the afternoon, so I have to change my schedule and take my holiday off to buy your product.

Claire: Yeah, and customers just won't. More ad more, customers will not put up with that. My husband said the other day, we had some garden furniture delivered. We got a text message to say, choose from these three delivery dates, so we chose the day and then it said, okay, choose between these three time slots and there were three two hour time slots, so we chose one. Then the delivery company phoned him and said that we'll be there in 15 minutes on the day that they were coming. It's like, that's brilliant. I didn't have to stay in for the entire day waiting for you to deliver something. Yeah, customers just will not put up with that. In this day and age, it's all about, the ease thing is interesting because not only is it about real time, customers are expecting things now.

We talk at work about, we can turn this around in a day or we can turn it around in 48 hours or whatever. All of those things are just different versions of not now. It doesn't matter whether it's an hour or whether it's 48 hours. It's not now. Actually, what customers are expecting is real time delivery. Particularly in a business like mine, where I'm not delivering anything physical, I don't have to send you something. I want confirmation of my payment and I expect an email now. I want my account number when I open my account to be there instantly. Yeah, we've definitely seen things like a time frame, that customers allow us to have, almost, have really shortened. It used to be acceptable for me to get you a new plastic in 10 days. There is no way a customer would wait 10 days now, for a plastic card.

Gareth: I been thinking a lot around how, this is off the interview slightly, but I've been thinking about how the need to, for companies, customer experience is not to exceed expectations, but almost to change what those expectations should be. You should be raising customer expectations, so it becomes the norm. If you're the one that's leading, in raising expectations, you're probably doing very well. The reason I mentioned [inaudible 00:13:44], has to do with what you were just talking about, I use Mondo, as a debit card now. I never knew how important it was getting instant notifications of what I just spent, so I can see exactly how much money I have in my account at all times. Now, my other cards, I don't do that. I actually find it quite like, oh, I'm not home at the minute, I need that. They've raised my expectations of what is needed.

Claire: Yeah, I agree.

Gareth: I recently got a survey on the role of marketing customer experience, found that by 2016, 89% of companies expect to compete mostly on the basis of customer experience versus 36% four years ago. What are your thoughts on that?

Claire: Yeah, that doesn't surprise me at all because ultimately, it is very difficult for most organizations to differentiate a product unless you are Apple. Although, tablets, iPad, you know, those are interchangeable or not, but ultimately product to product, they're pretty similar. The differentiating factor becomes the person that I deal with and the interaction that I have from the service level, so that doesn't surprise me at all.

Gareth: According to that same research, fewer than half the companies see their customer experience capabilities as superior to their peers, but two thirds expect their capabilities to be industry leading or more successful than their peers within 5 years. How do you feel about that?

Claire: That's a fallacy isn't it because there is no way that I would say our service, for example, is probably slightly above industry average but I certainly wouldn't say we were capable of becoming industry leading within the next 5 years. For a couple of reasons, really. One is, customers will hold me in competition with organizations like First Direct. My customer base is entirely different. I have no desire to offer the kind of service that First Direct offer, but customers don't know that.

Secondly, the cost involved to deliver industry leading, I don't know that we need to be industry leading. I don't think we aspire to be industry leading, which might sound a little bit defeated, but I don't think you need to be constantly striving to be the best. We need to be good enough for our customers.

Gareth: Excellent.

Claire: I think it's unrealistic to think the we could get from where we are now to industry leading in 5 years.

Gareth: Yeah, also, like you said, the cost involved, are you actually going to see that much revenue gained from being industry leading as opposed to just being above average. If you're good enough or better, that's probably enough to get most people to come to you.

Claire: You can take our stats on the way that we deliver our customer experience or our customer service, in our contact entered, is a majority of our footprint is offshore. We're a relatively small UK card player. Our cost of onshoring, everything that we currently offshore, is worse in the region of 10 or 11 million pounds a year to us. That, on our operating costs offline, that's a huge number. We can't afford to bring all that back on shore. We wouldn't be able to operate if we did, and so we make a choice that says, actually, we're confident that we can get to where we need to get to with an offshore footprint.

Gareth: Mm-hmm (affirmative).

Claire: We can't get to a First Direct, whose had a completely onshore footprint, but who service a completely different customer base than us. You almost can't compare us. We have to get comfortable with what it is we need to offer to satisfy our customer's needs. We need to meet that and not really worry about everybody else is doing.

Gareth: Wonderful. I am now going to take you through that presentation. What I'd really like is your feedback as we go through. What would you change? What's missing? Thoughts, recommendations. If you hate it. If there is anything. I really want just everything that you get on it and feel free to be brief with the listings that you feel are incorrect or missing on here.

Claire: Okay.

Gareth: Have you got the presentation up?

Claire: I have.

Gareth: Wonderful. We're just going to look quickly at how I did my research, the literature part of that, then some of the findings. Then, the actual model and the way that works. I've been going through, doing a study on customer experience and the literature around it. I've identified key themes and key topics within it. Then, classified those topics against those themes. What that's led me to is a framework and a series of questions that you should be able to use as an organization. That will then score you in the different areas of the framework, to give you a snapshot of where you are at the moment in customer experience. If you have, for example, your scoring very strongly in technology, but actually, culturally you need some work, it should be able to tell you that, so you can identify where there are challenges in the organization in the chain of delivering customer experience so that you can have that. The goal is to be able to compare that to the industry your in or to the market in general so you can start your benchmarking where you are.

Claire: Okay.

Gareth: The way, this goes back to what we were talking about earlier. I said I'd move back to this. The customer experience pyramid model, for us to use. You go from this mid to need up to enjoyable. What I wanted to do is get away from this pyramid idea because what happens happens at the top, the top of the pyramid, I often feel is that wow piece. Too often you hear, you have to delight our customers. We have to wow our customers. That's the easy bit, almost to do because, it doesn't involve, like you said, getting the hygiene factors right. It's the exciting bit. It's not sustainable as a business practice because taken to it's logical extreme, if my goal is to wow the customer. I could give away a Porsche in order to retain a 5 pound subscription client because I've wowed them. I think you have to reign that in, so what I've tried to do in the framework is actually, it's not a pyramid. It needs to be done around a level basis, where you have level one two and three which is slightly more, not completely linear, but slightly linear saying level one is you're getting the basic things right. Level two is you're delivering a customer experience and Level 3 would be at the top of the industry, good customer experience delivery.

Claire: Okay.

Gareth: Any thoughts on that.

Claire: Yeah, I agree. I think that, definitely the wow isn't sustainable and in every industry, isn't necessarily possible or necessary. Yeah, I agree with all of that. I tend to not really think about, as an organization, whether we are at level 1 or level

2 or level 3. I think what you were saying, I think perhaps what you come onto later in your presentation is, we think about it as being almost pillars rather than a pyramid. Having a customer experience model that follows a design implement listed and philosophy. Actually, I don't measure myself against levels. I measure myself against what the customer is telling me they need. I think that's what you're saying. You need to identify what your customer's expectation is and meet it. If your customers expectation is x, you can measure yourself as to whether you're a level 1, 2, or 3, against that, but everybody's levels are going to be different.

Gareth: That's real interesting. I guess, why I come at it is, it's going to be the survey is slightly more generic in that, anybody could take this and find out what their levels are, but I guess what you're saying there is actually that varies across industry.

Claire: Yeah, because you're telling me that I do some survey and it tells me that I'm at level 2. That's great. I might be happy with level 2. I might actually have no aspiration to get to level 3 whatsoever. I might actually think that level 1 is okay and therefore, I'm actually disappointment that I'm in level 2 because I'm over investing. That's not what's necessary for my business. I guess the interpretation is down to the user, but these things can always be difficult because everybody presumes, makes the assumption that I've got to get to level 3 because that's the top of the pyramid. Actually, maybe that's not true.

Gareth: Yeah.

Claire: There has to be some assessment of what's appropriate for your organization at any given time.

Gareth: Yeah, I fully agree. That's really useful feedback. Where I was trying to go would be the level 3, would be what is the best, is the customer experience that you should be delivering for where you are in the industry, so actually it does vary and everybody should be aiming for level 3 because that means that it's just good customer experience, not that it's industry leading.

Claire: Yeah, okay. That makes sense.

Gareth: Yeah. I wonder if that would become more clear as we go through the questions? If it doesn't, actually, that's real useful feedback. With the next piece then, what I wanted to do was to get away from just people, process, and technology which is fairly commonly used. Actually, there's some real important pieces in the delivery or, in having a customer experience focused organization. They are culture, you need to have a customer centric culture to then feed your operations and your processes, to make those customer centric. Which then dictates the process and the service, the product and service you can deliver and that feeds out to the technology that you would choose. You need to make sure that you have a customer centric or customer experience, the right technology for delivering your customer experience. Then, I've included the customer because I didn't want to leave those out in terms of measurement. We'll get to how you actually listen for those, in that section.

The reason that it's colored is that I wanted to get this content of having an emotional sense in the business. You then have to go through rational stages, but because you're dealing with an emotional customer at the end, if you have a purely rational culture, whereby, for example, in the core sense that it's getting off the phone as quickly as possible, actually you're going to miss out on that capability, the ability to deliver the customer experience because you're already focused on operational efficiency, rather than actually caring about the customer.

Claire: Yeah, absolutely. That's interesting because that's ... I said we focus on pillars. If I sent you the slide that I build my customer experience model on. I have pillars and running underneath it, I have culture and technology because without the technology to deliver and without the business culture that runs through the entire organization. Where everybody thinks customer experience is their job and not just my department. You would never deliver any of it because ultimately, your operations people say, all they focused on are their efficiency metrics and their cost base. They probably wouldn't choose to do some of the things that actually you need to do to meet customers emotional needs. I think concentric circles is a good way of representing that.

Gareth: Wonderful. The next stage is then, for us to have a look at how I've organized the questions for determining the scores within those different areas. Within culture, some of the key words that were coming up around culture measurement, empowering your employees, having board level oversight or at least senior level oversight. We can ignore the quotes in there for the moment. Then it gets to the questions, where you'd say, level 1, your base level would be customer experience to company value to a senior persons responsible. Then we go up through to the top level where, if you are really a customer centric organization the customer experience is linked to company incentives and training recruitment and HR is guided by the strategy.

Claire: Yeah. The only, I like question 3, as in we have a central customer experience team. You have to be careful with that in that there is an interesting interaction between that and question 1, where customer experience is a company value because if customer experience is truly [inaudible 00:27:25] and there's truly a company value, sometimes you can get to the point where actually you don't need a central customer experience team because everybody is building customer experience in to that individual process.

I guess that's the journey we've been on. Where, when my team started, we used to sign off on everything. Letters that went out. Texts that went out. Emails that went out. The whole kit and kaboodle. We were almost like a gate keeper for it. Over time, and it's probably taken us 3 or 4 years, what we are now is a facilitator. I don't see everything. I don't have knowledge of everything that goes on in the organization, but my team go and do pieces of work with process owners because ultimately every individual process owner within our business is responsible for the customer experience of their process. They will engage my team to do service blueprinting, end to end journey reviews. That kind of, bits of work. My team now, will go in and facilitate that interaction, but will very rarely come away with any action to actually do to improve the experience. That's sent to the process owner.

I think that the function of that central customer experience team probably changes as you get to be able to answer number 1, much more solidly. If it's embedded as a true value, the function of your centralized customer experience team can be different.

Gareth: Interesting. I wonder whether it would be worth swapping those questions over and actually moving company value up slightly higher. It might, it's probably fairly rare a company has customer experience and their company value, a stated company value. If you were going through these levels, I'd say the customer experience team might be a more likely starting point then.

Claire: Yes, possibly, although I think you'd be surprised how many companies will say, we have customer experience as a stated value, but that's different too. Maybe value is the wrong word. Customer experience is part of the culture because it's very easy to have it as a value, right? We've all seen organizations where they put up posters on the wall.

Gareth: I'm pretty sure [inaudible 00:29:49] has it on there you know.

Claire: Yeah, I'm going to stick it on the wall and say we've got customer experience as a value. That doesn't actually mean anybody gets to talk about it or anything gets done. We were guilty of that in the past. When I took this job on, I had a conversation with my CEO, which was I'll do it, but I may be doing it, if we're serious about it, I'm not doing it if all I'm going to do is put some maps out and tell everybody that the customers are the heart of everything we do because that's just [inaudible 00:30:15].

You've got to, I think, if customer experience is truly embedded in the culture. I would put that higher than question 1. If the organization is stating that it is important, that's a good starting point, but the two, for me, are very different.

Gareth: Okay. The top piece of our customer experience maybe the company incentives, do you think that's fairly involved, as needed?

Claire: Yes, I would say that training equipment and HR being guided by the extracted probably more advancement linking to customer incentives. It's really easy, for example, to link customer experience to call center incentives, for example. Much more difficult to link it to management incentive. Getting an organization to think through what people I need to hire if I'm trying to drive advocacy? How do I need to train the people? Is my HR consultant involved in those sort of conversations? I think that, for me, is pretty advanced.

Gareth: The on to the operations piece, so this was looking more around measurement and the strategy piece. The question here were, we've got to define customer experience strategies as being the base level. That's a good one.

Claire: Yes.

Gareth: Right where we continue to optimize the customer experience.

Claire: Yeah. You've got, it's interesting, you've got, we measure customer experience and we measure customer satisfaction. Can you just explain to me what your interpretation of what the difference is.

Gareth: The customer satisfaction is always the, at the end of some sort of transaction there, is how satisfied were you with what just happened. Whereas the customer experience is more, something like an MPS, but I don't know that MPS is the only, part of my research is leading towards there is a unified CX metric or weather it has to be a basket, but it's more, how do you feel around the whole of the interactions with the company.

Claire: Okay.

Gareth: I think, to use a slight example, I feel like I probably have quite a good customer experience with Tesla, but I've never bought on because they're brands amazing. I read about them. The website looks incredible and I feel something emotionally connected even though I've never transacted.

Claire: Yeah.

Gareth: It's that kind of thing.

Claire: Okay. In that case, it makes sense. The biggest one for me in there, is listening to the customer. I would almost, and to take action based on what we hear, to the end of that sentence, which makes it an incredibly long sentence. There are organizations that listen to the customers but do nothing with it.

Gareth: That's interesting because one of the things that I think is missing form the onion, the model. I don't know what you think is the need for feedback loops in there.

Claire: Yeah.

Gareth: And that action piece is that fever where we listen and then we do something with it.

Claire: Yeah absolutely. That's one of the things that we were doing. We were listening in hundreds and hundreds of different places and not really looking together, any of that listening for it to be able to become effective in terms of what we did about it. We made quite a bit of change there. Listening and taking action, I think is really important and you've got it in the right place I think.

Gareth: Okay, excellent. Then the product and service. You mentioned this earlier and I really like it. It's one of the things I think if there was a basket of CX measurements, MPS being one. Customer effort score. How easy are you to do business with. I can have great interaction with the sales guy, but when it comes to invoicing, it's absolutely horrific. My overall customer experience is terrible. That comes easy to buy in.

Claire: Yeah and we ask, we choose where we ask these questions. We measure differently so we have what we call touch point surveys, which is what you just described after I've interacted with you, I'm going to ask you a bunch of questions cause you've just put the phone down or you've just been on the app with, or on the website, whatever it might be. That's where we would ask these, because ultimately, we're not contacts in the contact center or trying to do something online is important to me. We don't ask these in our relationship survey where we survey three and a half customers a quarter. There, we're most interested in their overall relationship with Capital One. We're more interested in ease when it's in the front of your mind, when you've just come back with us. In each different channel, how easy is that?

Gareth: Yeah.

Claire: Yeah, but customer [inaudible 00:35:22] score, I agree with you. I don't think there is one lens through which you can measure customer experience. I think it is a basket of scores. Not least, because NPS is so incomparable to anybody else. Really your NPS is your score. I can't even compare mine [inaudible 00:35:41] score with the US equivalent of my organization. I can't. I constantly talk to the CEO, about you cannot put our NPS on the graph next to the USs on the graph, next Canada. You just can't do it because they're not comparable.

That a frustration, for me, with NPS. That's where if you have a basket of metrics, I think you can start to build up a better picture of what's going on.

Gareth: That's interesting. Why can't you compare NPS scores?

Claire: Because NPS is so, there is a big cultural impact to NPS because there's a couple of really good white cases on NPS. There's been a lot of research done that has proven that you will score more highly on NPS just because of culture in certain countries. The US ranks a lot higher on that table than the UK does.

They're just generally, more happy than we are. Therefore, their NPS scores will always be higher. New Promote Score can be influenced massively, depending upon who and where you ask it. One of our main competitors Bankquist, operate in the exact same market as we do. Publish their Net Promotion Score on their website, last time I looked it was 78. Mine is 45.

Gareth: 78 is higher than Amazon and Apple.

Claire: Yeah, exactly, but when I tell you that they ask it at the point that they just accepted a new customer and given them credit. They lend to people, like we do, who think they're not going to get credit. It's hardly surprising that their recommendation is really high because I've just got given credit, which I never thought I was going to get in a month of Sundays. Clearly, I'm going to recommend you to everybody I know. Whereas I as my Net Promotion Score to a cross section of customers. Some of who have been through a collections experience with us. That is never going to be comparable. If I asked everybody two days after they got accepted for credit, I probably would have a higher Net Promotion Score.

Gareth: Yeah.

Claire: You have to be careful about how you compare the two.

Gareth: Yeah. On the product piece. Question 2 is a bit odd. I put, we have a complex product service offering and what I meant is that we have a complex service but it's a product. It's simplified in its way that you experience it, but I didn't quite write it right in this. I'm still trying to work out exactly about how it's phrased, but that's kind of, what I was getting at.

We understand the expectations of our customers. We then serve them in the way that they want and the way they expect. Then we understand their values and we're easy to do business with. With the levels of your products and service.

Claire: Yeah, I think that's fine.

Gareth: The technology piece is around segmentation, self service, multichannel, being able to switch between channels and so the questions are there to stack up. We an track the customers across multiple channels, then we can collect quality feedback and then we offer a personalized customer experience that flow up through. If you can personalize a customer experience, that's the nirvana, if you like.

Claire: Yeah. It depends on what you categorize as personalization as well because if think about my interaction with my electricity provider. I don't know if they're personalized service comes into it. My electricity comes in, I pay for it. That's a difficult one because we talk a lot about personalized service. I think that, as a long as you offer that channel that the customer wants to operate on for the majority of the things that they would want to do. You're never going to be able to do everything, every customer wants at the completely personalize level, but I get where you're coming from. It is higher up there, food chain, for sure.

Gareth: I've been having some real interesting conversations recently. We're taking my <vendor> hat off completely because we do personalization. Actually there's a question around whether personalization is what people want. We often say, that customers expect personalization. Has anyone actually that aware that they're getting a personalized serviced because it should be there in the background.

Actually, some point, I don't want personalization. I want to know that I got the best deal and I don't want to think that Amber got a different deal to me because you'd know more about me. I want to know that I got the best one.

Claire: Exactly. I hear a lot of talk now as well about, we did a customer focus group last week and there are lots of customers saying, they actually are starting to get creeped out by how much following me around in the internet is being done. It's like, I look at a product and the next day I'm on Facebook and it happens to pop up in the advertising at the site. The Facebook, and actually I don't like that because that makes me feel like somebody is watching me. Yet, we would say that's kind of personalized marketing, almost.

Yeah, I think we have to be careful with that as a progressive thing because lots of customers are starting, I'm starting to hear that come through and I'm starting to hear customers react to it.

Gareth: Yeah, interestingly, I've been starting to hear it from clients as well saying actually, we played around with personalization and what's the next bit. We actually, I think probably, segmentation rather than personalization is the key. Getting broadly who I am but not necessarily one to one with me.

Claire: Yeah, absolutely. Our business, that is absolutely true. Segmentation is the thing that our business model is built on. If we don't get segmentation right, then the NPV of the product your on is probably not right. It won't perform well for you and it won't perform well for us. It's never going to be entirely personalized because there aren't enough permentations with a credit card for that to be able to happen. Broadly you'll be in the right bucket and that's probably good enough.

Gareth: Yeah, again, it comes down to what we've been discussing, right, like, to get you broadly in the right bucket, there's a certain expense to get it absolutely tailored for you, is quite expensive in terms of tech costs.

Claire: Yeah, very expensive, absolutely and not worth the payback.

Gareth: On to the final piece then, the customer. This is around emotional engagement, so I wanted to say, I just changed my mind I think. This like this two way interaction where you understand the customer and the customer understands you. Our customers understand our values. We understand what they intend to do. We measure referrals. We management their expectations. They enjoy using our service and then we can measure their emotional engagement.

Claire: Yep. Measuring emotional engagement is difficult.

Gareth: Yeah.

Claire: Everyone is trying to do it. Yeah, its difficult. I think customers understanding our values is an interesting one because actually, that's some of what we're starting to think is a differentiator, particularly in financial services. We have this mission of change banking for good. We want customers to understand that we're trying to be different to the other financial services providers. We want them to understand that. I would agree that sits in there.

Enjoying using our services is an interesting one because if you think about something like Apple or the John Lewis that we talked about, actually I enjoy going into John Lewis. I'm wondering around. I might not transact, to like, your test, for example. You enjoy using their website but you're not a customer. It's beware a transactor. You definitely want customers to enjoy it. That's where your recommendation comes from there. That drives your emotional connection.

Gareth: Yeah. What I've been trying to get in that enjoy language, is the emotional connection, but someone pointed out the other day, what happens if it's a funeral director that's taking your survey. It depends on how you convey emotional engagement without delight, wow, and joy. They're all very positive emotional engaging words. I wonder whether you just don't use enjoy. Whether you say, it is emotional engaged or something. I don't quite know where to go with it.

Claire: Yeah, emotional engagement is the nirvana, isn't it, because once you have a customer emotionally engaged, they're a lot less likely to leave. Also, we'll forgive you, the argument state. I think that's what it buys you. It buys you some kind of good will in the bank.

Gareth: Absolutely. I just had this exact same discussion as part of my research with some who mentioned Tesla as their example of good experience. He said, actually, Tesla really messed up loads of the time, but because I know, I love my car and because I love the brand. I know what they stand for is pushing the boundaries of what's possible. I forgive them but they don't pick up the phone when I try to call them.

Claire: That's like, that's the classic Apple model isn't it? We'll push our product and code, that doesn't work and we know it doesn't work. We know it's got bugs in it, but people will still stay outside the shop to get the latest iPhone. They will still download the upgrade because they want the latest and operating system, knowing it's got bugs and being prepared to be hacked off with it for a couple of months until somebody fixes it.

Whereas an organization like us, obsess over, get everything right before we release it to customers because we don't have that good will in the bank and they will not forgive us.

Gareth: I wonder if I can build something like that into the model in recommendations.

Claire: There is probably something about forgiveness because of the level of forgiveness your customers are willing to give you.

Gareth: I'll just go on to that, how willing your customers are going to forgive you. That's quite nice.

Claire: Yeah.

Gareth: Finally, that all feeds into a score and it would break down into a dashboard that would say you scored this is different areas and you can use that to say, okay, we need to maybe look into what's happening in this area or look at what's happening to this area. What's your overall feedback, thoughts, any?

Claire: I like it. I think it's good. I think you've got the build up of the questions right. I like the fact that you've split it down into product, technology, customer. Having things like training and HR and those kinds of things in there. Their questions but generally in these sort of models, don't get included. I am a firm believer in you have to have that kind of entire organizations in on this. Otherwise, it's never going to be effective. Yeah, I like it. It's good.

Gareth: Thank you. One of the reasons that this all came about and why I wanted to do it is, I was looking over these customer experience scorings and things like Lush continually winning. I realized loads of it is just that it's marketing customer experience. It's not operational customer experience, if that makes sense.

Claire: Yeah.

Gareth: It's customer, it's carrying out the customer marketing point of view and I want to delve further into how you actually do it as an organization.

Claire: Yeah, and I think that's interesting and it's something that we're going for at the moment. We're bringing in, like everybody else, we're starting to divide our business into product owners and we've got designers and we've got software engineers and all this, it's like, that's all well and good. You can go out and design great products and you can build up, but ultimately, if the customer needs something they're going to contact operation. That's where our customer experience needs to be right. The whole thing has to link together. A lot of it is marketing based and ultimately the interaction the customer has in marketing is pretty short lived.

Gareth: Yeah. Thank you so much for your feedback and you're input. I really really appreciate it. I will make sure that I get you a copy of the thesis when it's finished as well.

Claire: That would be great. I'd love that.

Gareth: Wonderful. Yeah, it's going to be, I'm submitting, the 1st of September is when I submit and then it has to be bound and published and all that sort of thing, so once that's done, I'll make sure it gets over to you.

Claire: That would be great thank you.

Gareth: Thank you and enjoy the rest of your day and your weekend.

Claire: Thank you and you, yes.

Gareth: Thank you, take care. Bye Bye.

Claire: Okay, bye.

Interview 12 - Joseph

Interviewee: Joseph
Interviewer: Gareth
Date and Time: 19th/July/2016
Location: London
Customer Experience Group: Producer

Gareth: What's your name please?

Joseph: Joseph

Gareth: What company do you work for?

Joseph: <producer>, a division of <producer> group.

Gareth: What is your job title?

Joseph: Global digital business director.

Gareth: What are you responsible for?

Joseph: Pretty much anything that <producer> I think [supposed 00:00:36] through a rectangular screen is the best way of phrasing it. Digital covering in a sense. Covering our e-business operations, transactional stores, lead generation, customer engagement, and customer service online, all the way through to our product portfolio where I'm responsible for the data and evidence driven improvement to improve our products.

Gareth: What does customer experience mean to you?

Joseph: From a digital perspective it means quite simply providing experience that's so good that customers prefer to use them compared to any other alternative.

Gareth: Have you seen an increase in customer experience being discussed both internally at <producer> as a need to focus on, but also have you seen it bit at an increase with your customers discussing it as well?

Joseph: Certainly internally at <producer>, and pleasingly, increasingly, so at the board level, which wasn't too prevalent before, but this business focus has certainly shifted. From a customer perspective, my internal customer definitely. Whether the same can be applied to the dialogue with our actual, our real world customers, I couldn't say, except to say I think they're far more sensitive to a good customer experience compared to a mediocre one now. Their expectations are certainly higher.

Gareth: Definitely. What I think is referred to as the expectation economy. It's this ever growing expectations being set by everybody in different industries as to what the acceptable level of good is.

Joseph: It's actually that. That bar's raising all the time.

Gareth: What do you consider to be the key elements in delivering good customer experience?

Joseph: Making sure it's unified fundamentally, that you've covered all elements of it. I think one of the mistakes many companies make is they will focus on one particular channel, oblivious to the fact that their customers will probably use three or four channels either individually or in sequence. If you don't have those channels aligned you're going to set up bottlenecks or poor experiences or a disjointed one across the board. The second one is fundamentally not understanding your customer. Copying a manual from industry to industry because it happens to be best practice doesn't tend to work because your customer is unique. They're your customers for a reason so you need to understand them whether that's to do with customer research, NPS, or deep analytics. If you don't you're going to hit a brick wall again.

Gareth: What are some examples of companies that you think are delivering good customer experience and why?

Joseph: I think a particularly good example is [Giftgap 00:03:41]. The reason why I think it's fundamentally that their model is based on a thriving customer community. I presume you're familiar with them?

Gareth: I know that they sell SIM cards but I'm not familiar with them beyond that.

Joseph: Forgive the mini lecture then. Basically the way that Giftgap worked, they were like an offshoot, I think like an R&D experiment [inaudible 00:04:07]. The fundamental model is that they give you a cheap SIM card which means you get cheaper phone calls and they undercut the [inaudible 00:04:15] and the O2's of this world. They grew at rate of knots and they've got an incredibly high NPS rating and if you like I will send you some material on what they do and why they're good. I think what they did was quite inspirational. Rather than having call centers, be it via phone, whether in India or whether in the UK or online email customer service responses. They let their community do it and their community is what drives them. They incentivize their community and they had influences within their community.

If you go to the Giftgap website it still fundamentally works that way but they have online message boards. If you go there and you ask something as a new question you tend to get a response whether you've got a fairly technical question like, "I've got an iPhone 5, can I get a mini SIM? Can it be Jailbroke and blah, blah?" You'll get a proper response within about 30 seconds which is miles faster than any call center or any professional forum who never get it back to you. The reason the community is incentivized, some people do it from the love of answering questions. Some people do it because they get Giftgap points and back in the early days when they first started out they actually gave out cash to the point where some kid managed to pay his way through Edinburgh University just by answering questions on the calls.

Fundamentally though the reason Giftgap is so good is because their customers are their customer support and there's a virtuous loop and a virtuous cycle there where because they're constantly monitoring their customers they're working out what incentivizes them. Their fundamental business models depends on what customers are asking them and then being agile enough to respond to it, means that they give their customers exactly what they want. It allows them to innovate slightly ahead of the curve as well to predictive and progressive analytics. Very, very clever.

Gareth: Where often do companies fall down? You mentioned that channel problem, are there any other places where you think actually people should focus on that and they tend to drop the ball and that's what gives you the bad customer experience?

Joseph: Yeah I think that or they're just too far removed from their customer. Someone like <producer> could be a case in point in the sense that he's got really good or multi-national company. How close can you really be to your customer, particularly in a world where social media response and social media engagement is an expectation now. If I'm working in London and I've got a centralized team in London how do I make sure my customers in the Philippines are getting what they want, or India or any other growth market. It's pretty easy to resource in the states where it's a huge business or pretty easy to thrive [inaudible 00:07:02] bigger business units or English is the first language. If you're a true global MNC how do you start to do that on a localized level? It's a huge challenge.

Gareth: Now a recent [Gartner 00:07:15] Survey on the role of marketing and customer experience said that by 2016, 89% of companies expect to compete mostly on the basis of customer experience versus 36% four years ago. What are your thoughts on that?

Joseph: One of the reasons I don't often read Gartner. To a degree I would agree with that really. I still don't think customer experience particularly in the B to B world is necessarily the differentiator. It is increasingly becoming so particularly as companies fight for a less established market. From a Lexis perspective and you may remember this, traditionally they focused on the head of their addressable market. Big law firms, a market which is not only saturated because those law firms buy <producer> and they buy the competitors any way they have to.

It's also contracting so the battle to efficiently capture the long tail, improve our margins by getting into that addressable market and converting them efficiently because you're not going to send an army of salespeople out there to go and do it, is where the battle is going to be won. To a degree that's where online customer experience in particular, as well as aligning all the channels behind it. Like your call centers, like your salespeople, like your onboarding programs, is really, really going to be the differentiator. If we can do that better than our competitors and the platform that you were instrumental in selling to me is the line to go and do that.

Gareth: According to that same research, fewer than half of companies see their customer experience capabilities as superior to their peers but two thirds expect their capabilities to be industry leading or more successful than their peers within five years. How do you feel about that? Is that achievable?

Joseph: Sounds like classic optimism when someone's doing a survey but from my perspective I would be optimistic about it if I'm half way through it.

Gareth: Interesting. Now I'm going to take you through that presentation now if that's okay. If you can just be as brutal as you like. Your feedback will all be going to the recommendations. I'm going to ask questions around the ordering of the questions, whatever your feedback is we'll get put back into there. Not that you ever would but don't feel like you have to pull any punches.

Joseph: Okay. The acronym looks like a roman numeral.

Gareth: What CXC or ...

Joseph: I keep looking at it going what's the number mean?

Gareth: It's actually been changed as well. Maturity Curves have this horrible feel to them which is like they're going to get old at some point or that you're ... it just didn't feel like the right word for it. It's actually become the customer experience competency framework.

Joseph: That rolls off the tongue.

Gareth: Yeah, it sums up what I'm aiming for. I couldn't think of any better names than your CXC score.

Joseph: That'll do.

Gareth: What I've done, I've been doing ...

Joseph: We spend ages coming up with acronyms for all the new crap we're doing.

Gareth: Yeah. <producer> of all companies should have reached a good acronym. I've been going through and doing all of my literature research and studying customer experience. I've been identifying key themes, key topics, I've been classifying those against each other. What I've developed is a survey that you would take. Basically you answer a number of questions on a scale of 1-10. They're weighted at different levels. They then spit out a score that shows you how ready you are or where your competency is around delivering customer experience.

Then you can drill down on that around the framework to say, "Actually we are very good for example in our technology. Our technology programs are very customer centric but actually our culture seems to be lacking. We're missing the tools that mean that we have a customer centric heart if you like." It's identifying the key points that actually we need to invest here, we need to change here to do exactly as you said which is line everybody up to be customer centric. To deliver the good customer experience instead of having people all over the place doing different bits with everybody saying, "We are customer centric but we're not actually having any sort of alignment behind it."

Joseph: Yeah. I can send you a deck but I actually gave, or actually the originator of this stuff. I actually gave at a [Script 00:12:37] conference in Melbourne last year. I called it digital revolution or digital evolution, with a cunning little laugh just because I like to be a smart ass. The notion of it once is I hate the term digital transformation. Transformation implies that you have some sort of metamorphosis and out the end pops the digital butterfly which is paint and bollocks. It doesn't work that way. It's a slow process, it's an evolution and it's something that doesn't really stop. It makes much more sense to do it that way. It also gave me an excuse to throw loads of animals into the presentation and do a pseudo-Darwin thing.

Point being is that the things that I've often identified in technology. Obviously it's necessary for the transformation but it's by no means the key step. If you don't get the technology right you don't have a foundation but you can have the technology and get nowhere close to the end game or the evolution at all. The fundamental challenge, the most difficult thing which will take up most of the time is changing the management processes and the culture, some of which would have been there for decades. That often means organizational shifts, it means people leaving, it means changing the way things work. That's incredibly difficult and time consuming and takes an awfully long time. I often call it at Lexis it's akin to continental drift. We'll make a mountain range eventually but Jesus it's taking it's time. That preamble again I guess is just some context for what we're about to go into.

Gareth: Wonderful. If you could share that that would be amazing. There's this Forester Pyramid that's out there and what I wanted to get away from was it's sort of like Maslo right but there's too many pyramids and ideas of wowing customers and ideas of delighting customers and that the customer you do absolutely anything to keep them happy. If you give this idea, like this pyramid here to someone and say, "This is what you need to do," most people will skip the hygiene factors at the bottom of that and go straight to the top and go, "We need to wow the customer." It's just not a sustainable business practice.

Taken to it's logical extreme it would be a customer service rep can give away a Porsche in order to save a $5.99 subscription customer. You wowed them, you delighted them, they were amazed but actually is it cost effective and actually have you don't all of the basics before that? What I wanted to move to was actually then a level system. Levels 1, 2, and 3 where level 3 isn't this sort of tipped wow nirvana but rather you are delivering good customer experience. Then below that is these are the levels you need to do to build up to get to that point. Rather than it being a focused tip that anyone can jump through it is, "What are you doing?" You could be doing different bits within the different levels so they can give you an overall score and that's where the waiting comes in.

Joseph: That's pretty smart in it's own right in a sense that one, it makes it easier to score as a competency framework which is where you're going but it's also pretty good to benchmark.

Gareth: Yep.

Joseph: Okay go ahead.

Gareth: Then those are the levels that the questions were based around and then I've built up this framework which is this onion model. I was trying to get away from people, processes, and technology which has always talked about and say actually there's more than that. You need to be talking about your culture as being customer centric. Once you get to the outside you actually need to be thinking about the end customer as well. They're often forgotten when we talk about customer experience internally. You still have to understand what's happening there. I've built up where culture needs to be customer centric. It then feeds into your operations and gives you the direction that feeds into the product and service that then feeds out to the technology and influences the technology you would choose which is then the interface to the customer. We have this blue inside and outside piece because the cultural piece is an emotional harp and you're dealing with an emotional customer.

If you were to get that wrong, for example, if you had a very rational culture then you'd end up something like a call center where you'd say, "We're all about operational efficiency and we're all about getting you off the phone as quickly as possible which is the complete opposite of what you want to achieve in a customer experienced focused environment. Do you understand the customer at the end on an emotional level as well? That's why you have that sort of differentiator across the onion.

Joseph: The only thing I would add here and maybe it's the assumption if it's within operations or products and service or something around brand. The reason being if you're speaking to a customer and you have a brown tone of voice which reflects your culture, someone like Virgin for example. The Virgin tone of voice, the way Virgin works. Have you ever seen [inaudible 00:17:57]?

Gareth: No.

Joseph: They're mail chimps which I'm sure you've heard of. There's a website called [inaudible 00:18:04] which was basically mail chimps, online personalities, how they use it to train all their customers so they're internal staffed. It's well worth a look and it looks at how mail chimp, the mail chimp personality which is reflected on the screen is reflected in those engagements, actually respond to the customer's emotional state. It's brilliant because it's basically a very early form of saying, "Look you're no longer going to meet your customer. You're no longer going to have that tangible handshake, the look in the eye, the shared dreams. Your entire relationship is going to be built through a screen that you have to work ten times as hard. That's very, very important. Particularly in terms of digital customer experience again because you're all basically donning relationship with these people through a rectangular screen or some sort of touch point.

It's quite nice having the cutesy flippant Virgin way of doing things like, "Hi Joseph, it's time to upgrade your broadband." That kind of crap when they send you direct mail. The problem with that tone of voice and all that sort of stuff is one, it can be inappropriate in a B to B context. The other issue is everyone's doing it now. Look at your direct mail, look at your just mail, they are all trying to be your bank and high gouge and all that sort of stuff. Because of that, the whole point of it, the whole impact of it is getting more and more diluted. [inaudible 00:19:38] brand, certainly and the way that everyone does things but for somewhere within this model possibly [inaudible 00:19:47] the onion or being all encompassing in it's own right would be your brand. Your brand is what the customer is emotionally responding to. That's what a real brand is and that sort of logo or any of the other sh*t that goes with it. Your brand is the emotional response that they get to it. That's quite subtle, quite powerful.

MEASURING CUSTOMER CENTRICITY FOR COMPETITIVE ADVANTAGE

I've seen some psychological studies of how people react to certain brands or they're actually don't brain studies on them. You look at the visceral anger that something like Monsanto or even McDonald's can produce in people. They don't actually feel angry but their anger senses flash and stuff like that. When you realize that I don't know if that's going to have an impact on whether they buy, whether they don't. Have you seen first moment of truth, zero moment of truth?

Gareth: No.

Joseph: Definitely have a look at zero moment of truth. The first moment of truth was a ton of research that Proctor and Gamble did in the 80s which was all about if you wanted to take shampoo or something you could go down the booth or something like that and you would look at the shampoo rack. They were all based on product price, placement, packaging, all that sort of stuff. They worked out that basically our minds make up, we pick which shampoo we want when we're looking at that stuff in the first aid section. You may spend two minutes perusing the things, you may spend time looking up and down at the bottles. Essentially, subliminally you've already made your choice.

Gareth: It get referred to as thin slicing by Blink who's that Martin Gladwell?

Joseph: It's actually not. yes[inaudible 00:21:32] you've basically made your mind up and after that you just rationally ... the rest of your brain is rationally trying to catch up to justify that initial decision. Then you get all the other things that go with it like buyers regret and all that type of stuff. The first moment of truth is all about winning that subliminal 8-second battle. The zero moment of truth, and I think there is a website literally called zero moment of truth.com was a load of Google research. The reason Google did it is if you win zero moment of truth, first moment of truth never happens because of the internet. Zero moment of truth when you think about it, and again guys I might have a deck on this because I was using it at Lexis to try and drive our case. It was basically if you want shampoo now, same analogy, you may just go in line and go, "Hi. I've got wavy hair and I'm a bit of a surfer. Just been dumped by my girlfriend in Canada but I need a shampoo." I know I'm being cruel.

You would maybe search or look at reviews and find influences and all this sort of stuff and then potentially buy it online or alternatively you've already made you choice. When you march into Boots you just go straight to the one that you've already picked. Zero moment of truth is based again on loads and loads of psychological triggers. I noted one of the books you had in your reading list was Influencing Our Persuasion.

Gareth: Yep, [Chavini 00:22:56].

Joseph: Probably the best web marketing book ever written. Although it was written in the 80s basically because if you want to build a highly converting store or website you need to use those principals.

Gareth: That's actually what a lot of the modules you see in digital experience are built around like social proof and all that sorts of things.

Joseph: [crosstalk 00:23:20] The Power of Reciprocity, every charity direct mail you get they give you a free gift. The example in the book about the [inaudible 00:23:26] is genius. I mean look how much those bastards are worth. Very valuable stuff so yeah basically end point, I would put somehow trying to brand in here.

Gareth: That's really useful. Is there anything else on that model? Does it make sense? Does it flow okay? Obviously we need to get branding?

Joseph: It flows perfectly and it's very logical that if you can change the culture of the business first that everything else will flow. The only problem is that it's by far the most difficult thing to change.

Gareth: Actually that's ...

Joseph: Now we get the technology first and I'm leveraging the technology to change the culture.

Gareth: It's kind of one of the goals of this is to say, "Right well look. We've scored quite high in other things, in technology for example, but we need to change the culture and actually that's going to be the hardest bit to do. Let's spend money doing that by talking to a change agent or whoever it might be, or a consultancy, instead of spending more money on making our products faster or making our technology better or actually let's invest in this area." It's kind of the goal of it.

Joseph: Correct. That makes perfect sense to me. It would have been useful.

Gareth: Then what we're doing I'm going to take you through the different sections of that framework and the questions it asks. Around culture a lot of the things here are keywords like empowered employees, expectation, having board level oversight of customer experience. If you go through to the cultural questions you've got a level one which is your base level customer experience and company value. That then builds through different layers up the same as the top one that you'd be doing. You'd ' be on your game would be customer experience is linked to company incentives.

Joseph: Okay. On a scale of one to ten where would we be? One?

Gareth: It would be interesting actually, once all this research is done, to actually get you to take the test and see where you score. For the moment I'm more interested in what your thoughts on the questions, are they ordered right, do they make sense, do you think they're actually indicative of a customer centric culture?

Joseph: Where is the question, which slide?

Gareth: Sorry it's on 29 I think it is. It'll have all three of the questions layered up.

Joseph: They just looked like statements. Going through looking at them as a scale, one escalating through six, the first thing I would say is actually phrase them as a question. I'm looking at going write these as statements, it's a lookout scale, great. Question one, is customer experience a company value? Then I could rate that because right now that's a statement to me. May seem fairly obvious but like I said you're sending this out blind to loads of people I'm looking at it going, "Okay where's my question. I can see it says question one but I don't see any question marks." That's based on me doing a very similar research exercise years ago to the one you're doing now by the way. People didn't understand I was asking them question. I had to start using Australian inclination. Assuming that they're phrased as questions though, yeah they make perfect sense. Customer experience is a company value I would say six and then thereafter on a scale of one to ten again you may want to be explicit about what that scale means. One being we have nothing, ten being yep been there, done it, got the t-shirt.

Gareth: You think if you had training, recruiting and human resource development being guided by CX and your customer experience is linked to company incentives, do you think that would be a pretty key indicator that you know what you're doing in customer experience? That's the top level right?

Joseph: Company incentives yeah. As a broad statement yeah. As a broad statement yeah but then you're done it. For example Lexis or <producer>, every executive including me is somewhere within our KPOs is something around the NPS. I don't know if you also read the NPS book as well. The yellow one, I can't remember it's name. We had that one sent out to us as part of the GSLTB with senior management team.

Gareth: Yeah it's called the ultimate question.

Joseph: That's the one and basically the idea is that really trying to embed that entire notion into everything that we do. It hasn't permeated all the way down through the business yet but I'm pretty sure that's ultimately what they want to do. Slide 29, logically speaking makes perfect sense all the way through. Finding recruitment and human resources development guided by the strategy and that's actually an interesting point. I've not seen that done anywhere. I know some companies I can't recall their names, it's a big American insurance company, they start employing chief experience officers. Literally nothing goes out to the customer, whether it's a letter, an email, an automated mail change, a website where at some point that senior experience officer or their team reviewing it and making sure that it fits in alignment with how they do business.

Gareth: One of the other people that I've interviewed as part of my research who works for a British finance company have exactly the same thing in place because it was the only way that they could actually ensure that the organization was aligned around customer experience was to say, "Look for the first two years nothing goes out unless it goes through us. Then once we've got you ready, we'll start dripping it out so you don't have to.

Joseph: Yeah. It's an elegant solution to what most companies have and it's an incredibly fragmented problem. Although that's one of the challenges I have is the sense that my [inaudible 00:30:08] covers the web platforms and stuff like that but there's still lots of fragmentation. I don't have email or CRM or anything else like that. I don't necessarily want it but if we wanted a genuinely aligned customer experience we would need some sort of mechanism to control that.

Gareth: Indeed. The next piece was ... unless you have any other thoughts on culture?

Joseph: No that's it for culture.

Gareth: Operations then is the key words in here were around measurement and being able to understand the metrics of what you're doing and being operational. If we go through then to the questions which are on slide 37, assuming I've already taken on board the fact that they have to become questions, this is then the base level, if you're just getting started what you should do is have a customer experience strategy and that then builds all the way through until we continually optimize the customer experience. That would suggest and actually it's one thing I think is missing from my framework. The need for some sort of feedback loop into it so that you can continually optimize.

Joseph: Yeah question 3 I put we listen and respond to the customer. Pretty easy to listen too.

Gareth: Actually that's come up before. That's great, you can put all these different surveys and everything out but unless you can actually do anything with that information what's the point.

Joseph: Yes and even if you do it let the customer know that you're doing it. Let them know they've been heard. That often isn't done. It's quite nice, even if it's six months down the line, you mentioned this, you complained about this, you said something about a call waiting time. We did something about it. Okay cool. That's good to know. It's good to know that I made a difference to your business even though I cancelled my insurance shortly afterwards. Thank you very much. What you're reaffirming and sometimes rekindling that relationship with a prospect is quite powerful. Question 3 we listen and respond. We measure customer experience probably continually. I think that's implicit in what you're saying but we continually measure customer experience to be a good one and then yeah we continually optimize it too. Maybe that's overkill, they're all continually. These are good, this question I'd put response.

Gareth: Then on your product and services I really like this. NPS is awesome but depending on where you deploy it depends on whether people are in a good mood, or whether they're responding. There's lots of tricks you can do to get round it. On it's own as a singular CX metric I don't think it stands but a lot of my research is pointing to, it's going down this road of actually is there a singular CX metric? What I'm slowly uncovering is actually there is more of a basket of metrics that would be useful. One of those I think should be customer effort score.

That is how easy do people find it to do business with you? You could buy from me today and have a great experience but when you get to invoicing and accounts don't do it properly and it's a nightmare. The hellistic effort has become very difficult to buy from me. You might have asked my NPS when you just bought and you'd be happy but this as a basket would be more indicative. That's where I'm going with product is how easy is it to use? How simple is it? Can people understand a complex offering?

Joseph: That's right and actually I've done a lot of work with this over the last six months so I set up a team broadly looking at our predictive analytics capability or at least looking at data driven development around the products but also broadly speaking my vision really is data driven decision making across the company. One of the big flaws with something like NPS like you alluded to is one is the lacking indicator. Usually the NPS survey goes out long after the actual customer experience. It does look at the overall [inaudible 00:34:35] of it so the product may be great but the saleswoman was a cow. Therefor you got a detracted score which tends to mask a lot of the things that are going on.

It's not to say NPS or the voice of the customer is not useful. It does have some severe limitations. One of the things we've been looking at and you said the word it's almost like an effort score. Using machine learning within our products. The beauty of machine learning if you start using things like decision tree algorithms is you can pinpoint pretty accurately where the red spots are. Also understand how recently after six, and also what magnitude impact they have on our overall customer experience metric. Kind of what you're getting at here is the same thing. We've done it through machine learning because we've got web analytics files, we've got customer surveys, we've got the ability to do it.

On a broader scale I'm not 100% sure what the methodology would be. At some point you would have to have some form of rigorous data collection and data cleaning. Like I said you probably can go one step beyond NPS and the real beauty of once you get to those [inaudible 00:35:53] the indicators is you can start using them to predict. If we did this what magnitude impact would if have on the customer experience. Okay if we did this, option B, would that have a bigger impact? It's quite powerful to do and if you ever look at companies like [inaudible 00:36:11] which may be a pseudo-competitor given you've got the survey and stuff like that. That's what they do, they've got that repeatable methodology. They look at what the responses are and how the responses have been made and they work out what's truly important to the customer or online to the customer experience.

When you're looking at the combination of the online and offline worlds and all the different channels and interactions that come between it, I can imagine that will start to get slightly complicated and you would need some fairly heavy duty machinery of the type that banks use to monitor all of your different interactions with them as a brand. Because interactions with brands are increasingly digital or even if you do it in person you have some form of digital interaction like if you go to a bank you put your card in to identify yourself and that kind of thing. This is becoming more and more possible. I don't mean to ramble this is just an area I'm really quite keen on at the moment. Hopefully that was useful.

Gareth: Indeed it is. Then on the questions around that then, you've got the layers which is page 45. Question 2 doesn't make any sense because what it was meant to say was we have a complex product offering but we've simplified it. I couldn't quite word it properly and it ended up coming out completely wrong. Ignore question two but the idea is that here with our product, and this has come up a lot in my research is this idea of expectation meeting, the ideal for customer experience is to meet expectations and not necessarily go beyond wowing them all the time which come s back to that pyramid piece. In order to actually do it properly you need to actually understand what the expectations of your customers are and then you build through until the top ones understand the values of of our customers are more easy to do business with.

Joseph: Yeah it makes sense. Going back to question 2 so is this like an analogies to Apple when they made their product portfolio much, much simpler compared to what it used to be? [crosstalk 00:38:22] or the nature of the products themselves?

Gareth: I was trying to thing of a good example. It's more like if you have an insurance product is a fairly complex product, or a mortgage maybe, it's fairly difficult in terms of it's different bits but you've made it easy to understand or you've simplified it despite the fact that it's complex so that the customer can understand it is kind of what I'm getting at.

Joseph: Yeah I think the Apple analogy is a good one. Again you probably know this, when Steve Jobs took over Apple again they did a three month order of that strategy and what was wrong. You can find this on YouTube. It's an hour long internal speech that he gave. He talks about the three things they needed to get right. One was their marketing. Their product portfolio when he took over was astonishingly complex. You could take their matrix when you looked at the options you could select when buying a new MAC had thousands and thousands of different options. It was analysis paralysis. It was geek heaven. The first thing he did was completely simplify the product line. He just got MAC book, iMac, whatever. I'm not a MAC fan but it's a pretty good speech.

Then he talks about their experience and their operations and then their supply chain. It's like on those three pillars that they started to rebuild Apple and that's where all the innovation and everything else came from. It might be worth looking at that because I think he phrases it pretty well. It's just basically simplifying their product for service lines. The actual computers themselves are still bewilderingly complex and obviously excellent at what they do and well designed but the actual product line in terms of understanding what you're getting from them was drastically simplified if that helps you.

The rest of this in terms of the order seems to work okay. I'm looking at question five, part of me thinks maybe that should be wedged with question three or four but ultimately that's your hygiene [inaudible 00:40:42] that we're easy to do business with. We are able to serve the customer in the way that they want. The definition of we're easy to do business with I think given you laid out the pyramid at the beginning that makes more sense but you have to make that connection back to the pyramid.

Gareth: Yeah and I wanted to add to you, being able to serve the customer in the way they want is actually quite complex from a product offering because you need to understand how they want it, when they want it and then be able to serve that. That's fairly difficult to do actually.

Joseph: Yep agreed.

Gareth: Maybe we swap three and five over.

Joseph: [inaudible 00:41:33]

Gareth: Yes. Technology then is around the voice of the customer, channel switching, self service pieces. Then the questions there are on page 51. It starts with we can track our customers across multiple channels. It builds into connecting or delivering a consistent experience across those channels and then the top one is we can personalize that customer experience in the channels.

Joseph: If you can do one you should be doing two. It's probably as good a reason as any to keep them separate because I think ideally [inaudible 00:42:15]. We can collect qualitative feedback. Qualitative feedback is actually easier than the first two.

Gareth: Okay so maybe you swap them out.

Joseph: Yeah it's a lot easier. Consistent experience across multiple channels, I would change the word consistent to unified. Presuming you have a Forester subscription, if not I can probably dig it up and send it to you, there's a pretty good paper on the difference between a unified and a consistent customer experience. Unified takes into account the context of what the user is doing. If they're using a phone, they don't necessarily want to consistent experience of what's on the laptop they want something which is unified. They know it's still your brand, they know they're still in the right place, they know what they're doing but they want to do it differently on the phone because they've got bandwidth requirements or the fact is they're on a phone rather than a laptop and a big screen. Consistent isn't that difficult to do. Consistent is getting your logos in the right place and having a patent library. Unified is pretty difficult and needs a good strategy. The Forester paper is called Digital Customer Experience Governance. That's basically what lays out what that means.

Gareth: Cool. I'll check it out. Just an interesting piece here, I've put in there the top being personalized customer experience. Actually I'm finding talking to a lot of companies at the moment as part of my research and just in general, I don't think that personalization is necessarily the goal. I think what people meant by personalization is actually advanced segmentation.

Personalization seems to have this personal being a core part of the word at one to one element. Actually the returns you would get on expense you would need to spend to get one to one aren't necessarily there. Actually what most people want is just to be able to do advanced segmentation and serve experiences to those different segments. Actually as a user, I'm not sure that personalization is quite what I want. I don't want to know that Joseph is getting a different deal to me, I want to know that I'm getting the best deal. I don't know what your thoughts are on that.

Joseph: Yeah you've heard a couple of little bits but I'm in agreement with you. Doing one to one personalization is a pipe dream at scale. Advanced segmentation is one good way of putting it. Dynamic cohorts would be another one. A customer, depending on their context, and again it can be can be done by a phone or a tablet, are they coming in the evening or are they coming in during the work time. Are they coming in as a customer or as an employee? As a buyer or the influencer? All of these things will impact what cohort they're in at any particular time and really good predictive analytics will pinpoint what cohort they're in based on analysis of historical data and then you can serve that experience up. It's not easy to do but it's much easier to do than a one to one relationship and it's far easier to scale.

It is generally personalized because again depending on what day or how that customer arrives or what their context is they are getting a response or an experience which is relevant to that state at that particular time which is a way of producing. That's basically how I would phrase it. Customers moving seamlessly between channels is a good one. I think that's a very good question because it comes back to what their preferences are and what their state is at the time and it goes back to one of my answers to your very first questions, how do I define a good digital experience? It's on that they prefer to use. They would prefer to use digital experiences rather than using call center, or rather than coming in personally. We know that we've got it right when they would rather come on and just use the digital experience. Like [inaudible 00:46:36] I would rather go click and collect or get it delivered than actually go in the store, that kind of thing that we know that you've won and you've done the right thing. If you can persuade it. You'll never persuade everyone obviously but that's the way to look at it. Hopefully that makes sense and you can hear me.

Gareth: Definitely. The final one then is the customer and this is around emotional engagement and expectation management and this two way relationship. They understand our values and we understand theirs and we can measure referrals from them, we can manage the expectations and we can measure emotional engagement. Why I wanted to get the customer understanding our values piece right was a story that I was told around Tesla.

Tesla, the people who drive them absolutely love them but actually according to owners I've spoken to they aren't actually ... they're still not MVP by any stretch but there are still a lot of bugs that need to be ironed out. Though because you understand the Tesla's values and what they're trying to do is revolutionize the way that cars work, you kind of forgive them and therefor you get this sort of leeway in terms of experience you still have a great time. Whereas someone like a utilities company you have a very different experience because you're just like, "I just want you to put the [inaudible 00:47:59] away and let me do it." That's why that values piece came in as the understanding. I don't know, hopefully that makes sense.

Joseph: It makes perfect sense and it comes back to why I said brand is so important in your model. People understand that about Tesla. You probably couldn't articulate what their brand or their mission statement is, or what their brand turns out, but we all know that's what Tesla is doing. Like I said if you've got a crap brand or you've got really anodyne mission statements or company value which incidentally <producer> has, then it's going to be very difficult for people to actually truly understand that. For example, an old company they had three core values which was independence, integrity and innovation. I used to laugh at that going, independence is important for what the company did but the other two, integrity and innovation, if you're a company with no integrity you're f****d. If you're a company that can't innovate you're f****d. They're both utterly meaningless, it's just total sh*t. Did you just go out and try and find two more words that began with I so you can have the full alliteration effect? It's meaningless.

Whereas a strong brand you already know in your own mind even if you don't have a big vocabulary what that brand is all about. Tesla is a great example frankly. I don't know what their mission statement is or what [inaudible 00:49:23] says or even what their brand statement is but yeah, I do know all about what Tesla is trying to do.

Gareth: Interestingly Tesla's customer experience is so good that I haven't bought their car but yet I would consider they have good customer experience. It's insane. I've used their website, I'm aware of their marketing and the press about them like that's an amazing customer experience. Like you said that's the power of their brand. I haven't even bought, I'm not even considering buying one.

Joseph: Yeah. Like I say it's an incredible branding experience. I had a good look at it because I thought ... you know Oslo is full of them and all of the counts in Oslo. [inaudible 00:50:06] having been in one I went, "This thing goes like sh*t off a shovel. It's great. I want to have a look at this." Besides the cost which is prohibitive in it's own right, but then the whole point is they reassure you with the model and the value, the thing that would stop anyone buying in this country at the moment is the lack of superchargers and the lack of government incentives to do it. The newest supercharger to me is in North Hampton about 35 miles away. I'd have to try and find a way to plug it in every day or eventually get a Tesla wall. Fair enough the UK and market and the government isn't particularly environmental but in places like Norway, bear in mind Norway is dark for six months of the year, they're everywhere. It's a success story and I think Norway is going to ban petrol driven cars at some point in the mid-2020s.

Tesla has kind of driven that. Tesla is the preeminent brand of doing it and Toyota and Nissan but Toyota and Nissan don't have that reputation for innovation and genuinely Toyota and Nissan have the hybrids whereas Tesla completely revolutionized how things are done. I think it's a fantastic example but again it's a brand. It's an emotional content with a brand. You mentioned Tesla to someone, what does Tesla mean to you? Providing they've got some sort of pseudo awareness of the car and presumably they're under 40 years old, they'll have a very good recollection of what it is.

MEASURING CUSTOMER CENTRICITY FOR COMPETITIVE ADVANTAGE

Gareth: Yeah. Okay. Wonderful. Then it spits out to your score and it would give you, you'd be able to drill down on this and you'd be scored in the different areas. You'd then be able to do comparisons so you'd be able to say, "Right. Can you compare where I am within industry or to the market which goes back to the expectation economy piece where you're competitors aren't necessarily your direct competitors anymore. It's everybody vying for people's attention. This should be able to bench mark you against the market as well is the end goal.

Joseph: Yeah. The benchmarking piece is important. Sorry I just realized I'm looking at the wrong ...

Gareth: I'm sorry I went down to slide 60 which is just kind of the end.

Joseph: It went to slide 45 as you were talking and [inaudible 00:52:37] so I'm looking at the 50 again. Yes makes sense.

Gareth: Good. Any other feedback, thoughts, bits and pieces, any other inputs?

Joseph: The brand piece I think is really important. Paradoxically is also going to be the most difficult because it's driven by emotion and because it's largely subjective it's probably a difficult one to put in your benchmark. I think it's important because customer experience fundamentally is about an emotional response to what you've done and a huge part of that is your brand. Somewhere in that onion model I think brand has to permeate out from culture, from a horizontal vector.

Gareth: It's interesting, I wonder whether you would put it ... because what I was trying to get is technology is where you interact with the customer but it's almost worth not having it as an onion or splitting some of the rings of it to say, actually a brand is as much of a touch point with a customer as a piece of technology is.

Joseph: Brand reflects the culture and probably again Virgin is probably the archetype MBA example of this. Virgin has all of those different groups, all those different brands, but they all upgrade under the same culture. You find Virgin Atlantic, the stewardesses have licenses to crack a joke with you that kind of thing. Then they all have that kind of interaction. They're trained to have that personality whereas you go on another airline it's obviously very different. Singapore has always rated among the best airline. Their stewardesses are super professional, super responsive. Their CRM is excellent. They know exactly who you are but Christ no they will never crack a joke with you. Don't even try.

        The Virgin way of doing things, like you say, everything about them [inaudible 00:54:46] saying that repeatedly, is by far their biggest asset though it's not necessarily represented that way on their balance sheet. Somewhere within our model I guess this is my main piece of feedback and I'm pretty keen when I did my visitation way back when it was on branding. It did focus on services marketing with airlines because airlines is that weird intangible between the tangible where you actually sit in the seat, you eat the food and all that sort of stuff but the differentiator in any airline is the service. What [inaudible 00:55:19], how hot the stewardesses? How good's the seat? Did they welcome you onboard the plane? Did they have the right newspapers? Was the lounge any good? Was that whole check in experience good, blah, blah, blah. For something like this where you're looking at something as important as a customer experience metric somehow in there something to do with brand is important. The challenge you would have is it's such a difficult thing to measure with the questions.

One of them could be what are three words, if I say our brand name to you whatever it may be give me three words. Then do some sentiment analysis on that. That's probably one way. You could probably work out whether something was negative sentiment or lukewarm or something or some sort of weighting. If someone said something like superior, luxury, and efficient when they see Rolls Royce that's clearly a good thing. When they say sh*tbox, unreliable, terrible for Ford then it's fairly obvious it's at the other end of the scale

Gareth: I should feed that back into the recommendations.

Joseph: The moment of truth by the way, you should have it in your inbox.

Gareth: Yep awesome. I will take a look at that. Thank you. Without this we'll put the brand piece into the recommendations.

Appendix G - Customer Survey Demographics

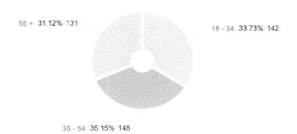

Figure G1: Demographic split for *age* in the customer survey (*above*)

Figure G2: Demographic split for *gender* in the customer survey

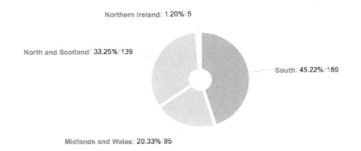

Figure G3: Demographic split for *region* in the customer survey

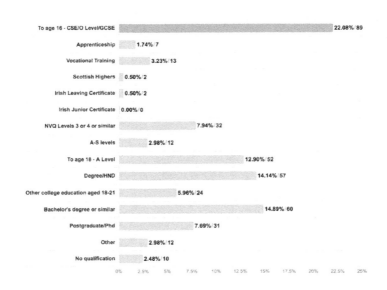

Figure G4: Demographic split for *education level* in the customer survey

Figure G5: Demographic split for *annual household gross income* in the customer survey (above)

United Kingdom: 100.00% / 421

Figure G6: Demographic split for *country* in the customer survey

Figure G7: Demographic split for *ethnic background* in the customer survey (*above*)

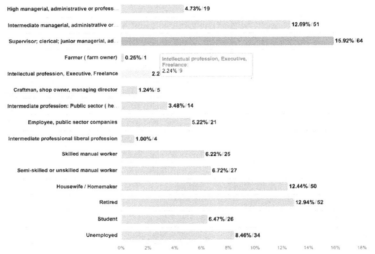

Figure G8: Demographic split for *employment* in the customer survey

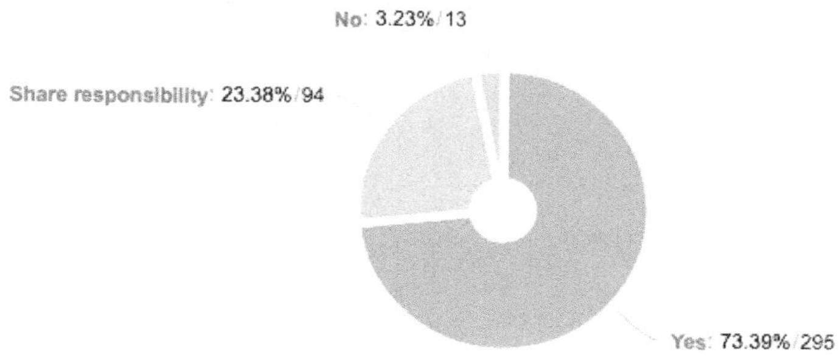

No: 3.23% / 13

Share responsibility: 23.38% / 94

Yes: 73.39% / 295

Figure D9: Demographic split for *responsible for household spending* in the customer survey

Appendix H – Raw Survey Data

Available upon request

Appendix I - Competing on Customer Experience

Source: Interview Findings

Part I

Practitioners were asked to discuss their thoughts on

> A recent survey on the role of marketing customer experience said that *"by 2016, 89% of companies expect to compete mostly on the basis of customer experience, versus 36% four years ago"* (Sorofman, 2014)

Interview findings

- 58% *agreed* with the findings and thought it was likely that *"companies compete mostly on the basis of customer experience by 2016"*. (Sorofman, 2014)
- 17% of interviewees *disagreed* and felt that it was unlikely this would be the case.
- 17% were *ambivalent* to if it would happen or not
- 8% did not answer the question.
- The findings are shown below in Figure 16.

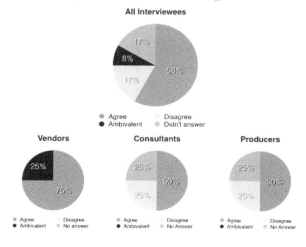

Figure I1: Findings from a practitioner interview question about the findings of a Gartner study

- Vendors were the most positive on the findings of the Gartner survey. 75% of them thought it was likely that companies would *"compete mostly on the basis of customer experience by 2016"* (Sorofman, 2014)

Part II
Practitioners were then asked to discuss their thoughts on

> According to that same research, they said *"fewer than half of the companies see their customer experience capabilities as superior to their peers, but two thirds expect these capabilities to be industry leading, or more successful within the next five years"* (Sorofman, 2014)

Interview findings
- 42% disagreed with this research and said that it was unlikely this would be possible.
- 33% did not answer the question.
- 17% were ambivalent and thought it might or might not happen.
- Only 8% that agreed it was likely.
- There was no noticeable differences between the practitioner groups.
- The findings are shown below in Figure 17.

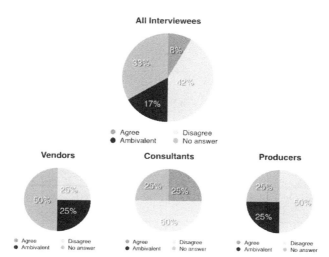

Figure I2: Findings from a second practitioner interview question
about the findings of a Gartner study

Appendix J - Results from Customer Survey

Table J1: Results from the customer survey question *what does customer experience mean to you?*

Response	% of answers	Response	% of answers
How Staff Deal with you	16.92%	Meeting Needs & Expectations	3.33%
Customer Service	11.54%	Loyalty	2.56%
Good experience	9.74%	Good Online/Offline Experience	2.05%
End to End Journey	8.72%	What I get from a business	2.05%
Don't Know	7.95%	Made to feel Value	1.54%
How I feel	7.44%	Access to Information	1.28%
Other*	6.92%	The Environment	1.28%
How you are treated	5.90%	Choice & Price	1.03%
What happens when I shop	4.62%	Marketing Jargon	0.77%
Buying/Purchasing	4.10%	Personalised Experience	0.26%

*includes responses that didn't directly answer the question

Figure J3: Results from the customer survey question *do you agree or disagree with the statement? Customer experience is something I consider when purchasing from a company for the first time*

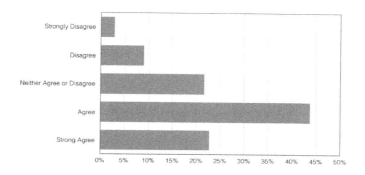

Figure J2: Results from the customer survey question *do you agree or disagree with the statement? Customer experience is something I consider when repeat purchasing from a company*

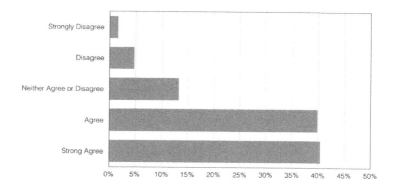

Figure J3: Results from the customer survey question Do you agree or disagree with the statement? *Bad customer experience is something that would stop me purchasing from a company*

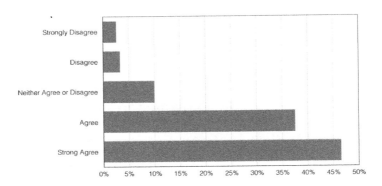

Table J5: Results from the customer survey question *what do you consider to be the key elements of a company delivering good customer experience?*

Response	% of answers	Response	% of answers
Friendly/Helpful Service	32.08%	Don't Know	1.41%
Other	10.07%	Good environment	1.41%
Customer Service	9.37%	Price	1.41%
Feel Valued and Understood	6.32%	Easy Returns	1.41%
Listening to the Customer	4.92%	Having Stock	1.41%
Delivery Times	4.45%	Loyalty	1.41%
Good Quality Products	3.98%	Good Website	0.70%
Meeting Expectations	3.75%	Good choice	0.70%
Efficient Service	3.28%	Good communication	0.70%

Easy to Purchase	2.81%	Value for Money	0.47%
Honesty	2.81%	Consistency	0.47%
Knowledgeable staff	2.58%	Having a good reputation	0.23%
Availability to speak	1.64%	Being Trustworthy	0.23%

Table J6: Results from the customer survey question *give examples of good customer experience.*

Response	% of answers	Response	% of answers
Friendly Staff	14.29%	Efficient Service	1.37%
Helpfulness	14.29%	Loyalty Discount	1.37%
Resolving Issues	14.29%	Amazon	1.37%
Other	7.69%	Easy to Use Website	1.10%
Knowledgeable Staff	5.77%	Marks & Spencer	1.10%
No Examples	4.95%	Enjoyable	0.55%
Quick Delivery	4.12%	Easy Purchase	0.55%
Going one step further	4.12%	Nationwide Building Society	0.55%
Don't Know	3.85%	Good Environment	0.27%
Good Returns Policy	3.85%	LG	0.27%
John Lewis	3.30%	Mamas and Papas	0.27%
Good Prices	1.92%	Pizza express	0.27%
Being Listened to	1.92%	Poundland	0.27%
Feeling Valued	1.65%	Wilko	0.27%
Quality Product/Service	1.65%	Tesco	0.27%
Customer Satisfaction	1.37%	Sainsbury's	0.27%

Table J7: Results from the customer survey question *where do companies fail when delivering customer experience?*

Response	% of answers	Response	% of answers
Customer Service	14.22%	Product Out of Stock	1.96%
Not Feeling Valued	11.52%	Difficult Returns	1.72%
Other	10.54%	No answer	1.47%
Unfriendly Staff	9.31%	Hard to use Website	0.98%
Rude Staff	6.62%	Ignoring Loyalty	0.74%
Unhelpful Staff	6.13%	Feeling Pressured	0.74%
Unknowledgable Staff	4.90%	Not Feeling Understood	0.49%
Delayed Delivery	4.90%	Not Meeting Expectations	0.49%
Not Feeling Listened to	4.90%	Price	0.49%
Don't Know	3.43%	Slow Service	0.49%
Breaking Promises	3.43%	Not Trustworthy	0.25%
Bad Communication	2.70%	Intrusive Staff	0.25%
Dishonesty	2.70%	Not getting an apology	0.25%
Non English Speaking Customer Service	2.21%	Getting order wrong	0.25%
Poor Quality Product/Service	1.96%		

Appendix K - Practitioner Interview Quotes

Table K1: Quotes from practitioners on the *definition of customer experience*

Interviewee	Quote
Robert	"an experience that causes them to have an ongoing relationship with us"
Lorne	"how individual experience your brand and your products and your services in a holistic manner across all channels, across all periods of time"
Matthew	"it's a rather broad definition" - "Is the product or service that they're using meeting their needs"
Lucas	"it's the experience you have when you're interacting with a brand as you're going through a decision making process to interact with the brand" and "how a brand and business deal with that entire life cycle is the full end to end customer experience"
Edward	"means that you're building a lasting relationship with your customers rather than treating them like numbers"
Paul	"delivering happiness"
Patrick	"It's the observed performance that the customer has with the company, minus the expectations"
Alex	"business that put their customers first. They think about how their customers are going to interact with the brand, with the product, and with the general operations of that business"
John	"it's creating content and committed customers which ultimately generate a sustainable profit for the business"

Michael	"means the measure of how we, as a brand, made the customer feel during their time of interacting with us across our channels"
Claire	"it's about establishing customers needs and then meeting them"
Joseph	"providing [an] experience so good that customers prefer to use them compared to any other alternative

Table K2: Quotes from practitioners on *have you seen an increase in customer experience being talked about both internally and externally?*

Interviewee	Quote
Edward	"absolutely - this is what really drives our product development and company"
Robert	"digital has enabled direct contact with consumers in a way that we never had before"
Joseph	"customer expectations are certainly higher"
Claire	"it's more and more becoming a differentiating factor - the service becomes the thing that differentiates us and if we get it wrong customers will leave"
Michael	"customer's expectations are that any brand, certainly a major brand, a big favour brand, should offer a superior customer experience"
Michael	"arguably the biggest part of the strategy is a focus on customer experience and customer experience improvement"
Alex	"we live in an age now we call this the expectation economy, where the customer has got a very low opportunity cost to move to another solution, brand or product. What's that created is a sort of a very impatient customer... Customers are extremely demand and a bad experience will lead that customer detracting and never coming back to you again"
Patrick	"the simple fact that we are a practice on customer experience is already quite a good revelation"

Table K3: Quotes from practitioners on the *key elements of customer experience*

Interviewee	Quote
Robert	"using customer insight at a planning stage of the product, understanding a customer's needs, understanding a customer's lifestyle as a conceptual stage, using consumer information [...] to help iterate and develop the product through its lifecycle"
Paul	"Understanding what the customer wants"
Lucas	"the product, the communications, the brand and the employee"
Matthew	"Data and information. Customer experience relies on, in my opinion feedback loops"
Lorne	"it's about turning and saying what is my ability to understand what customers really go through their points of pain, their points of delight, know their underlying motivation, and then your ability to take that insight and return it to better experiences"

Table K4: Quotes from practitioners on *where do companies fail at customer experience?*

Interviewee	Quote
Robert	"we see a lot of people who collect a lot of data but they don't analyse the correct data points, or they analyse but then they don't act on it"
Joseph	[when] "they're just too far removed from their customer"
Claire	"it's the companies that don't get the basics right"
Michael	"broken promises basically. If you set an expectation or you say to somebody, I'm going to do this, and you don't deliver on that, that is just bad customer experience"
Paul	"not delivering on their promise"
Matthew	"At the CXO level because they know the strategies but they are just implementing technology or are they really changing the organisation, the culture throughout the organisation to be more customer experience"
Lorne	"lack of insight. They don't actually know what their customer think. They have very basic metrics on that. They have poor use of data"
Robert	"it doesn't work if you don't have a CEO who is obsessive about the consumer"

Table K5: Quotes from practitioners on a *Gartner study part I*

Interviewee	Quote
Lorne	"rubbish"
Joseph	"like your call centers, like your salespeople, like your onboarding programs, it really is going to be the differentiator"
Claire	"that doesn't surprise me at all because ultimately, it is very difficult for most organisations to differentiate on a product"
Michael	"I think they're probably overcooking it"
John	"I think the statement of expect to compete on customer experience versus will compete on customer experience is probably a casm"
Alex	"It's not like they are choosing to compete on customer experience. I think they're forced to compete on customer experience"
Matthew	"100% of our clients who we're talking about are using that language now"

Table K6: Quotes from practitioners on *a Gartner study part II*

Interviewee	Quote
Matthew	"it seems like customers and clients should be a little bit more focused on shorter term value delivery to customers"
Lorne	"which isn't reMichaelstic"
Joseph	"sounds like classic optimism but from my perspective I would be optimistic about it. I am half way through it"
Claire	"that's a fallacy isn't it because there is no way that I would say our service, for example, is probably slightly above industry average but I certainly wouldn't say we're capable of becoming industry leading within the next 5 years"
Alex	"it's just not going to happen. It's going to require transformation. I think if businesses want to become customer experience first, they need to change their culture. They need to change their organizational structure around the customer" certainly wouldn't say we're capable of becoming industry leading within the next 5 years"
Lucas	"then you have to ask the question of how many of them have a good measurement framework in place. They see it has being industry leading, what are they actually comparing it against"

Table K7: Quotes from practitioners on *the framework and the levels*

Interviewee	Quote
Robert	"in lay persons terms level one is effectively survival. Level two is transacting well and level three is having a relationship"
Claire	"I agree. I think that, definitely the wow isn't sustainable"... "we think about it as being pillars rather than a pyramid" "I don't need to measure myself against levels. I measure myself against what the customer is telling me they need" "everybody's level is going to be different"
Michael	"I would agree with all of those. I think the reason I'm not feeling the linear thing is ideally I think it probably would be a gradual thing in understanding the values of that real utopia"
Michael	"the reason I'm not feeling the linear thing is ideally I think it would be a gradual thing in understanding the values of that real utopia"
Joseph	the only thing I would add here and maybe its the assumption that it's within operation or products and service is something around the brand"
Joseph	"that pretty smart in its own right in a sense that one, it makes it easier to score as a competency framework .. it's also a pretty good to benchmark" Joseph - "you may want to be explicit about what that scale means'"
Michael	"what you're maybe saying is that if you are doing some stuff that's in level three but you're not doing stuff in level two, then your stuff in level three isn't as effective as it could be"
John	"I'm not convinced that ranking is right for your study"
John	"we're saying for each of the different areas these are the six things that you should be doing, if you're doing the top two and the bottom for that doesn't mean you're very

	mature it means you have skipped a few steps" .. 'could you argue, you kind of have to do one to four in order to do five and six correctly"
John	"I might be tempted to simplify it. I might out technology, products and services in the same ring made a 3rd each" .. "I might be tempted to say operations, then the next layer is technology, product and service in the same ring"
Lucas	"this falls down if you're in any kind of disruptor's mindset - you don't need to feel any kind of optimal foundation, you can go straight to the top level and come at it from a different angle"
Patrick	"it's more black and white kind of...either your delivering or not"
Alex	"you're seeing a lot more companies emerge that are literally, the product is a brand, the brand is the product, it's all blurring"

Table K8: Quotes from practitioners on *the need for extra levels and questions*

Interviewee	Quote
Matthew	"it's maybe that under each one of those questions you have in there there's another set of five questions to further diagnose"
Lorne	"now you've just suddenly boxed this three into two. You're not getting very differentiated"
Michael	"you give them a mid point, as in if it's a one to seven scale, you can sit on the fence of it. If it's sort of even you can sit on the fence. That would be a factor to consider"
Michael	"it may be worth trying to...have extremes scores I guess. What I'm trying to say? I'm just trying to think of a survey where if you said zero is this and then is that, then they are just going to give a score at some point in between"
Lorne	"do you not need four levels? Is there just a baseline? Rather than try and squeeze them down, it's almost like baseline, level one, level two etc"
Alex	"I feel like the questions are very high-level. I feel like, will you get enough sort of variance in the model from the questions that are pretty high level"
Edward	"because it's a slightly ambiguous question, the answer is likely to be ambiguous. Therefore the derivative action is likely to be less effective"

Table K9: Quotes from practitioners on *emotions*

Interviewee	Quote
Robert	"that's a very emotional call for the consumer"
Edward	"like the simplicity thing, you can actually miss out on that emotional connection with simplicity so it has to be smart simplicity when it matters for simplicity and immersive when necessary"
Edward	"that what it comes down to, its the appearance of control that provides you a more emotional investment in the relationship with the product"
Claire	"there is probably something about forgiveness because of the level of forgiveness your customers are willing to give to you"
Claire	"emotional engagement is the nirvana, isn't it. Because once you have a customer emotionally engaged, they're a lot less likely to leave"
Claire	You definitely want customers to enjoy it. Thats where your recommendation comes from there. That drives your emotional connection"
Michael	"Based on three key phrases that we want to the customers to say. We wanted them to say "I understand. It works. Then we want them to say I'm impressed....It works well that's because I'm consuming the product or service I expected to work, and then the emotional, I'm impressed"
Alex	"like the virgin experience The culture is at the core, that their job is to serve the customer... British Airways is a bit more rational about serving the customer, rather than emotional. It leads to more friction"
Edward	"the interesting questions are the core questions, like, how do you get people to emotionally connect culturally to a better experience"

Edward	"you shouldn't strive to be happy all the time because happy is an extreme emotion. You should strive for contentment"
Matthew	"the emotional piece is interesting"
Lorne	"derisk it [the framework] just suggests there's this big divide between internal emotional culture and then there are barriers of operation products, technology and then the customer"

Table K10: Quotes from practitioners on *culture*

Interviewee	Quote
Robert	"companies that are genuinely customer centric are borderline obsessive about their customer. They're borderline obsessive about collecting data, about analysing it and about learning from it"
Lucas	"This is where actually culture drives operations comes in. At this level, if the culture isn't driving that customer experience is listened to in operations is not going to happen"
Claire	"If customer experience is truly embedded in the culture. I would put that higher than question 1"
Claire	"if customer experience is truly a company value, sometimes you can get to the point where you don't actually need a central customer experience team because everybody is building customer experience into that individual process"
Alex	"if you have a central CX team, then you're not taken CX seriously"
Alex	"I'd like to switch four and five over. I think "we empower people to make decisions in the best interest of the customer" is actually pretty complex thing to do, to actually empower people to like now what should I give this customer". Think recruitment is a more fundamental thing"
Paul	"yeah I can't help thinking thats [employee empowerment] probably in Level 3 because that's quite something"
Paul	"I'm just thinking for that Level 1, when the customer experience is a company value, whether even that level 1 would be in there or not. Some level 1s might not have that.... I don't think a lot of companies have got their company values right"
Edward	"something that says "okay we're not just doing it lip

	service. Question 2 is we can still do lip service. Question 3 is we actually made an investment"
Robert	"you need to reframe question three as, we have a customer experience team that is situationally appropriate for our business and our business model"
Edward	"my gut is it feel like you want to ask a more precise question on question 3, something about the size and the scope or something of the team"
Lucas	"why does it have to be a single individual person who's responsible for that? I'm more inclined to agree with the notion that there should be people throughout representing different departments at that senior level"
Lorne	"You don't want to have central customer experience"
Robert	"my question is whether a centric customer experience team is a prerequisite for that? Actually I think you could find examples of organisations where customer experience is proudly decentralized, but is very good"

Table K11: Quotes from practitioners on *operations*

Interviewee	Quote
Robert	"and on of the key things there is not just to measure customer experience and that you continually optimize but there is a constant feedback loop between the two"
Matthew	"are people willing to change the operations because so many times technology is not the reason most of our projects fail even though they are technology projects. Its are people willing to change their operations"
Matthew	"are they willing to change the operations. Are the operations flexible and agile." "are our operation agile.

	That's the basic"
Matthew	"that one is interesting because you don't have anything here about how agile the organisation is to change operations to adapt to the customer experience"
Edward	"we measure customer satisfaction but do you measure the whole cycle of customer satisfaction?"
Edward	"I do think there may be something beyond on this which is continuously optimizing the customer experience"
Edward	"how do you measure customer satisfaction in a non customer service kind of scenario for it not to become a popularity question. Question 2, I think there is a lot laced into question two where it has to be done carefully"
Paul	""we measure customer experience, we listen to the customer, we measure customer satisfaction" for me they're probably all the same"
Paul	"As a bare minimum, we have a defined customer experience strategy, and probably understand the customer experience journey. So question 4 into level 1"
Paul	"we understand the customer journey should probably be on level 1"
Alex	"the ultimate is when you're reporting on your customer experience. If you're a public company, you're actually reporting on customer experience, as a public company metric"
Lorne	"In order to delight, you've got to do more than optimize. If this is like nirvana, i'd almost say optimizing customer experience sits at this level [mid level]" .. "i would say that level one is like we measure customer satisfaction and listen to our customers. I think those, to me, are the basics"
Joseph	"question 3 I would put we listen and respond to the customer"

Claire	"the biggest one for me in there, is listening to the customer, I would almost add..and to take action based on what we hear.. to the end of that sentence"
Michael	"the full 360 takes in everything into product development and suddenly NPS becomes, or whatever is set for that faction, becomes the most valuable for product development"
John	"I've always assumed [customer experience journey] is the best starting point"
John	"so they don't actually listen to the customer, they get feedback from the customer but they don't actually listen"
John	"maybe measure customer performance or something, make it more generic"
Alex	"your question one and two. I would be more like we have to find how each part of the business is interacting with the customer experience"

Table K12: Quotes from practitioners on *product/service*

Interviewee	Quote
Robert	"...because they're three successful businesses who are competing fundamentally for the same thing as us. Consumer attention. They are not only doing that really well and absolutely killing it but they're also sufficiently large and sufficiently influential they they set a consumer expectation around what good looks like"
Lorne	"everybody has to be easy to do business with, everybody has to understand the values of their customers..if you're not there, you're not going to be successful and be able to operate"

Lorne	"thats your baseline. If it's around products and service, again I would say it's more about if you continually innovate and adapt our products and service, based on working with our customers to understand their needs and to understand their evolving needs..that's got to be there at the top:
Lorne	"I'd actually question too, we have a complex product [question two] and question five, easy to business with, are pretty much the same thing"
Matthew	"question 4 is interesting. When you talk about customer experience and surveys and you get feedback from the customer. That's one way to look at it but then there's other companies that say "well my customer only knows what they have experience so far. If I can give them a completely different experience, something they're not expecting maybe that's what I should be doing? Do I know better than my customer?. I think that was Apple's thing right?"
Lucas	"in order to become a customer you would have to have be easy to do business with. That would be a lower level protocol"
Lucas	"if you weren't easy to do business with, them many people wouldn't be using your products because you weren't easy to do business with"
Edward	"that what it comes down to, its the appearance of control that provides you a more emotional investment in the relationship with the product"
Edward	"like the simplicity thing, you can actually miss out on that emotional connection with simplicity so it has to be smart simplicity when it matters for simplicity and immersive when necessary"
Alex	"when you break the problem down you help guide people through the purchase process of your solution. Buying a car is like that. It's a complex thing to buy a car. It's a complex thing to buy a car. It's expensive. It's got lots of features so you need the problem broken down for you"

Alex	"my question here would be, as a product business, how do you use your customers need to influence what you build?"..."It's not necessarily about building exactly what your customer asks for, but it's about interpreting their needs and then solving a problem for them. I think that a connected customer and product innovation that's really important"
Joseph	"I'm looking at question five, part of me thinks maybe that should be wedged with question three or four but that's ultimately your hygiene factor"
Joseph	"the actual computer themselves are still bewilderingly complex and obviously excellent at what they do and well designed but the actual product line in terms of understand what you're getting from the was drastically simplified"
Joseph	"the first thing he [Joseph Jobs] did was complete simplify the product line
Michael	"it's creating new expectations"
Michael	"Customers or consumers don't even know that they want it. It kind of happened. If you know what I mean" ... "you don't even know that you need it.. that to me is customer centric product services. I feel like somebody who's way more intellectual than me has already told me what I want, or he has told me what I need from a product or service. That to me is true customer centricity"
John	"you can marginMichaelse your position in the marketplace by making things so effortless and easy for customers. Customers no longer value it and then they go somewhere else because it wasn't something they reMichaelsed that they should have valued anymore"
John	"thats a lot to do with how much impact that particular purchase has on you, if it's a low impact piece then I want the effort to be particularly low, your effort can get confused with assumptions" .. "I think this is one of those time bombs that will go off at some point where we've made it so easy for customer that they didn't actually

	reMichaelze what they were signing up to and then there's a lot of compensation claims to be made on the back of it"

Table K13: Quotes from practitioners on *technology*

Interviewee	Quote
Robert	"Interesting within my own business one of the key things this year is a strategic theme is the single customer view. The idea that we can take disparate data sources and identify an individual across all of them and respond to it so I think that's absolutely right.
Robert	"it's interesting that in question three you specifically say qualitative feedback as well as quantitative....being able to say something qualitative feels much better than them just mining my data and trying to get insight from me"
Robert	Consistent experience is an interesting one, to a certain point. I actually don't want a consistent experience across multiple channels. All I want is an appropriate experience across multiple channels"..."I would consider situationally appropriate rather than consistent across multiple channels there"
Matthew	"that potentially where the technology comes in as well is if I have Salesforce for some of these things, how quickly can I change a process in Salesforce. Are my content delivery, my content management or content delivery peices? How agile is that really?
Matthew	"question three. Talking about customer experience from a product standpoint is, again, that think of am I just asking them or am I designing the product in a way where they are telling me through their actions"
Matthew	"now people expect recommendations because there is so much content out there. There's so much stuff out there they expect a company to hold their hand to curate their experience through whatever product or service. It's kind of just the new norm to some extent"

Matthew	Matthew - "Six [personalisation] is increasingly in level 1 or 2. Its if people are expecting it"
Joseph	"customers moving seamlessly between channels is a good one. I think that's a very good question because it comes back to what their preferences are and what their state is at the time"
Joseph -	"Consistent isn't that difficult to do. Unified is pretty difficult and needs a good strategy" Michael - [moving seamlessly from channel to channel] - "that's customer centric. Thats removing friction"
Joseph	"Consistent experience across multiple channels, I would change the world consistent to unified"
Joseph	"If you can do [level] one then you should be doing [level] two. It's probably as good a reasons as any to keep them separate because I think ideally we can collect qualitative feedback is actually easier than the first two"
Claire	"segmentation is the thing that our business model is built on"
Claire	"that's a difficult one because we talk about lot about personalised service. I think that, as long as you off the channel that the customer wants to operate on for the majority of thing that you they would want to do. You're never going to be able to do everything"
John	"Question 1 is a high bar but I thinks it the right sort of positioning"
Michael	"personalisation tests wouldn't perform as well as just a good segment group"
Michael	"it's all about relevancy. Maybe you could argue relevancy is another way of saying personalisation but if it's simple and relevant then I don't need it to be highly personalised"
John	"the only one I would challenge is six as being the pinnacle.. quite a lot of the time the thing that customers

	aren't looking for is personMichaelsation"
Alex	"[level 3] I think here you want to says it's all about continuity. It's all about wherever the customers, whatever touchpoint the customer is interacting with, what's the continuity from the last place they were at. That the holy grail, advance off that"
Alex	"You have to think about, what do I need to know about my customer, at any touchpoint? I think that's a really fundamental thing"
Alex	"You've got to have a profile schema. You've got to have a way of defining the profile of the customer across all these different touchpoints"
Alex	"the fundamentals are just going to join things together, be able to create...that's really hard to do. I'd say qualitative feedback is more fundamental"
Alex	"question 6 is all about can offer a personalised customer experience into every touchpoint"
Alex	"[level 1] is we can collect and analyse data from all touchpoints. I'd switch 2 and 3 around"
Lucas	"potentially at level 3 we cover a unified strategy which is able to create a customer experience seamlessly across all those different audience segments. Question 1 and 2 is probably do we understand what our customer segments are. Level 2 is we understand what those customers, each of those segments expect from us and we have way of deploying communications in order to satisfy their needs. Then 3rd level is we have a holistic unified way of delivering that and we are doing it on a modus operandi basis"
Lucas	"I would potentially say those 2 are 2 different separate things. When you get into the qualitative data and providing a consistent experience, that is much more into customer experience. I'd probably say questions 1 and 2 is much more about audience reach. I'm not sure how audience reach and customer experience directly correlate"

| Lucas | "this [question 3] is quite tightly covered almost a feedback loop into the operational later and how much is listened to is then considered by the culture of the business" |
| Matthew | "Maybe its framing, maybe it's saying it wrong [personalisation]. They expect the service or product to be relevant to them and if it's not relevant then maybe it's because you're not peronsMichaelsing" |

Table K14: Quotes from practitioners on the *customer*

Interviewee	Quote
Edward	"what is my overall scheme of the customer interaction? Am I the gas bill or am I Nike"
Edward	"I think baked into this is emotional enjoyment. For the gas bill it's much different than if you're trying to delight somebody. I think the first level you sort of have to be what's the correct or the best expectation or the most reasonable expectation, and it has to be a pretty cold assessment of your place in the world. Then layered on top of that these questions can be honed correctly"
Robert	"I changed the order of questions one and two around personally because I thinks it's quite possible for a business to understand what's customers intend to do even if those customers don't understand its value. This implies a certain hierarchy and I think those go the other way round"
Robert	[question 3] - "You can absolutely measure referrals but ... there's a sort of level beyond that which is, we feel sufficiently confident that we bade the growth of the business around customer recommendation"
Robert	"an adequate business does that [meets expectations] but surprise and delight are the hallmarks of an exceptional business"

Robert	"maybe instead of managing expectations in here what we do is move back down to a lower level and then maybe we have something like, we can meet the expectations of our customers and surprise and delight when is required"
Lorne	"I'd say we measure advocacy. There's lots of ways of doing advocacy, one of which is referrals"
Matthew	"Yeah the emotional piece is interesting. We've done some work just around content of what emotions does content illicit in individuals and that's a whole other sort of analytical piece of really understanding, but at a much deeper level that before and requires different skill sets"
Daivd	'that [question 2] seems like it should almost be at a higher level.If you're anticipating people's needs. That's a pretty mature capability.
Lucas	"I'm not sure about measuring emotional engagement. I think that's basically an impossible thing to do"
Matthew	"swapping that one [two for five] people should enjoy it no matter what"
Edward	"Exceeding expectations are key. I think the early questions are we understand our customer expectations and then maybe questions two is something like, we understand our place in our customer life or workflow"
Michael	"it's hard to get customers to understand our values. If that's a prerequisite to moving on to levels 2 and 3 then I think a lot of companies will fall straight to level 1"
Alex	"I think there are other, more fundamental metrics around just like, our customer buy from us again. It's like repeat purchase and things like that"
Alex	"we measure loyalty"
John	"maybe enjoyment is the right word"
Michael	"enjoy is a good phrase, good word, good way of looking at it. I would also think about delight and stuff like that"

Joseph	"it's a brand. It's an emotional connection with a brand"
Claire	"there is probably something about forgiveness because of the level of forgiveness you customers are willing to give you"
Claire	"Also, we'll forgive you, the argument stage, I think that's what it buys you. It buy you some good will in the bank"
Claire	"emotional engagement is the nirvana isn't t because once you have a customer emotionally engaged, they're a lot less likely to leave"
Claire	"you definitely want customers to enjoy it. That's where your recommendation comes from. It drives your emotional connection"
Claire	"customers understand our values is an interesting one because actually, thats some of what we're starting to think is a differentiator, particularly in financial service"
Michael	"thats almost irrational. It works, well that's because I'm consuming the product or service I expected to work, and then the emotional, I'm impressed"
Michael	"we used to talk about almost the steps to customer experience delight. Based on key phrases that we want customers to say. We wanted them to say..I understand. It works...then we want them to say...I'm impressed

Table K15: Quotes from practitioners on *the need for different models for different industries*

Interviewee	Quote
Robert	"it's completely situational. If you think about banks, mobile phone networks, other institutions that typically interact with their customer through a call center...from a framework point of view, it look at different sectors or different use cases and say level 2 in this section means

	this, in this sector means something quite different and set some sectoral norms that you can use for benchmarking"
Edward	"what is my overall scheme of the customer interaction? Am I the gas bill or am I Nike"
Edward	"I think baked into this is emotional enjoyment. For the gas bill it's much different than if you're trying to delight somebody. I think the first level you sort of have to be what's the correct or the best expectation or the most reasonable expectation, and it has to be a pretty cold assessment of your place in the world. Then layered on top of that these questions can be honed correctly"
John	"They run a global study and they were finding that organisation would say "we're not enjoyable" Walt Disney would definitely want enjoyment in there but it's not in there because they also have SSE and they have in there T-Mobile, it's not going to be enjoyable it it. If they had it in there as one of the variables then it would skew organisations that weren't able to deliver an enjoyable experience"
Lucas	"I wonder if there's actually another one here, actually something like business model,, or what is the most important attribute of the business which defines the order"

Table K16: Quotes from practitioners on *the need for feedback loops*

Interviewee	Quote
Robert	"one of the key things there is not just to measure customer experience and that you continually optimize but there is a constant feedback loop between those two"
Lucas	"almost a feedback loop back into the operational layer and how much is listened to it then considered by the culture of the business.. this is where actually culture drives operations comes in"
Matthew	"customer experience relied on, in my opinion, feedback loops"
Lorne	"one of my thoughts was to put a feedback loop around the outside if you like em the customer feeds back into the culture"
Robert	"you could almost say that a link between [culture and operations] is a prerequisite"
Edward	"the problem with level 1 doesn't imply that you're actually doing anything for your customers because you can take all this analysis and you could just sit it on a shelf somewhere. You try to contract your customers, you can collect, analyse customer data but it doesn't mean you're doing anything about it. I think it's an inherent part of doing something about it but I would want the action to be at level 1"
Alex	"my question here would be, as a product business, how do you use your customers need to influence what you build?"..."It's not necessarily about building exactly what your customer asks for, but it's about interpreting their needs and then solving a problem for them. I think that a connected customer and product innovation that's really important"
Lorne	"thats your baseline. If it's around products and service, again I would say it's more about if you continually innovate and adapt our products and service, based on

	working with our customers to understand their needs and to understand their evolving needs"
Michael	"the full 360 takes in everything into product development and suddenly NPS becomes, or whatever is set for that faction, becomes the most valuable for product development"
Claire	"listening and taking action, I think is really important"
John	"i would perhaps put a note to say this works both ways, it can push from the outside in or it can be pushed from the inside out"
Alex	"in here, it would be something like, we have a feedback mechanism, or we have a feedback loop with our customer for developing our product"
Alex	"I think it's [feedback loops], absolutely critical"
Patrick	"there are a few links between your levels that either reinforce themselves if they're all there, or kind of hinder the impact if they are not"

Table K17: Quotes from practitioners on a *central customer experience metric*

Interviewee	Quote
Lucas	"do you understand what metrics you're actually measuring customer experience by?"
Claire	"I don't think there is one lens through which you can measure customer experience. I think it is a basket of scores"
Michael	"NPS [is it] is a measure of customer experience. Out and out, pound for pound, it is a measure of customer experience. You can always nitpick in the methodology and all this type of stuff but at the end of the day it's a single metric"

Alex	"the EBITDA of customer experience? It's tough, I don't know. That one's still being defined"
Paul	"a sort of office 5 star score would be great. If you had an office 5 star thing going out to all our clients once a week or once a month, then you could keep tabs on how they're feeling"
Paul	"I tend to feel that something like that might be quite skewed by their last interaction and whether it's been product related. No I wouldn't recommend you. I've had a bad experience because of the product. It's not you. It's the product"
Edward	"the metric has to take out the notion of popularity of brand in order to get to the real question of are they giving a superlative customer experience and customer service. I don't know what that metric it"
Edward	"there isn't a unified customer CX metric. Quite often the customers voting sort of thing turns into a popularity contest"
Lucas	"by investing in the customer experience, actually that means we're going to have a higher lifetime value in the business and therefore the business value in the long term for shareholders shouldn't be be impacted negatively'
Lucas	- "having a customer experience as 1 metric has been useful. If for examples profits have decreased quarter on quarter but at the same time customer experience metric has increased significantly, that's a very powerful thing for a CEP to go and tell their customers"
Lucas	- "at the moment we leave it down to each individual customer to define what their goal is...I can imagine a team where actually there is a single guiding CX metrics which we could use to some kind of composite of these things"

Table K18: Quotes from practitioners on the *overall feedback on the model*

Interviewee	Quote
Lorne	"there is a lot of really good stuff in there. I think it all makes sense"
Robert	"make totals sense. Its very structured. Its simple enough for a busy person to understand which is always a helpful thing"
Joseph	"the brand piece is really important. Paradoxically it is also going to be the most difficult because it's driven by emotion and because it's largely subjective it's probably a difficult one to put in the benchmark"
Michael	"you give them a mid point, as in if it's a one to seven scale, you can sit on the fence of it. If it's sort of even you can sit on the fence. That would be a factor to consider"
Michael	"it may be worth trying to...have extremes scores I guess. What I'm trying to say? I'm just trying to think of a survey where if you said zero is this and then is that, then they are just going to give a score at some point in between"
Michael	"my observation would be operations. What does operations actually mean....if i'm running a business, I can talk about the culture. I can talk about the technology. What exactly is operations?"
John	"I think getting the algorithm that sits behind this is probably the most important thing" Michael - "the framework is good. I think the transition from culture to customer is a good one"
John	"just measuring it is one thing but actually to say that we had a problem, we fixed it in a way that was best for the customer and good for the business and then we delivered it, that then moves the dial on from being strategic reviewing to actionable review. If you feel that's covered then that's find but I am not getting a sense of that coming through"

John	"one of my observations is that there's nothing in here in terms of what you have actually delivered because a lot of it is around structure and culture. I could really do well on a lot of this but I haven't delivered much. I haven't actually achieved much and got stuff out there"
John	"one of the biggest areas of frustration I find with clients is the ability to actually launch something, to make a change, have it in place"
Alex	"I feel like the questions are very high level, I feel like, will you get enough sort of variance in the model from the questions that are pretty high"
Matthew	"you are asking a lot of good, questions in there. It's maybe that under each one of those questions there another set of five questions to further diagnose"
Lorne	"I full agree that the culture is at the heart of it. But it's almost like you've got your customer on the outside, then you've just got one big circle which is culture, and inside that... I also think that there is no logic to me in why you're stacking it up in that particular order. why is operations, product and service. Why is technology touching the customer? Wheres is you'd say, the customer experience, the whole of our organisation is driven by culture and there are three parts sitting insider that, almost like a venn diagram approach"
Lorne	"One of my thoughts was to put a feedback loop around the outside if you like. The customer then feedback back into the culture. But you are right that doesn't get rid of those step issue. I would be tempted to put culture. The customer and the culture as one big spot and the 3 others as enablers"
Lorne	"my concern there is it feels like the culture of the organisation is dis-intermediated from the customer by all these pieces of the puzzle. It's more visual representation to me"
Robert	"my company is historically bad at customer experience and getting better at it, which is fine. Being able to say "we

	score X, the sectorial average for our business is Your main competitor is Z" and being able to compare those three number immediately makes it a very real thing which I think it good

Appendix L - The Customer Centricity Measurement Framework and Scorecard

The Framework

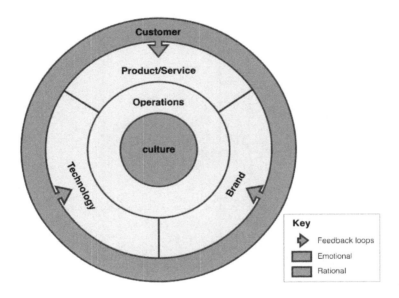

Figure K1: The Customer Centricity Measurement Framework

The Scorecard
Culture

Do you agree or disagree with each of the following statements?

The responses would be strongly disagree, disagree, neither agree or disagree, agree or strongly agree on a 5 point Likert scale (Joshi et al. 2015)

Table L1: Statements for the *culture* layer of The Customer Centricity Scorecard

Level	Statement Number	Statement
1	1	A senior person is responsible for customer experience
1	2	The customer experience is the focus of every team
2	3	We empower employees to make decisions in the best interest of the customer
2	4	"Training, recruitment and human resources development are guided by the CX strategy" (Klaus, 2015)
3	5	Customer Experience is linked to company incentives
3	6	Customer Centricity is a company value
4	7	*Further research needed on additional questions for additional layers*
4	8	*Further research needed on additional questions for additional layers*
5	9	*Further research needed on additional questions*

		for additional layers
5	10	*Further research needed on additional questions for additional layers*

Operations
Do you agree or disagree with each of the following statements?

The responses would be strongly disagree, disagree, neither agree or disagree, agree or strongly agree on a 5 point Likert scale (Joshi et al. 2015)

Table L2: Statements for the *operations* layer of The Customer Centricity Scorecard

Level	Statement Number	Statement
1	1	We understand the customer experience journey
1	2	We listen to the customer and act on what they say
2	3	We measure customer experience
2	4	We have a defined customer experience strategy
3	5	We continually optimise the customer experience
3	6	Customer centricity is included in the business model
4	7	*Further research needed on additional questions for additional layers*

4	8	*Further research needed on additional questions for additional layers*
5	9	*Further research needed on additional questions for additional layers*
5	10	*Further research needed on additional questions for additional layers*

Product/Service

Do you agree or disagree with each of the following statements?

The responses would be strongly disagree, disagree, neither agree or disagree, agree or strongly agree on a 5 point Likert scale (Joshi et al. 2015)

Table L3: Statements for the *product/service* layer of The Customer Centricity Scorecard

Level	Statement Number	Statement
1	1	We are easy to do business with
1	2	We simplify a complex product/service offering
2	3	We understand the expectations of our customers
2	4	We understand the values of our customers
3	5	We are continuously develop our product and services on the needs of our customers

3	6	We *expand* the expectations of our customer
4	7	*Further research needed on additional questions for additional layers*
4	8	*Further research needed on additional questions for additional layers*
5	9	*Further research needed on additional questions for additional layers*
5	10	*Further research needed on additional questions for additional layers*

Technology
Do you agree or disagree with each of the following statements?
The responses would be strongly disagree, disagree, neither agree or disagree, agree or strongly agree on a 5 point Likert scale (Joshi et al. 2015)

Table L4: Statements for the *technology* layer of The Customer Centricity Scorecard

Level	Statement Number	Statement
1	1	We can collect qualitative feedback from our customers
1	2	We can collect and analyse data from all touchpoints
2	3	We have a customer driven segmentation strategy
2	4	We can deliver a channel appropriate experience across multiple channels
3	5	Customers can move seamlessly between channels
3	6	We can offer a personalised customer experience
4	7	We have a single view of the customer
4	8	*Further research needed on additional questions for additional layers*
5	9	*Further research needed on additional questions for additional layers*
5	10	*Further research needed on additional questions for additional layers*

Brand
Do you agree or disagree with each of the following statements?
The responses would be strongly disagree, disagree, neither agree or disagree, agree or strongly agree on a 5 point Likert scale (Joshi et al. 2015)

Table L5: Statements for the *brand* layer of The Customer Centricity Scorecard

Level	Statement Number	Statement
1	1	The *brand* statements are an area for future research
1	2	
2	3	
2	4	
3	5	
3	6	
4	7	
4	8	
5	9	
5	10	

The Customer

Do you agree or disagree with each of the following statements?

The responses would be strongly disagree, disagree, neither agree or disagree, agree or strongly agree on a 5 point Likert scale (Joshi et al. 2015)

Table L6: Statements for the culture layer of The Customer Centricity Scorecard

Level	Statement Number	Statement
1	1	Customers enjoy using our service
1	2	We understand our customer real goals
2	3	We manage the expectations of our customers
2	4	We reward customer loyalty
3	5	We measure customer advocacy
3	6	We have emotional engagement with our customers
4	7	*Further research needed on additional questions for additional layers*
4	8	*Further research needed on additional questions for additional layers*
5	9	*Further research needed on additional questions for additional layers*
5	10	*Further research needed on additional questions for additional layers*

Appendix M – A Single Customer Experience Metric

Interview findings

Although there was not a specific question asked about a single customer experience metric it was a topic that was discussed often in the interviews.

- The idea of a *single customer experience metric* was discussed by 50% of the interviewees. From those that discussed it 33% agreed with the concept of a single customer experience metric. 67% disagreed with the concept and felt that one would not be possible. These results are shown in Figure 24.

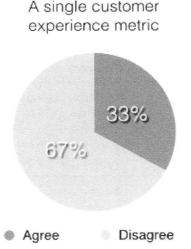

Figure M1 Results from the practitioner interviews on whether interviewees agreed or disagreed with the concept of single customer experience metric

Interview Discussion

The discussion of the single metric for customer experience was a common one in the practitioner interviews. The findings suggest, however, practitioners disagree with the concept either for practical reasons, that is it would be difficult to agree to a single measure, or for reasons of usefulness, there is a need to measure the many components that make up customer experience to be able to manage them all. The reason for this is that customer experience is seen as hard to measure. Palmer (2010) says the *"problem in developing an operationally acceptable measure of customer experience is the complexity of context specific variables"* and the findings from the interviews would suggest that these are the challenges practitioners also see in a single customer experience metric.

The challenge in measuring customer experience is that, as the customer survey and the interviews show, partially *customer created*. Measuring the customer created customer experience is difficult it is *"out of the control of the organisation."* (Verhoef et al. 2009)

Customer centricity leads to enhanced customer experience delivery and it is *"in the control of the organisation."* (Verhoef et al. 2009) This means that its measurement would be more straightforward. This is where the Customer Centricity Score would be used, to provide organisations with a single metric for aligning the business to deliver enhanced customer experience.

GARETH EVANS

"We are perishing for want of wonder, not for want of wonders."
G. K. Chesterton

Made in the USA
Las Vegas, NV
12 December 2023

82650586R00193